JOHN WILKES BOOTH

JOHN WILKES BOOTH

BOOTH

Beyond the Grave

W.C. Jameson

TAYLOR TRADE PUBLISHING
Lanham • New York • Boulder • Toronto • Plymouth, UK

Published by Taylor Trade Publishing
An imprint of The Rowman & Littlefield Publishing Group, Inc.
4501 Forbes Boulevard, Suite 200, Lanham, Maryland 20706
www.rowman.com

10 Thornbury Road, Plymouth PL6 7PP, United Kingdom

Distributed by National Book Network

British Library Cataloguing in Publication Information Available

Library of Congress Cataloging-in-Publication Data

Jameson, W. C., 1942-
  John Wilkes Booth : beyond the grave / W.C. Jameson.
    pages cm
  Includes bibliographical references and index.
  ISBN 978-1-58979-831-1 (cloth : alk. paper) — ISBN 978-1-58979-832-8
(electronic) 1. Booth, John Wilkes, 1838-1865. 2. Assassins—United States—
Biography. 3. Fugitives from justice—United States—Biography. 4. Lincoln,
Abraham, 1809-1865—Assassination. I. Title.
  E457.5.J349 2013
  973.7092—dc23
  [B]

2013008412

Printed in the United States of America

Contents

Preface   *vii*

ONE   *Introduction*   *1*

TWO   *Who Was John Wilkes Booth?*   *6*

THREE   *Plots to Kidnap*   *14*

FOUR   *Plot to Assassinate*   *42*

FIVE   *The Assassination*   *51*

SIX   *The Attack on Seward*   *62*

SEVEN   *Escape*   *67*

EIGHT   *Flight, Pursuit, and Death of John Wilkes Booth: The Traditional Version*   *72*

NINE   *Flight from Washington*   *86*

TEN   *Surrattsville*   *89*

ELEVEN   *Dr. Samuel Mudd*   *94*

TWELVE   *The Swamp*   *99*

THIRTEEN   *Reenter Boyd*   *107*

FOURTEEN   *The Crossing*   *113*

FIFTEEN   *The Diary*   *118*

SIXTEEN   *Closing In*   *124*

SEVENTEEN   *The Killing at Garrett's Farm*   *127*

EIGHTEEN   *The Body*   *140*

NINETEEN   *Tracking John Wilkes Booth*   *158*

TWENTY	*The Return of the Assassin*	*163*
TWENTY-ONE	*Booth's Secret Families*	*169*
TWENTY-TWO	*The Strange Case of David E. George*	*174*
TWENTY-THREE	*Analysis*	*182*
	Bibliography	*201*
	Index	*207*
	About the Author	*223*
	Acknowledgments	*224*

Preface

◆◆◆

Virtually every American knows the name John Wilkes Booth. Surveys have confirmed that for most citizens of the United States, as well as residents of much of the rest of the world, the infamous actor and his associated deed are synonymous with the word "assassination." Mention the name "Booth," a noted thespian of the mid-nineteenth century, and all but a sheltered few associate it with the murder of President Abraham Lincoln, April 14, 1865.

Even now, according to author David M. Robertson, the enigmatic, attractive, manipulative, and violent Booth "continues to command the American imagination in a way not fully explained by the fact of his life or his notoriety."

Indeed, to this day, John Wilkes Booth remains a looming, gnawing enigma, among the most complex and puzzling in American history. Rising well above the confusing and tangled web of mysteries embracing the actor, his escape, and his alleged death are the ones associated with the distinct possibility of his survival.

As a child, I remember the few occasions when family members brought up the subject of John Wilkes Booth in hushed tones accompanied by furtive glances at the doors as if the speakers feared someone might be listening. During those rare times that I chanced to enter a room filled with adults having such conversations, the subject was immediately dropped and another substituted. I was too young to understand or even care about the family secrecy surrounding this. When I was ten years old and in the fifth grade, I was subjected to an elementary school lesson in history that included information on the tenure of Abraham Lincoln as president of the United States and his role, as they said in those days, in freeing the slaves. We also learned that Lincoln was assassinated in his prime by Booth, an actor who was eventually killed several days afterward. So said the teachers and the textbooks.

On arriving home that afternoon, I excitedly related portions of the day's history class to my mother and a visiting guest. When I got to the part about John Wilkes Booth, I was shushed and sent to another room. Later, after the visitor departed, I was reprimanded for bringing up the subject of Booth and instructed never to do it again. When I asked why, the answers stunned me then as they stun me today. I was told Booth was kin on my father's side. To many, especially my mother, any family association with the assassin was considered socially unacceptable, and the matter was not to be discussed. In addition, the actor was never spoken of by tacit agreement among relatives because, they believed and I was told, John Wilkes Booth was never captured or killed by government authorities but escaped to live for many years afterward.

The prospect of being related to a famous assassin generated a mixed reaction in a ten-year-old. On the one hand, I was honor bound to maintain the secret. On the other, the revelation that Booth had escaped generated in me a burning curiosity about the man and his life and times, a curiosity that has not abated in the decades since. Beginning at that young age, I read everything I could find about Abraham Lincoln, the Civil War, the politics of that era, and John Wilkes Booth. The more I read, studied, researched, analyzed, questioned, and considered the traditional histories on these subjects, the more I came to realize a number of things that caused me to appreciate what I now perceive to be the truth of what I was told as a youngster: John Wilkes Booth was not captured and killed by federal agents as we were taught in our history classes. He escaped.

ONE

❖❖❖

Introduction

What is the truth about John Wilkes Booth? What really happened to the man who many historians contend is the world's most famous political assassin?

History records that Booth, on the evening of April 14, 1865, assassinated President Abraham Lincoln. Of that there can be little doubt since dozens in attendance at Ford's Theater in Washington, D.C., witnessed the killing and the escape of the actor. History also records that, following a twelve-day pursuit, Booth was finally trapped in a barn on the northeastern Virginia farm of Richard Garrett. Shot while resisting capture, the mortally wounded fugitive was dragged from the structure, which had been set on fire, and later carried to Garrett's porch, where he died a short time later.

Unlike the killing of Lincoln, this particular event was layered with doubt and confusion. Almost from the moment the dying man was pulled from the barn, it was being whispered among the soldiers present that he was *not* Booth. As events of the next forty-eight hours unfolded, the complications and contradictions concerning the identity of the man did not abate. Instead, they swelled to such proportions that government authorities were put to the task of writing and issuing informational releases on the matter. Rather than quash the rumors of Booth's escape, they only added to the mystery.

More doubt and contradiction surfaced during the subsequent inquest, identification, and burial of the body, all borne of obvious governmental fumbling, ineptitude, and deception. Conspiratorial overtones strongly hinted at government duplicity and cover-up regarding the identity of the body being passed off as that of the assassin. I am troubled by those who find conspiracies everywhere and am loath to invoke one here. The sad truth, however, is that elected politicians and appointed officials have long demonstrated that such are not uncommon in Washington, D.C. Many of the facts related to the conspiracy to assassinate the president and the fate of Booth will likely never be known.

What most people know or think they know of the capture and killing of John Wilkes Booth has been derived primarily from interpretations of government documents written well over a century ago. Critical examination of these records, as well as their representations and interpretations by scholars and writers over the years, reveal obvious and in some cases embarrassing elements of contradiction and beclouding. William Hanchett, himself a historian, blames "professional historians for writing some truly bad books about the Lincoln assassination." Historians, in fact, do not even agree among themselves as to what actually happened relative to the assassination of the president and the escape of Booth.

In recent years, we have been exposed to information that reveals that much of the history we were taught in school and exposed to in books and on television was not true. A number of recent books have pointed out that much of the history that has been served to us was, if not bogus from the beginning, written from the viewpoint of one or a few people with little to no fact-checking or represents certain political or religious points of view.

I learned this the hard way while conducting research and investigation for the book *Billy the Kid: Beyond the Grave.* I discovered that what most of the public knew about the outlaw came from one source—Sheriff Pat Garrett, who claimed to have shot and killed the Kid. Over the years, historians, writers, and researchers merely repeated in one form or another what Garrett said and inflicted little to no research of their own into the matter. Far too much western history suffers from this malady. Garrett, it was learned, rarely told the truth about anything, and someone else wrote most of his book, *The Authentic Life of Billy the Kid.*

After over five decades of writing, formal study, and pertinent experience, I have come to realize that a complete and honest study of history (as well as many other subjects) requires research, investigation, and reconstruction. I learned that the terms "research" and "investigation" are often used interchangeably among historians, professionals as well as hobbyists. My experience has been that many of them research but seldom investigate.

Research is the systematic pursuit of knowledge and information. When one is researching, one is looking for facts. It is, however, a useful skill to be able to separate the truth from what someone has simply written or reported, and this is not always easy. Unfortunately, as was often demonstrated in the Billy the Kid research as well as that associated with John Wilkes Booth, materials that had been previously published were interpreted as the truth simply because they were found in print in book, journal, magazine, or newspaper. Few questioned the validity of what they read.

Investigation is related to the solving of a mystery or conundrum. I may conduct research relative to a particular historical event, but I also investigate its provenance. I have approached issues from a number of angles, including history, chronology, geography, and more. During the course of several projects, I have attempted to prove something wrong as often as I try to prove it right. Further, I never start with an answer and work backward, handpicking evidence, to support my conclusion. Unfortunately, far too much historical research and writing manifests this tendency. In addition, there are times when I seek the assistance and contribution of trained investigators to help me interpret the evidence. Throughout years of research and investigation, I have sought and received the services of state police and sheriff's department detectives and crime experts, the Federal Bureau of Investigation, and private handwriting experts.

"Provenance" is a term often brought up in historical research. I have seen writers criticized for lack of provenance by so-called historians. Provenance refers to the origin or derivation of a historical fact (or artifact). It is important to trace a statement or fact to its source. It is also important to know whether that source is reliable. I have had the experience of witnessing so-called experts criticize the provenance of a statement or contention made by someone. These reputed experts, however, were guilty of blindly accepting and employing information and reputed facts gleaned from government documents that were clearly spurious.

Richard Nixon, along with a slew of other elected and appointed officials, has taught us to never take for granted that anything they state or write is true. A great deal of government documentation, we have come to learn, is automatically suspect. In the case of materials associated with the Lincoln assassination and John Wilkes Booth, I started by searching for internal consistencies. The documentation, along with subsequent interpretations thereof, often revealed inconsistencies, even chaos. When I encounter chaos, I look for patterns. The actions and conclusions offered by the elected officials of the time were at best contradictory, at worst dishonest, and likely both.

With investigation comes inductive and deductive reasoning. The goal of the investigator goes well beyond finding some historical information and writing an article or book. The goal is to develop or locate proof or at least some substantial evidence that is used to assist in arriving at the intended goal. To a true researcher and investigator, mysteries, such as those associated with John Wilkes Booth, invite solution.

Following research and investigation, one is ready for reconstruction. By now, the researcher should have at his or her disposal all of the available facts, some of which may vary, depending on provenance. Using inductive and deductive logic, he or she is now in a position to re-create events, geography, transportation or travel routes, and more. Only when the reconstruction phase of a project is completed, along with an analysis, should one undertake the final report. In the end, what one comes up with may differ markedly from the standard and long-accepted versions, as happened with Billy the Kid and John Wilkes Booth. One is now in a position to tell the truth or a version of the truth based on the work that has been done. There may be many truths associated with a particular event. The goal of the researcher is to provide the truth based on the quality and amount of substantive information that has been located and investigated.

Following intensive research and investigation, along with an infusion of logic and reasoning, it is difficult to come away from an in-depth experience with Booth-related documents and publications without a number of doubts, including what actually occurred; doubts about the role of highly placed elected and appointed government officials; doubts relative to the number, identity, and role of the conspirators; and doubts concerning the identity of the body that was said to be that of John Wilkes Booth.

Adding to these doubts are the relatively recent discoveries of a number of important documents. Compelling and revealing information in the form of papers and diaries has been located in private collections, materials that provide additional insight into the events of the pursuit and capture of the man identified as Booth. This recent information, along with a critical reexamination of the traditional historical materials, provides sufficient reason to challenge the general and long-held assumption that John Wilkes Booth was killed by government agents in Virginia. It can be argued that a greater body of evidence not tainted by governmental machinations exists that supports the notion that Booth escaped and that a Union spy, a Booth look-alike, perished at Garrett's farm.

In the following pages, a case will be presented that (1) the government's account of the capture and death of John Wilkes Booth is riddled with inconsistencies and contradiction, (2) Booth was never captured, and (3) the assassin lived for another two or more decades in Europe, India, and elsewhere, eventually returning to the United States, where he passed away, perhaps as a suicide.

TWO

✦✦✦

Who Was John Wilkes Booth?

Beyond his specific identity and notoriety as the man who assassinated President Abraham Lincoln, very few people have any knowledge of the complexity and depth of the curious, tragic, and enigmatic figure of John Wilkes Booth. Even fewer are aware of the bizarre sequence of events and circumstances related to the pursuit and alleged killing of the man believed to be Booth, events and circumstances that remain a mystery to this day.

John Wilkes Booth was a successful and popular actor in his time. It has been written that he was one of the finest thespians ever to grace the stages of New York, Baltimore, Washington, D.C., and elsewhere. His performances filled theaters, and the press treated him well in reviews. In spite of Booth's theatrical success, however, many have dismissed him as a mere lunatic. Some historical accounts have referred to him as a crazed actor. Labels applied to Booth over the years by a number of researchers and writers have included "Satanic genius," a "mad zealot," a "villain from the cradle," a "half-demonic creature of savage instincts," and a "vulgar cutthroat activated by a thirst for notoriety." In *The Great American Myth*, author George S. Bryan referred to Booth as a ham actor, boisterous, lazy, devoid of talent, ranting, coarse-grained, shy, trivial, and vain.

Others have claimed that Booth at various times was an emissary for the Roman Catholic Church, an officer in the Knights of the Golden Circle, and a hired accomplice of Vice President Andrew Johnson. Save for his membership in the Knights of the Golden Circle, however, there exists no evidence that any of these descriptions fit the man who was John Wilkes Booth.

Booth was, among other things, a passionate and patriotic son of the American South who gave himself wholeheartedly to the southern cause with a devotion and fervor unmatched. Booth's niece, Blanche

6

de Bar Booth, was once quoted by the actor's biographer John Francis Wilson as saying that Booth was "loved for his kindly nature, his generosity, and the qualities of a refined gentleman convinced that he had good reason to slay Lincoln, and he was not alone in his thinking."

John Wilkes Booth was a child of Junius Brutus Booth and Mary Ann Holmes. He was the fifth of six children of that union who survived to maturity. In all, Junius fathered ten children, but since he and Mary Ann were not married at the time, all of the American-born Booth offspring were technically bastards.

Junius Brutus Booth was born in London in 1796. By the time he was seventeen, he was performing regularly in theaters throughout England and receiving wide acclaim for his work. The elder Booth arrived in America in 1821. One year later, he purchased a farm near Bel Air, Maryland, twenty miles from Baltimore.

Junius soon became one of America's most noted Shakespearean actors, was regarded as the most prominent stage performer of his day, and performed throughout much of the eastern part of the United States. He remained popular with American audiences for three decades. In addition to being a superb performer, Junius was also considered to be a linguist, playwright, scholar, and philosopher. He was also a hopeless and pathetic alcoholic.

John Wilkes Booth was born on May 10, 1838, in the small town of Harford, Maryland, three miles east of the Bel Air farm. He was the second youngest and was named after John Wilkes, the eighteenth-century British reformer and political agitator who made a strong impression on Junius. Wilkes opposed practically everything about the rule of British King George III and served for a time as the British representative of a Boston-based revolutionary group.

Called "Johnnie" by his father and siblings well into his adult years, young John Wilkes Booth was brought up by Junius to respect and champion the ideals of liberty and to never tolerate any kind of tyranny. The elder Booth raised his children in aristocratic luxury on the Bel Air farm's 150 acres. He constructed a brick English-style cottage he called Tudor Hall, planted an orchard and vineyard, and supervised the construction of stables, a large swimming pool, and slave quarters. Junius was always kind and liberal with his slaves.

In this environment, young John received a proper education as well as instruction in riding. In time, he even broke and trained his own horses. John was sent to schools in and near Baltimore but spent summers on the estate. He attended St. Timothy's Hall at Catonsville, an

Episcopal academy with a military curriculum. There, he learned to shoot rifle and pistol. According to all reports, he became an excellent marksman.

Author George S. Bryan wrote that Booth's fellow students remembered him as one who sought notoriety and who often spoke of doing something of sufficient impact that he would always be remembered and recognized. At St. Timothy's, Booth met Sam Arnold, a fellow student who was to play an important part in his future.

Booth grew up spoiled and snobbish. He manifested an air of elitism unlike most of his playmates, and he was often moody and sullen. Booth seldom concealed his distaste for the family's black slaves, and he never deigned to engage in conversation with the hired help, black or white. Although he often listened to and enjoyed the music of the blacks, he held them in contempt as human beings.

At times, Booth also demonstrated a vicious temper. Once, during a play rehearsal when a promoter was lagging behind schedule, Booth grabbed a piece of wood from a nearby set and flung it hard at the man, barely missing his head and causing serious injury.

Booth deplored immigrants of any kind, particularly Irishmen. He attended meetings of the Know-Nothings and the American Party, two organizations opposed to foreign immigration and the political influence of immigrants and Roman Catholics.

John's brothers were Junius Brutus Jr., Edwin, Joseph, Frederick, and Henry Byron. His sisters were Asia, Rosalie, Mary Ann, and Elizabeth. Junius Brutus Jr. and Edwin were both fine actors but never received any instruction from their famous father. Joseph had a brief fling with the stage but lacked the skills and presence of his famous parents and siblings.

Although he was only thirteen years old when his father Junius died, John learned much about the craft of acting at his father's side. As he gained theatrical prominence in later years, many commented that he had obviously inherited a fine and rare talent from Junius Brutus Sr. Brother Edwin once stated that John could have become one of the most brilliant actors in the world.

Booth made his acting debut in 1856 when he was seventeen years old. It was a minor role in *Richard III*. By all accounts, it was a disaster—he suffered a severe case of stage fright and forgot his lines. The performance was so bad that the audience booed him and the newspapers panned his performance. Booth sulked for days and swore he would never act again.

John Wilkes Booth
Library of Congress, Prints & Photographs Division, LC-
USZ62-25166

Two summers later, however, Booth performed as Horatio in *Hamlet* in Richmond, Virginia. On this occasion, he garnered cheers and raves. In 1860, Booth joined a theatrical company that toured throughout the South. His performances were spirited and dynamic, and he soon played to packed houses and enthusiastic responses. Women screamed during his curtain calls and often threw roses on the stage at his feet. Booth's career as an actor was on the rise. Popular though he was, Booth's performances were always overshadowed by those of his brother and late father. Booth was openly jealous of Junius and Edwin.

As a young man, Booth manifested a passion not only for acting but also for politics. He often worked himself into a lather over the topics of secession, slavery, and President Abraham Lincoln. Booth sided strongly with the South, supported withdrawal from the Union, and considered abolitionists to be tyrants. He often spoke of the Confederacy as "his country." So violent and angry were his politics that brother Edwin forbade political discussions when John came to visit.

Between 1861 and 1864, Booth was in great demand as an actor and toured extensively throughout the North, the South, and Canada. He was paid around $20,000 per year, an impressive sum at the time.

During April 1863, Booth played his first engagement in Washington, D.C., at Grover's Theater. The play was *Richard III*. Among the large and fashionable audience that attended the April 11 performance was President Abraham Lincoln.

In addition to his growing celebrity status, Booth was quite handsome, and he became a favorite with the ladies. After a string of successful performances in Washington, women began following him through the streets asking for his autograph. They were drawn to him, as writer Theodore Roscoe says, "like pins drawn to a magnet."

Booth reveled in the attention. He even dressed the part: a fawn waistcoat, a long black coat with velvet lapels, trousers with heel straps, a wide-brimmed hat, an expensive and prominently displayed cameo, and a bamboo walking cane.

Booth is believed to have had many lovers and, though shrouded in mystery, at least one wife. He was known to consort with a noted prostitute of Washington named Ella Turner, also known as Ella Star, Nellie Starr, and Fannie Harrison. In Manhattan, Booth lived for a time with Sally Andrews. He was believed to have promised marriage to a woman named Ann Horton. Some researchers have suggested that the widow Mary Surratt was among Booth's romantic flings. Surratt was ultimately executed for her role in the conspiracy to assassinate President Lincoln.

Booth also had romantic and apparently sexual inclinations toward actresses Fanny Brown, Alice Grey, Effie German, and Helen Western. In fact, photographs of these four women, along with a fifth (some say a sixth), were found among Booth's possessions following the assassination. One of the photographs was of Lucy Lambert Hale, the daughter of Senator John P. Hale, a noted prowar and antislavery advocate. Booth and Lucy Hale were, in fact, engaged to be married even while he was dallying with actresses and prostitutes.

Others were taken with Lucy Hale, including a twenty-four-year-old Oliver Wendell Holmes, a Union officer and future Supreme Court justice. Lincoln's personal secretary John Hay was also enamored of the young lady. In an interesting historical twist, it was discovered that another Union officer, Robert Todd Lincoln, the president's twenty-four-year-old son, was fond of Lucy. By March 1865, the engagement of Booth and Lucy Hale was common knowledge, although she continued to maintain contact with Hay and the young Lincoln. One evening, Booth spotted Hale dancing with Robert Todd Lincoln and flew into a rage.

Evidence suggests that Booth was secretly married to Izola Mills D'Arcy in 1859. Mills, a devoted southerner, was believed to be active in smuggling medical supplies, such as quinine and morphine, into the South.

When it came to women, Booth also possessed a dark side. He was once reported for rape in Philadelphia. In Syracuse, New York, he was severely beaten in an adultery incident.

For a time, Booth worked clandestinely for the South and its hoped-for success. He once admitted to his sister Asia that he was a secret agent, a spy, and that he entered the Rebel underground during the winter of 1863. When the opportunity arose, Booth smuggled bandages and medicine, mostly quinine, to the southern troops. He was known to many of them as "Dr. Booth." During this period, Booth himself may have started using drugs.

In addition to medicine, Booth carried important information to southern leaders. To what degree he engaged in official spying, if any, is not known, and the truth about Booth's alleged espionage activities is yet to be documented.

Booth's passion and support for the South grew dramatically during the early 1860s. Asia's husband, John Sleeper Clarke, regarded Booth as monomaniacal on the subject of the South and refused to engage in discussions with him. Older brother Junius also expressed concern for John's unbridled enthusiasm for the southern cause and his vitriol against the Union and President Abraham Lincoln. More and more, it seemed, Booth blamed the country's growing problems on the president. He despised Lincoln and all that he stood for.

John Wilkes Booth was just under five feet eight inches tall, slightly above average for the time. Author David Miller Dewitt described the actor's face as "remarkably handsome." Sister Asia wrote that he possessed his father's "finely shaped head and beautiful face." Booth's head was topped with thick, wavy, glossy, jet-black hair. A moustache decorated his upper lip, one that turned down somewhat at the ends and provided him with a certain roguish air. Although Booth has often been described as having piercing and penetrating black eyes, Asia wrote that his were large, expressive hazel eyes similar to those of his mother, eyes set deep under heavy lids.

Author George Alfred Townsend said of Booth,

> He had one of the finest, vital heads I have ever seen . . . one of the best exponents of vital beauty I have ever met . . . health, shapeliness, power in beautiful poise, and seemingly more powerful in repose than in energy. His hands and feet were sizeable . . . and his legs were stout and muscular. . . . From the waist up he was a perfect man; his chest . . . full and broad, his shoulders gently sloping . . . his arms . . . hard as marble. [He had] a fine Doric head, spare at the jaws . . . seamed with a nose of a Roman model.

Booth's hands were noticeably large, and he was, according to research, right-handed. As a child, wrote his sister Asia, he tattooed his initials "JWB" on the back of one of his hands in India ink. Unfortunately, Asia did not specify which hand bore the tattoo, an omission that was to contribute heavily to a deep mystery in later years.

Booth also possessed a number of scars on his face and body. One of the most prominent was the result of a deep wound on his forehead from being struck as a youth by a thrown oyster shell.

Booth was quite athletic and, according to writer Bryan, "well-knit and well proportioned." He was an excellent horseman, swordsman, and gymnast. David Miller Dewitt wrote that Booth was "noted for extraordinary leaps on stage."

Offstage, Booth was a gentleman, charming, high-minded, cultured, eloquent, gracious, kindly in manner, a good listener, generous with his money and time, and, as Bryan states, "devoid of petty vanity."

Writers Bill O'Reilly and Martin Dugard describe Booth as "an exceptional young man. Blessed with a rakish smile and debonair gaze, he is handsome, brilliant witty, charismatic, tender, and able to bed almost any woman he wants—and he has bedded quite a few."

That John Wilkes Booth, at twenty-six years of age, killed President Abraham Lincoln is not open to question. This is certain and unassailable fact. The events following the assassination, however, are another matter. Although the escape, pursuit, and alleged death of the assassin have been extensively researched and written about hundreds of times since 1865, there remains overwhelming doubt relative to what, in truth, actually happened to John Wilkes Booth. The official report is one thing, but the evidence is something else altogether.

THREE

♦♦♦

Plots to Kidnap

During the first week of March 1864, Union Brigadier General Judson Kilpatrick led a raid into Richmond, Virginia, for the stated purpose of releasing over 100 federal prisoners held there. Kilpatrick assured President Abraham Lincoln during a meeting on February 13 that the Confederates were expecting nothing and that the plan had an excellent chance of success.

The strategy called for Kilpatrick to approach Richmond from the north with a large cavalry force accompanied by artillery. Colonel Ulric Dahlgren was to lead another contingent of cavalrymen, all dressed in Confederate uniforms, across the James River and attack Richmond from the south. After freeing the prisoners from the Belle Isle Prison, Dahlgren was to rejoin Kilpatrick's troops at about the time Richmond was being attacked.

Following a positive beginning, things began to go terribly wrong for Dahlgren. During the early part of the raid, his soldiers destroyed a sawmill and a number of gristmills and sank several boats loaded with grain. In addition, canal locks and a coal mining operation were disabled.

Rather than terrify the southerners into flight, however, Dahlgren's raid served only to infuriate them. Grabbing whatever weapons they could find, the Virginians took to the woods and began sniping at the Dahlgren force, picking off men at an alarming rate. So great was the resistance that the colonel ordered a retreat.

By the time Dahlgren and his command reached the Rapidan River, they found it flooded from recent rains and impossible to cross. As he pondered the best course of action, a scout informed him that southern marksmen were closing in and inflicting serious casualties. Dahlgren decided to lead his men downstream in search of a ford. Within minutes, they rode into an ambush. Dahlgren, along with twenty of his troops, was killed. One hundred more were captured.

On Colonel Dahlgren's body, two sets of papers were found that some historians claim eventually led to the death of Abraham Lincoln. The first was a letter written by the colonel himself, stating that, after freeing the captives, he would lead his force into Richmond, destroy the bridges behind him, and exhort the released prisoners to burn the city and not allow Confederate President Jefferson Davis to escape.

The second paper was a handwritten yet unsigned order that stated that once inside Richmond, Dahlgren was to destroy the city and kill Davis and all of the members of his cabinet. When news of these documents spread throughout the southern countryside, Confederates were furious. Lincoln, who had been seeking peace with the South, was puzzled by the documents, for he had made no such orders.

There were two immediate and unfortunate results of the failed Dahlgren raid. First, the peace negotiations that were secretly being held in Nashville, Tennessee, were scrapped. Second, the Lincoln administration and leadership were cast into doubt, with members of the president's own party already making plans to abandon him in the upcoming election in favor of Salmon P. Chase.

Contrary to the perceptions of most Americans at the time and since, President Abraham Lincoln was more disliked than he was loved. It has been argued, in fact, that he was the most hated man in America during his tenure as president. He was hated not only by southerners but by a surprising number of northerners as well.

According to Lincoln researcher and author William Hanchett, the president was despised for attempting to force the South to remain in the Union, for usurping cherished congressional rights, for pursuing a policy regarding slavery that would lead to the Africanization of the United States, for degrading the presidency, for shedding so much blood, for making so many widows, and for creating so many fatherless homes.

Lincoln, in truth, had been marked for assassination on the very day he was elected. Southerners loudly and often boasted of traveling to Washington to slay the president. At various times during Lincoln's tenure as the country's leader, dozens of Confederate soldiers, viewing him as an obstacle to southern independence, volunteered to kill him. Some southern citizens even took out ads in local newspapers offering to accomplish the deed. Dozens of plots to kidnap or assassinate Lincoln had been known since 1861.

Abraham Lincoln
Brady National Photographic Art Gallery, Library of Congress,
Prints & Photographs Division, Civil War Glass Negatives and
Related Prints Collection, LC-B8171-1321

Although some were convinced that Lincoln was a great president
and leader, those who hated him perceived him as vulgar, unrefined,
uneducated, obscene, vicious, and brutal in habits as well as filthy, a
boor, a coward, a drunk, and a clod.

As early as the first week of August 1864, U.S. Marshall Ward
Lamon informed Lincoln of recent rumors of assassination attempts.
Lamon, Lincoln's former law partner, was regarded by many as the
president's best friend. According to writer Margarite Spalding Gerry,
Lincoln responded to Lamon's concerns by telling him, "Assassination

is not an American practice. If anyone was willing to give his own life in the attempt to murder a president, it would be impossible to prevent him." What Lincoln could not know at the time was that the most serious threat to his life was from a man he knew of but had not met—John Wilkes Booth.

During the early part of 1864, a group of planters assembled outside of the small quiet community of Bryantown, Maryland. Over drinks, they discussed strategies pertinent to ending the war. The meeting was called by Patrick C. Martin and included two physicians—Dr. William Queen and Dr. Samuel Mudd.

During the meeting, one of the participants suggested that the best way to end hostilities was to kidnap the president and turn him over to Jefferson Davis. At first, the idea was rejected as being reckless and foolhardy, but as the discussion proceeded, interest in such a plot grew. After a time, most agreed that if Lincoln could somehow be removed from office, the war might quickly come to an end.

Eventually, the idea of kidnapping Lincoln took on a life of its own, and the planners began to seriously consider a scheme. The first question raised was related to finding a suitable individual to commit the act. Several names were suggested, but all were rejected for a variety of reasons.

Finally, Martin told the others that he knew a man who would be capable of arranging and accomplishing a kidnapping. When the participants expressed interest, he told them the man was named John Wilkes Booth. By way of providing credentials, Martin told those assembled that Booth was a Maryland native, was passionately loyal to the South and the southern cause, had demonstrated his allegiance to the South in a number of ways, and was very eager to become involved. More discussion followed, and by the time the meeting was concluded, all agreed that Martin should arrange a meeting with Booth to discuss the proposed abduction.

During the war, hundreds of Confederate soldiers who escaped from Union prisons fled across the border into Canada. For the most part, they remained in that foreign country, living among the natives and awaiting the cessation of hostilities so that they could return to their homes.

In April 1864, Confederate President Jefferson Davis appointed Jacob Thompson and Clement C. Clay as special commissioners to

Canada. Thompson was from Mississippi and had been the secretary of the interior in the cabinet of former President James Buchanan. Clay, a former Alabama state senator, was currently serving as a senator for the Confederate States of America. The two appointees joined other Confederates already operating in Canada, among them Beverly Tucker of Virginia and George N. Sanders of Kentucky.

In Canada, the southerners had orders to work for the defeat of Lincoln in the approaching fall election by buying up influential newspapers. They were also to encourage the Rebel soldiers living in Canada to conduct raids against American towns just across the border.

In June, three months after the failed Dahlgren raid, Colonel William A. Browning, the private secretary to Vice President Andrew Johnson, visited Washington, D.C. During his stay in the capital, Browning ran into an old acquaintance, the actor John Wilkes Booth. Booth asked Browning about the Dahlgren raid and was told that the Confederates faked the papers found on the colonel's body in an attempt to bring embarrassment to the Union.

Booth then surprised Browning with a comment about the ongoing and secret peace negotiations. Shocked, the secretary asked the actor how he knew of such things. Booth merely replied that he had many

Jacob Thompson
Library of Congress, Prints
& Photographs Division,
Brady-Handy Collection,
LC-DIG-cwpbh-02849

Beverly Tucker
Library of Congress, Prints
& Photographs Division,
LC-USZ62-61751

friends in the South. With such connections, Browning suggested to Booth that he might be able to find a role for him in helping to reestablish the peace discussions. Booth replied that he was not interested.

Weeks later, Booth learned that his wife, Izola, had been arrested in Tennessee for smuggling medical supplies to Confederate soldiers. Although Booth was engaged to Lucy Hale, it is believed by many that he was married to Izola D'Arcy Mills. Recalling Browning's earlier offer, he sought an audience with him. After Booth informed Browning of his predicament, the secretary made arrangements for the actor to meet with Vice President Andrew Johnson. Johnson, in turn, told Booth that he could easily arrange for the release of his wife but that he wanted something in return. He asked for Booth's help in reestablishing the peace negotiations. Booth agreed and told Johnson that he would need passes to travel to Richmond as well as passes signed by Confederate authorities in order to return. Johnson assented.

Weeks later, Booth returned from Richmond in a rage. He confronted Browning and, furious, told him that while he was in the South, he learned that the papers found on Dahlgren were *not* forgeries and that the intent had been to kill Confederate President Davis and destroy Richmond all along. Browning tried to pacify the angry Booth, but the actor's fury was palpable, and he accused the vice president's secretary of lying and deceit.

Fuming, Booth turned and strode away from Browning, an anger smoldering in his breast. He felt betrayed and used by a man he thought he could trust. Rather than cooling off, the incensement and rage continued to grow, slowly at first but soon with an intensity that gradually consumed the young actor.

On August 9, 1864, the Democratic National Convention made preparations to nominate General George B. McClellan to run against Lincoln. Booth, according to researchers Balsiger and Sellier, followed the progress of the convention closely and wrote in his journal that he believed the election of McClellan would help bring the war to an end.

Around this time, Booth was growing convinced that his service and contribution as a spy and as an occasional smuggler of medicines and bandages to the southern camps was not enough. He wanted to do more and craved greater participation. Like others, Booth often entertained the notion of kidnapping the president.

During this month, Booth was stricken with a bacterial infection called erysipelas, a skin infection. The symptoms include fever and chills as well as painful lesions with raised borders manifested mainly on the legs, cheeks, and bridge of the nose. The affliction forced the actor to cancel several stage performances, but Booth applied his free time to refining his kidnap plot. In time, he recovered but continued to devote his attention to the plans, immersing himself in his once-in-a-lifetime quest.

During the final week of September 1864, planter Patrick Martin sought and received an audience with Booth. At the time, Martin outlined a workable kidnap plot and discussed with Booth the possibilities of what might happen should McClellan be elected.

Martin also informed Booth that an adequate amount of gold would be made available for recruiting the right men for the job. He further convinced the actor that he would be generously compensated for his efforts. Martin also assured Booth that he could expect cooperation from the higher levels of the Confederate government in Richmond. Booth told Martin he would give some thought to the proposition and that he might even draft a letter of inquiry to President Jefferson Davis himself.

Edwin McMasters Stanton, President Lincoln's secretary of war, was by all accounts a rather strange man. Judged by today's standards, according to writer Theodore Roscoe, Stanton would be considered

Edwin M. Stanton
Library of Congress, Prints
& Photographs Division,
LC-USZ62-40603

psychotic. Once, on learning that a young woman he was fond of
had died from cholera, Stanton went to the cemetery and dug up her
body. He told investigators that he was afraid she had been buried
alive. Several years later when Stanton's own daughter died and was
buried, he had her corpse exhumed, placed in a different casket, and
stored in his bedroom.

Stanton was born in Ohio in 1814. When he was thirteen years of
age, his father died, and the family was thrust into financial difficulties. Life was not easy for the young Stanton, but in 1831 he was able
to enroll at Kenyon College and remain until his money was depleted
two and a half years later. He read law on his own and was finally
admitted to the bar in 1836. He soon won a reputation as a competent
and efficient attorney.

According to historians, Stanton was bellicose, unfit, temperamen-
tal, and prone to savage moods. It was said that Stanton was unable to
retain his composure long enough to form rational and equitable judg-
ments. Author David Miller Dewitt stated that Stanton would "boil
over with rage whenever the course of affairs did not run to his liking."

In his memoirs, Ulysses Grant said of Stanton, "He cared nothing for the feelings of others. In fact, it seemed pleasanter to him to disappoint than gratify. He felt no hesitation in assuming the function of [President Lincoln] or in acting without advising him."

Stanton made no secret of his dislike for Abraham Lincoln. When they first met, Stanton, then a noted lawyer, treated the younger Lincoln as though he were a mere bumpkin, refused to dine with him, and called him a long-legged ape. After Lincoln was elected president, Stanton often referred to him as an imbecile.

On October 5, 1864, a Confederate prisoner, Captain James William Boyd, was transferred from Hilton Head, South Carolina, to the Old Capital Prison in Washington, D.C. The transfer was a move specifically ordered by Secretary of War Stanton.

Boyd had enlisted in the Confederate army two years earlier and, as a result of often-demonstrated competence and leadership, was soon given the responsibility of overseeing Secret Service operations in western Tennessee. Eventually, Boyd was transferred to Virginia, where he served in the same capacity. He was ultimately identified and captured by the National Detective Police in August 1863, formally charged with spying, and sent to the provost marshal's stockade in Memphis, where he was subjected to questioning for weeks.

During his incarceration, Boyd learned that his wife was sick and probably dying. At the time, she was living in Tennessee with their seven children. Boyd agreed to cooperate with the National Detective Police if he would be released for a specified time and allowed to visit his ailing spouse. A deal was made. Using Boyd's sick wife as leverage, the Federals convinced the Confederate Secret Service captain to join the Union side.

Boyd was placed on the Federal payroll and given the responsibility of reporting on Confederate prisoners' escape plans. He was moved often and may have spent time in as many as five different prisons as an undercover agent. Shortly after being sent to Port Lookout, Maryland, an old ankle wound on his right leg developed a severe infection. In need of having it drained and treated, Boyd arranged for a transfer to Hammond General Hospital on May 20, 1864.

While incarcerated at the Old Capital Prison, Boyd learned that his wife had died. He wrote a letter to Stanton requesting a transfer to Tennessee, where, he said, he was willing to serve as a spy. He informed Stanton of the death of his wife. He also wrote that his seven children were living on charity and that he wished to be near them.

On the day after receiving Boyd's letter, Stanton had the spy brought to his quarters. There, the secretary of war informed him that he would be freed if he would accept an important assignment. After listening to Stanton explain what he wanted accomplished, Boyd agreed to the duty: he was to kidnap President Abraham Lincoln.

Boyd was forty-three years old and slightly above average in height and possessed wavy, reddish-brown hair and a scraggly mustache. Facially, Boyd bore a remarkable resemblance to John Wilkes Booth. The two men also shared the same initials.

Weeks after meeting with Martin, Booth finally convinced himself that he should contact Jefferson Davis and sent him a letter via courier. As a gesture of good faith, Booth also shipped 1,000 ounces of quinine to the Confederate hospital at Richmond.

Booth eventually received instructions to travel to Montreal. On October 18, he checked into St. Lawrence Hall and met with Clement Clay and Jacob Thompson. Clay was currently serving as a senator for the Confederate States of America and was involved in the secret peace negotiations. Thompson was now the head of the Confederate Secret Service in Canada. On arriving at the Lawrence, Booth was surprised to discover that the hotel was swarming with southern agents and politicians.

During a breakfast meeting with Clay and Thompson, Booth was told that the South could certainly use his help if he were willing to undertake a dangerous assignment. Clay and Thompson informed Booth that they wanted him to organize and arrange for the kidnapping of President Abraham Lincoln. They agreed to allow the actor to select fifteen trusted men to assist him. They provided Booth with $20,000 in gold to cover the recruitment expenses. Thompson suggested that Booth contact a man named John H. Surratt Jr. for help in organizing a force capable of completing the job.

Booth accepted the assignment, and Thompson informed him that he was now part of the Confederate Secret Service. Booth was provided the uniform of a Confederate colonel. He placed the uniform in his trunk.

A short time later, Booth returned to Washington. Within one week, the $20,000 in gold promised by Thompson was clandestinely delivered by a messenger from the Union's judge advocate general's office. Now with the financial resources and the authority to undertake the mission, Booth began making earnest plans to kidnap the president.

While Booth was outlining his approach to take Lincoln, yet another plot to kidnap the president, as well as the vice president and the secretary of state, was being discussed and formulated by members of Lincoln's own party. Their intention was to make the abduction appear to be a Confederate scheme, and their aim was to imprison the abductees in the basement of the Washington mansion of Thomas Greene, brother-in-law to Confederate General L. L. Lomax. While the president was shackled, fake charges of treason were to be filed and impeachment procedures undertaken.

On or about November 1, Booth was in New York. Using some of the money provided by Thompson and Clay, he purchased carbines, revolvers, cartridges, ammunition belts, canteens, and handcuffs. All of these items were stored in a Washington boardinghouse owned and operated by Mary Surratt, the mother of John Surratt.

By early November, National Detective Police Adjutant William R. Bernard learned about Booth's plan to kidnap Lincoln from a number of informants and federal spies. He immediately informed Stanton. The secretary of war decided to wait and see how the plot developed and perhaps make an attempt to capture Booth and his accomplices. With careful planning, he considered, he might also nab some high-ranking Confederate officials.

One of the Union's principal informers was Captain James William Boyd, currently residing in the Old Capital Prison. The prison was located just beyond the east grounds of the capital. Until 1819, the building had been occupied by the U.S. Congress and was thereafter referred to as the Old Capital. When Congress was moved to newer quarters, the place was turned into a boardinghouse for senators and representatives. When the Civil War broke out, it became a military prison.

It is believed that Boyd learned of Booth's plans for kidnapping from Rebel inmates during the course of his normal duties as a prison spy. Little did Boyd or anyone else know at the time that he was soon to become deeply and inextricably involved in the tragic events of the future.

In late November, according to George S. Bryan, Booth traveled into southern Maryland to Bryantown, where he presented a letter of introduction from Patrick Martin to Dr. William Queen. Booth reputedly suggested to Queen that he might be interested in purchasing some land in Charles County.

Queen introduced the actor to a number of residents, including Dr. Samuel A. Mudd. Mudd, thirty-one, owned a prosperous farm in

Dr. Samuel A. Mudd
Library of Congress, Prints
& Photographs Division,
LC-USZ62-15116

the county, one that he inherited from his father and one to which he devoted a great deal of time and energy while he also conducted a small medical practice. Mudd took Booth on a tour of the nearby countryside and introduced him to other residents. During the tour, Booth purchased an old, one-eyed bay saddle horse from a neighbor.

Mudd and Booth met once again on December 23. During this visit, the two men were walking toward the H Street boardinghouse of Mary Surratt when they happened to encounter her son, John. The younger Surratt was in the company of Louis Weichmann, one of Mrs. Surratt's boarders. Mudd introduced Booth to Surratt. John Surratt, a committed southerner, spent time traveling between Canada and the South arranging deals for weapons, ammunition, and medicine.

After exchanging conversation and philosophies relative to the present political administration, Booth and Surratt agreed to begin recruiting a kidnap force. Booth was overjoyed to find Surratt eager to participate in the project.

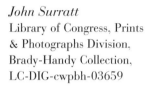

John Surratt
Library of Congress, Prints
& Photographs Division,
Brady-Handy Collection,
LC-DIG-cwpbh-03659

Weichmann was a government employee and a self-appointed informant. As he gradually learned about the plot to kidnap the president, he passed information on to Captain D. H. L. Gleason, a War Department officer.

During his stay in Washington, Booth visited a shooting gallery to practice his marksmanship. Close friends remarked that Booth was an excellent shot.

Booth soon made a trip to Richmond, where he met with former Louisiana Senator Judah Benjamin. Benjamin had served, at various times, as Confederate attorney general, secretary of state, and secretary of war. Benjamin introduced Booth to Confederate Vice President Alexander Stephens, and together the three men went to see President Jefferson Davis. Davis provided Booth with a $70,000 draft and asked him if he would use it to arrange the movement of southern cotton to northern speculators. He also requested assistance in moving northern meat to the armies of the South.

Benjamin arranged a meeting between Booth and bankers Jay and Henry Cooke in Philadelphia. The two financiers introduced Booth to several other men—senators, political bosses, lawyers, and cotton brokers. As the conversation progressed, it became increasingly clear to Booth that many of Lincoln's close friends and presumed allies were speculating in cotton and gold with the South. Among them, according to information uncovered by Balsiger and Sellier, was Lincoln's trusted friend Ward Lamon.

Lamon, who was responsible for obtaining Lincoln's signatures on numerous documents during the course of a week, told those assembled that it was a small matter to get the president to sign cotton passes. Lincoln, he said, seldom looked at what he was signing. Booth later recorded an entry in his diary relative to the fact that each of the men at this meeting had business dealings with the Confederate States of America and, as long as a profit could be made, would continue to do so.

Booth asked the men how he could be of service. In response, Jay Cooke handed him two letters, both written in code, and asked the actor to deliver them to Confederate agents Beverly Tucker and Jacob Thompson in Montreal. Booth took the letters and left for Canada.

As Booth was signing the register at St. Lawrence Hall for the second time, he was startled to see Confederate agent Tucker leaving the hotel in the company of Colonel Lafayette Baker, chief of the National Detective Police, the precursor to the Secret Service. Booth went immediately to the room of Confederate agent George N. Sanders and reported what he saw.

Sanders excused himself and returned several minutes later with Tucker. Booth, uncomfortable not knowing what was going on, listened in silence as the two men spoke with one another. Presently,

Lafayette C. Baker
R. Whitechurch, Library of Congress, Prints & Photographs Division, LC-USZ62-49959

Canadian Secret Service chief Jacob Thompson arrived carrying a black leather satchel. Booth eventually produced the coded letters and gave one each to Thompson and Tucker.

After the letters were decoded, Thompson handed Booth the satchel and told him it contained $50,000 in banknotes and the $15,000 in cash, all of which was to be delivered to California Senator John Conness. There was an additional $20,000 to be delivered to Senator Benjamin Wade, a staunch critic of McClellan and close friend of Secretary of War Stanton. The rest of the money, explained Thompson, was to be used by Booth for recruiting men.

Booth returned to Washington with the satchel, deeply confused yet exhilarated at the promise of adventure and notoriety. Delighted to be involved in advancing the cause of the South, Booth was nevertheless amazed at the machinations and deceptions of the Washington politicians.

On December 11, Ward Lamon repeated his warning to the president that his life was in danger and that he needed to take more precautions against kidnap and assassination. Lincoln, however, continued to attend the theater with little or no provision for his safety.

Lincoln truly enjoyed the theater, and at the time Washington had several: Grover's on Pennsylvania Avenue, Canterbury Music Hall, Oxford Hall, Seaton Hall, and the most popular, Ford's Theater on Tenth Street.

Along with others, Major Thomas Eckert, general superintendent of the Military Telegraph Corps and aide to Stanton, also received information of Booth's role in the kidnap plot. Eventually, Lincoln was provided with an armed escort of cavalrymen when he went on trips. William B. Webb, the Washington chief of police, appointed four officers to guard the president: all the men—Alphonso Dunn, Thomas Pendel, Alexander Smith, and John Parker—were armed with revolvers and ordered to stand between the president and danger at all times.

John Parker was an odd choice to guard the president. Formerly with the Metropolitan Police, Parker was a known malcontent, prone to use coarse language, and was of questionable character. Throughout his brief service as a D.C. policeman, he had an unimpressive, even puzzling record. He had been twice charged with conduct unbecoming an officer, willful violation of police regulations, sleeping on duty, insubordination, and visiting a brothel. Parker, like Captain Boyd, was destined to play a significant role in future events.

According to Balsiger and Sellier, Booth, on returning to Washington, delivered the packets of money to Conness and Wade. During his meeting with Conness, the senator told Booth he was aware of the plans to kidnap the president and suggested he could be of some assistance. He also told Booth that not only the president should be abducted but also the vice president and the secretary of state. Booth expressed surprise at this development and asked why, but Conness told him only that the reasons were to remain confidential for the time being.

Booth reasoned that Conness was in league with the Radical Republicans who wanted to control the government and exploit the South. He was also well aware that Conness had a great deal of money at his disposal. Booth did not particularly like the planters because their goal in removing Lincoln was profit motivated. Conness's plan, determined Booth, would go a long way in bargaining for the release of Confederate prisoners. Booth actually cared little for Conness and even less for his politics, but he agreed to cooperate and asked the senator how he planned to help.

Conness replied that he and his accomplices were quite intimate with the daily schedules and movements of the men targeted for kidnap. Booth was told that if all three could not be abducted, the president must be the first. At one time, Booth was completely unaware of the Radicals' plan to seize control of the executive branch, take charge of reconstruction, prevent the Democrats from dominating Congress, and deny the inauguration to the southern-leaning McClellan.

Convinced that Conness's plan could be successful, Booth began enlisting the help of others. He quickly recruited two of his boyhood friends—Samuel Bland Arnold and Michael O'Laughlin. Booth had known O'Laughlin while living at Bel Air. O'Laughlin was twenty-four years old, employed as an engraver, and known to have a serious drinking problem. Arnold was a classmate at St. Timothy's. Both men had served as Confederate soldiers, and O'Laughlin once assisted Booth in smuggling quinine and other medicines into the South.

Booth explained to his two friends that he planned to kidnap Lincoln. In fact, Booth had two plans, each based on opportunity. One would be to capture the president on the road during one of his visits to the theater at the Soldiers Home, located three miles from the White House. The other plan, which Booth considered the better of the two, would be to grab Lincoln while he was attending a play at Ford's Theater.

Samuel Bland Arnold
Library of Congress, Prints
& Photographs Division,
Civil War Photograph
Collection, LC-DIG-
cwpb-04213

Booth also acquired the services of David Edgar Herold and George Andreas Atzerodt. Herold was an unemployed man of twenty-three years of age who lived with his widowed mother and seven sisters. Herold had no particular skills other than that he was intimate with many of the roads of Washington and southern Maryland. Herold once worked as a clerk in a drugstore but was currently unemployed. He spent most of his days wandering the streets of Washington and most of his nights standing outside the theaters. Although an adult, Herold was regarded as far more of a boy than a man. Family friends described him as callow and a bit of a simpleton. He has been described by writer Dewitt as "light and trifling, unreliable" and easily manipulated. During his trial subsequent to his later capture, Herold was referred to in court by his lawyer, Frederick Stone, as having the mind of an eleven-year-old boy. Subsequent research, however, revealed that Herold had been educated at Charlotte Hall Academy and that he may have attended Georgetown College for a time. Georgetown was then—and still is—a highly regarded institution of higher education.

Atzerodt was a German immigrant and worked as a carriage painter in a coach-building shop established by his brother, John, at Port Tobacco in Wicomico County, Maryland, on the Potomac. Atzerodt owned a boat that he kept there and sometimes used to ferry southern-

David Herold
Library of Congress, Prints
& Photographs Division,
Civil War Photograph Col-
lection, LC-USZ62-121530

George Atzerodt
Library of Congress,
Prints & Photographs
Division, Civil War Photo-
graph Collection, LC-
USZ62-22995

ers and mail bound to and from Richmond across the Potomac River. He was also a smuggler and known to transport contraband. Atzerodt was a rough-looking, solid man who spoke with a heavy German accent. According to Dewitt, he was "fierce in appearance and talk, but cowardly at heart." According to Roscoe, he was "earthy," "a clod," "a lout," and "crude," and he ate with his knife. Although Atzerodt was recruited by Booth to be a member of the kidnap plot, the German's motivation was related more to getting paid for his services than to any commitment to the southern cause.

With the recruitment of Herold and Atzerodt, Booth studied a number of possible escape routes. After rejecting several possibilities, he settled on a flight across the Navy Yard Bridge that crossed the Potomac River at the end of Eleventh Street. Once decided on this route, he then planned several alternative ones.

Booth then recruited Edman "Ned" Spangler. Spangler was a part-time stagehand, sceneshifter, and carpenter at Ford's Theater. He also groomed Booth's horse and once worked for the Booth family. Spangler has been described by Roscoe as a "composite of ignorance, incompetence, poverty, sloth, turpitude, distemper, and alcoholism." Should Booth decide to snatch Lincoln while the president was attending a play, Spangler could prove to be a valuable asset. He could control the lights and, as he knew the stage, could help transport the president through the dark. It is believed that Booth paid Spangler off with drinks.

Booth also recruited Lewis Thornton Powell, who went by several aliases, including Payne (sometimes spelled Paine), Wood, Hull, Kincheloe, and Mosby. Powell, the youngest of Booth's henchmen, had served as a soldier in the Confederacy and rode with Mosby's Raiders. He was from Tallahassee, Florida; the son of a Baptist preacher; and one of nine children. Powell was known to be a hard-shell fundamentalist and an avowed racist. Roscoe stated Powell had the strength of a giant and the "instincts of a panther."

Powell fought at Antietam, Chancellorsville, Richmond, and Gettysburg. He was wounded at the latter, taken prisoner, escaped, and rejoined the Rebel army. In January 1865, Powell, after losing two brothers at Murfreesboro, made his way to Alexandria, where he took an oath of allegiance to the United States.

Powell was a fan of the theater and would attend performances when he could afford a ticket. The first time he ever saw a play was one evening while he was stationed in Richmond. John Wilkes Booth

Edman "Ned" Spangler
Library of Congress, Prints
& Photographs Division,
LC-USZ62-22994

*Lewis Powell aka
Lewis Payne*
Library of Congress, Prints
& Photographs Division,
LC-B8171-7772

was the featured actor and made a lasting impression on the young man. Following the performance, Powell initiated a conversation with the actor. The two men, so different in so many ways, became friends. Powell later arrived in Washington. He was homeless, penniless, and dressed in rags but was taken in by Booth, who provided him with food, clothing, and money.

Powell was tall, heavily muscled, and extremely strong. Coarse dark hair was parted low on the left side of his head, his eyes were dark, and his complexion was ruddy. One side of his face had been disfigured as the result of a kick from a mule. It has been concluded by a number of researchers that Powell was deranged, even psychotic.

Not only had Booth given Powell money and a place to live, but he provided the former Confederate soldier with a plan whereby he could exact revenge on the hated Yankees. In Booth's scenario, the muscular Powell was the only man strong enough to carry Lincoln.

Ultimately, the members of Booth's kidnap conspiracy included Arnold, Atzerodt, Herold, O'Laughlin, Powell, John Surratt, and Ned Spangler. In addition to these men, it is believed that the actor received promises of aid from Dr. William T. Bowman, John C. Thompson, Samuel Cox, and Thomas Jones.

In time, Louis Weichmann, the friend of John Surratt and a resident of Mary Surratt's boardinghouse on Sixth and H streets, gleaned bits of the plot and reported the names of those involved to Captain Gleason, the War Department officer. Weichmann also specified that the plotters intended to spirit Lincoln out of Washington by way of the Navy Yard Bridge. Gleason immediately relayed this information to Army Intelligence Headquarters, but they ignored it.

Weichmann's motives for reporting Booth and his conspirators to officials have long been debated. Some refer to Weichmann as a patriotic and concerned citizen. Others point to the fact that Weichmann once attempted to court Mary Surratt's daughter, Anna, who also resided at the boardinghouse. Anna, however, was infatuated with the charming and dashing Booth. Once, while Weichmann was conversing with Anna in the parlor of the boardinghouse, she became offended at something he said and slapped him hard across the face. It has been speculated that the rebuffed Weichmann sought vengeance against Booth and the Surratts as a result of his rejection by the girl.

Booth was enjoying his role as the leader of the kidnap plot. He envisioned himself a hero in the abduction of the president of the United States and the ultimate release of the Confederate prisoners. The actor's ego swelled at the possibilities of fame far greater than what the stage could ever deliver. His craving for recognition and notoriety burned within, and he continued to feed the fire.

Booth had played Ford's Theater on numerous occasions. For several afternoons in a row during December 1864, he entered the building and undertook an intense study of how the kidnapping should progress. He determined that, once the lights were lowered, Lincoln could be grabbed in his private box with his hands cuffed, lowered to the stage, carried bodily out into the alley, placed in a carriage, and spirited toward the Navy Yard Bridge and Maryland. Despite often-expressed discouragement from his coconspirators, particularly Arnold and O'Laughlin, Booth was convinced that such a plan could work. Rather than becoming discouraged by the others, he grew even more excited and eager.

David Herold was given the responsibility of assembling a team of horses to be used as a relay, if necessary, on the southern bank of the Anacostia River near the Navy Yard Bridge. John Surratt was sent to tell Atzeroldt at Port Tobacco to have a flatboat at the ready to receive the carriage bearing the kidnapped president.

Booth gathered materials he believed necessary to carry out the plot: handcuffs, ropes, and a gag. He arranged to have them stored in a room at the National Hotel. He also provided for a carriage to be pulled up in the alley next to the stage door at a signal from one of the recruits.

As the plan evolved, Booth decided that he and Surratt, on the dimming of the house lights, would enter the presidential box, grab Lincoln, gag and handcuff him, and then lower him to the stage using ropes. From there, he was to be lifted by Powell and rushed out the backstage door, placed into the carriage, and transported to Maryland. Booth decided that the evening of January 18, 1865, would be the best time to take the president.

Men and equipment were readied, and minute by minute the tension mounted. That night, however, it rained and stormed, and Lincoln chose not to attend the theater.

During the first week of March 1865, Booth was surprised and stunned to discover that he was being removed as the leader of the plot to kidnap the president. His sources informed him that he was to be replaced by a Confederate officer now in league with the Union. The following morning, Booth met with James V. Barnes, speculator and cotton broker, and vented his frustration.

Booth was outraged by his dismissal as the leader of the plot. His chance for glory was gone, vanished, and his actor ego was reeling at the cancellation. After all of the work he had invested in the plan, to be treated in such a manner made him furious. Booth exploded at Barnes, pacing and screaming and telling him repeatedly that he refused to be replaced. He claimed that the entire plot was his own creation, a product of his investment of time, energy, and money, and that he refused to step down as leader.

Barnes, who stood to gain significantly in cotton contracts if the Radical Republicans took over, told Booth there was nothing that could be done. He also stated that the Confederate States of America were going to fall and would be of no help whatsoever.

Steaming with rage and anger, Booth cursed Barnes and Lincoln. Red-faced, incensed, and indignant, the actor stormed out of the room. Booth's hatred for the president now grew in intensity such that it twisted his face in wrath and anguish. Although Booth tried on several occasions to learn the identity of the man who had been assigned to replace him as the leader of the kidnap plot, he was unsuccessful. That man was Captain James William Boyd.

In front of others, Booth tried to pretend that his removal was not affecting him. From some of his own well-placed sources, he learned that the new leader planned to take Lincoln not to Richmond as the actor had planned but rather to Bloodsworth Island in the Chesapeake Bay, where he was to be killed by Union agents.

Booth seethed because everything had been taken away from him. He now believed it imperative that he had to get to the president before the others. He saw it as his duty, and he would not give it up. He was determined not to allow this chance at eternal fame to be snatched away from him.

By February, things were not going well for the South. The Confederates were losing their last vital port at Wilmington, North Carolina. After burning, looting, and destroying a significant portion of the state of Georgia, General William Tecumseh Sherman was doing the same to South Carolina and was on his way to North Carolina. The Confederate command of Jubal Early was about to be wiped out by General Phillip Sheridan, and Grant was threatening Richmond.

On March 4, Lincoln was sworn in as president for his second term. The inaugural activities were held in the eastern portico of the Capitol

Building. Booth, having obtained a pass from New Hampshire Senator John Hale, was present at the ceremony.

After being given the oath of office by Chief Justice Salmon P. Chase, Lincoln gave his address. As the president spoke, Booth managed to gain a position immediately above and behind him. He was looking down on Lincoln as he completed his address.

According to Benn Pittman in *The Assassination of President Lincoln and the Trial of the Conspirators*, Booth proclaimed to a friend several days later that he had "an elegant chance . . . to kill the president . . . if I wished."

By March, Captain James William Boyd had returned from Canada, where he met and reviewed kidnap arrangements with several ranking officials. After moving into a residence in Maryland, he began making preparations to implement the plan he had been assigned to carry out. Relative to his mission, Boyd discreetly made inquiries about specific routes and roads. During this time, the wound in his right ankle was giving him trouble. It was not healing properly, forcing Boyd to move about on crutches.

Booth determined that his plot to kidnap the president was still viable, and he continued to curse the circumstances that had led to his dismissal. With bruised ego and growing anger, he decided to go ahead with his original mission, a plan that he was convinced would catapult him ahead of his rivals, one that would make him known to the world.

Booth revised his plot somewhat. His new plan began to take shape during the second week of March. He decided that he would grab the president at Grover's Theater on the evening of March 15. On March 13, however, the actor read in the newspaper that Lincoln was ill. Booth presumed the president would be unable to attend the theater, so he canceled the preparations. As it turned out, Lincoln recovered sufficiently to go to Grover's Theater.

The next day, Booth summoned O'Laughlin, Surratt, and Powell and informed them of his latest plan. He arranged for Powell and Surratt, accompanied by their dates, to attend the performance of *Jane Shore* at Ford's Theater on the evening of March 15. The tickets were for seats in the presidential box. During intermission, Booth visited his accomplices, and together they thoroughly examined the configuration, layout, ingresses, and egresses.

It is believed that while Booth was examining the theater, David Herold traveled to Surrattsville, ten miles southeast of Washington in

Prince Georges County, Maryland. There, he went to Surratt's Tavern, owned by Mary Surratt, where he met with Atzeroldt and John Surratt. Before leaving, the three men deposited a bundle of guns and other gear with proprietor John Lloyd, who hid them in an upstairs room.

Late one evening several days later following a performance, Booth met with Arnold, Atzerodt, Herold, O'Laughlin, Powell, Surratt, and James Wood in a back room of Gautier's Restaurant. Booth unrolled a floor plan of Ford's Theater and explained his kidnapping strategy. Most of those at the gathering were stunned at the sheer boldness of the plot and voiced concern that it was too dangerous and unrealistic and had little chance for success. Surratt argued that the government was aware of a plot to kidnap the president and suggested the plan be scrapped for the time being.

At this, Booth's ego took yet another blow. He was still reeling as a result of being replaced as leader of the northern kidnap plot, and he was determined to get to the president before his replacement.

Booth was also infuriated with the lack of cooperation he was getting from his fellow conspirators and even angrier that they dared to question his decisions. He was gradually losing control not only of his accomplices but also of himself.

The following morning, Booth learned that Lincoln was to attend a play at 2:00 p.m. at the Seventh Street Hospital. The entertainment was designed for the wounded soldiers being treated there. The skies had been growing dark and menacing all day, the wind was picking up, and the temperature was dropping rapidly.

Booth, accompanied by Arnold, Atzerodt, Herold, O'Laughlin, Powell, Surratt, and Wood, were mounted and riding toward the hospital by 1:30 p.m. All were armed. They reined up in a grove of trees adjacent to a curve in the road. From this vantage point, they could observe the approach of anyone travelling toward the hospital.

According to Roscoe, Booth, accompanied by Surratt, would ride out into the road in front of the presidential carriage when it came around the curve. The rest of the conspirators were to assume a position behind the carriage. Surratt was to grab the coachman, divest him of his clothes, and replace his own with them. Arnold, Atzerodt, Herold, O'Laughlin, and Wood were to occupy the cavalry escort while Booth and Powell cuffed and gagged Lincoln.

As the men awaited the presidential carriage, a hard sleet began to fall. Sitting astride their horses, they were growing cold and uncomfortable and anxious for something to happen. Presently, the sound of an approaching vehicle was heard, and each man tensed as they waited in silence. Suddenly, Booth and Surratt spurred their mounts out onto the road and were quickly followed by the others, who took positions behind the carriage. As he peered into the window, Booth was startled to discover that the occupant was not Lincoln at all but rather Salmon P. Chase.

Foiled again, the conspirators fled. Like the previous two kidnap attempts, the third was a failure. Booth learned the next day that Lincoln had been attending a ceremony at the National Hotel, where he presented a battle flag to the governor of Indiana.

Shortly after the third failed kidnap attempt, Arnold and O'Laughlin decided to leave Booth. They were growing concerned that the actor's expanding ego and sometimes loose and overzealous approach to abducting the president would get them all in trouble. They told him that they believed the plan was a losing proposition and recommended that he abandon it. Booth refused to listen to the advice from his two friends, and he continued to pursue his scheme with renewed vigor.

Booth and his remaining conspirators made yet a fourth attempt to kidnap Lincoln. Unfortunately for them, the president was surrounded by a contingent of armed cavalry—yet another setback.

On March 19, Conness provided Booth with some information about Lincoln's movements. Gathering his remaining associates, the actor rode to a predetermined location to await the passage of the president, but he never appeared.

Frustrated and angered by the repeated failures, Booth grew increasingly discouraged and began drinking more than normal. He was often seen in Taltavul's Tavern, a restaurant and saloon adjoining Ford's Theater, consuming large amounts of brandy and growing irascible and humorless.

On the morning of March 20, Booth received word about another movement. He assembled his men and, hidden among some trees, waited for the president at a selected ambush site. As they lay concealed some distance from the road, word was delivered to Booth that the authorities were aware of his plan. The men fled, and Booth began to suspect he was being set up.

During the next few days as he fumed over his sixth failure, Booth found fault with everyone but himself. He was growing suspicious of those around him and was certain someone was plotting his undoing. His suspicions eventually centered on Conness, whom he had distrusted from the beginning. Gradually, Booth convinced himself that the California senator wanted him out of the picture altogether.

A few days later, Booth, armed with a carbine and accompanied by Powell and Surratt, acted on information provided by an unknown source. The three men took up a position in a grove of trees alongside a road a short distance from the White House. Presently, a group of horsemen came cantering down the road. The three conspirators immediately recognized Lincoln, who was surrounded by an armed escort. It is not clear whether the original intent of the three men was to kidnap or assassinate. In any event, Booth raised his rifle and fired. The bullet struck Lincoln's hat, knocking it from his head. Powell fired twice, missing both times—one more failure.

In addition to becoming frustrated, Booth was now growing desperate. He was seeing his opportunities for fame and notoriety fading.

Several days following the last attempt at the president, Booth, while in the company of Powell, was paid a visit by Colonel Everton J. Conger. Conger told Booth that he knew of the attempt to ambush the president, accused him of being reckless, and called him a fool. He reminded him that he had been dropped from the kidnap plot too.

Angrily, Booth informed Conger that he was now acting on his own. He told his visitor that it was he, Booth, who had designed the plan to abduct Lincoln and that he intended to see it through. Conger responded by telling Booth in no uncertain terms that if he did not remove himself from the scene, he and his friends would be eliminated.

On April 2, the Union army took Petersburg, Virginia, and Richmond was only hours away from falling. Booth fumed. His original plan and motives for kidnapping the president were now completely useless. While meeting with the speculators in New York, Booth blamed National Detective Police commander Lafayette Baker. Booth insisted that once the South had fallen, Baker would likely betray the businessmen, arrest them, and perhaps even have them killed. He insisted that something must be done and soon. The speculators told Booth to return to Washington and await further instructions.

Lafayette Baker bothered Booth. Named by Stanton to be chief of the nation's Secret Service, Baker established offices in the Treasury Building and, with help from the secretary of war, formed an army of some 2,900 secret agents and developed a sophisticated intelligence network.

Although a relatively unknown historical figure to most Americans, Baker is regarded by scholars as one of the more powerful Union figures who worked behind the scenes during the Civil War. Baker was thirty-eight years old, average height, and slender with gray eyes and a full beard. He never drank alcohol and was never known to use profane language. He was considered a superb horseman and an expert marksman. Even Baker's foremost detractors regarded him as an excellent detective.

Baker was also egotistical, ambitious, and considered by most to be untrustworthy. As chief of the National Detective Police, he introduced for the first time in America's law enforcement history the concepts of midnight raids, entry without warrant, summary arrests, and imprisonment without bail. Baker's National Detective Police was also credited with unbridled corruption, including bribery and blackmail. Baker himself was known to lie, cheat, and employ whatever means necessary to accomplish his goals. He once admitted that he had Secretary of War Stanton's telegraph lines tapped. Many of his contemporaries hated him for his deception and intimidating practices.

On April 9, General Robert E. Lee surrendered to General Grant at Appomattox. The war was now over. Booth was stricken with the news, crushed. He believed that Lee never should have surrendered, that he committed a gross error in judgment, and that victory was inevitable. He was now convinced that politicians would swoop into the South and strip it bare. He lamented in his diary that "all we have planned and striven for has come for naught . . . I believe Eckert, Baker, and the Secretary [Stanton] are in control of our activities."

Booth was persuaded that Stanton believed that removing Lincoln would ensure his remaining in office as secretary of war. With the war over, Stanton would be concerned that Lincoln might not need him any longer. Booth believed that if Stanton remained in office and was placed in charge of reconstruction and the military government of the South, he would become the most powerful man in the country. As the nation's most influential man, Stanton then stood an excellent chance of being elected to the presidency. The faithful Eckert, Stanton's assistant and chief of the War Department Telegraph Office, would most assuredly accompany Stanton in his rise to power.

Lafayette Baker would likewise advance his prestige in government since he would be in charge of Secret Service operations in the South as well as the North. Although essentially unknown to the American public, one of Baker's chief duties was the protection of the president.

Booth was nervous because he knew that Baker was aware of his plans to abduct Lincoln, and the actor was not certain whether the National Detective Police commander was friend or foe.

FOUR

♦♦♦

Plot to Assassinate

On April 10, 1865, Lafayette Baker sought an audience with Secretary of War Stanton and told him that he had obtained information about a plot to assassinate President Lincoln. The information was based on secret ciphers provided by Major Thomas Eckert. Eckert, in charge of federal ciphers, had years of experience decoding Confederate messages. Baker told Stanton that the attempt was to take place on April 14. Stanton, however, told Baker that he did not believe the information was accurate and dismissed him.

The next day, Stanton called Baker back into his office and told him that he was in possession of information that linked him, Baker, to the assassination plot. Baker, of course, denied it.

The following morning, Baker met with National Detective Police agent Earl Potter, who told him that he believed Stanton was insane and that the secretary hated Lincoln. Baker replied that he was convinced Stanton was ultimately responsible for the assassination plot that had recently been uncovered. He also expressed the concern that, if it happened, he, Baker, would be blamed for it.

Booth, disheartened by the surrender of the South, was now deeply concerned for his own safety and may have feared for his life. Among the lost pages from Booth's diary that were found in 1977 in the possession of Stanton's descendants, the actor wrote that he was now determined to kill the president and that he "shall lay the body of this tyrant dead upon the altar of [Stanton]. If by this fact I am slain, they too shall be cast into hell, for I have given information to a friend who will have the nation know who the traitors are."

A short time later, Booth received another message from the New York speculators. After reading it, he made an entry in his diary that mentioned a new plan. More important, he was to be in charge. On the morning of April 12, Booth was seen in Deery's Saloon drinking heavily, one brandy after another.

That evening, President Lincoln delivered a speech from the Executive Mansion in which he promised citizenship for the freed slaves. In the audience were Booth and David Herold. Booth, enraged at the president's message, turned to Herold and stated, "That means nigger citizenship. Now, by God, I'll put him through." He returned to Deery's and, as was now his pattern, drank more.

In today's terminology, Booth would have been regarded as a white supremacist. He was rigidly proslavery and was persuaded that the abolition movement was the real and only cause of the Civil War. He was convinced that slavery was natural and condoned by God.

Captain James William Boyd was keeping busy acquiring riding stock in Prince Georges County, Maryland. During this undertaking, Boyd learned that a retired Confederate officer named Thomas H. Watkins attempted to rape the wife of one of his close friends. Boyd took sudden leave of his duties to search for Watkins. When he found him, he shot him in the back of the head, killing him instantly. A soldier named John H. Boyle was blamed for the crime, but Boyd eventually confessed his guilt. As a result of this mix-up, a few historians have confused Boyd with Boyle. Although Boyd's superiors learned about the murder, they did nothing. His current assignment, they reasoned, took precedence over having him arrested for killing Watkins.

Booth continued to drink more and more, and the liquor continued to fuel his southern passions, which flared and sometimes exploded. He grew increasingly and visibly frustrated. He loudly blamed Lincoln for everything bad that was happening, and his hatred for the president only deepened.

On the morning of April 13, Booth encountered a fellow actor named E. A. Emerson. The two men spoke briefly about Lincoln and the surrender of the South. During the conversation, according to Emerson, Booth referred to Lincoln and stated, "Somebody ought to kill the old scoundrel."

After rising at 7:30 a.m. on the morning of April 14, Booth had breakfast in the dining room of the National Hotel. Following his meal, he walked to the barbershop, where he was shaved between 9:00 and 10:00. While at the barbershop, he encountered Henry Johnson, his black valet, as well as O'Laughlin and Surratt. Booth, O'Laughlin, and Surratt returned to the National Hotel, arriving around 10:30 a.m., where they conversed privately. According to a statement made later by O'Laughlin, Booth told the men that the next time Lincoln attended a play at Ford's Theater, a soldier would enter his box during the intermission at the end of the second act and tell him that his presence was needed at the War Department. The guards, said Booth, will be lured away, drugged, and replaced by others friendly to the cause.

Outside the theater, Booth continued, the president would be placed in a carriage and escorted by a troop of cavalry to the homes of Secretary Seward and Vice President Johnson, both of whom would be forced to join Lincoln in the vehicle. The carriage would then be led out of Washington to Maryland by way of the Navy Yard Bridge through Surrattsville and Bryantown and on to Benedict's Landing on the Patuxent River, an arm of the Chesapeake Bay. There, the three were to be loaded onto an awaiting ship.

Booth, now excited and very animated, was revived by this plan that he believed was daring, risky, dashing, and original. Important to Booth, it was also dramatic. In his current state of mind, the actor envisioned himself a national hero.

Booth told O'Laughlin and Surratt that following the abduction, the prisoners would be hidden at an unspecified location. Booth would then proceed to Europe, where he had arranged for bank credits in England and France. He informed his two coconspirators that he had made arrangements for a ship to pick him up at Port Tobacco and take him to the Bahamas. Six weeks after the abduction, he told them, arrangements would be made to have the two men rendezvous with him in England.

Booth excused himself from O'Laughlin and Surratt, went to the home of Mrs. Surratt, and visited with her for several minutes. It was Good Friday, and she was preparing to attend services at St. Patrick's Catholic Church. As the two spoke, Mary spotted Louis Weichmann eavesdropping on their conversation. Mary ordered Weichmann to go retrieve her horse and buggy. For reasons not clear, Booth presented Mary with a telescope wrapped in brown paper. Moments later, Booth left the boardinghouse and walked to Ford's Theater, arriving just before noon.

Ford's Theater was a rather impressive three-story brick building located on Washington's Tenth Street. Originally a Baptist church, it was abandoned in 1861 and neglected. In 1861, John T. Ford, a Baltimore producer, envisioned its possibilities as a theater and leased

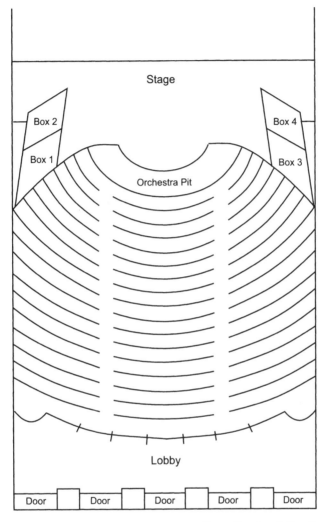

Orchestra and parquet seating (first floor) of Ford's Theater

the structure, named it the Athenaeum, and featured plays. It burned to the ground in December 1862, and Ford rebuilt it to his own specifications.

Ford's Theater reopened in August 1863 and was regarded as one of the top theaters in the country. Before long, it became one of Washington's most popular showplaces. Abraham Lincoln, seeking diversion

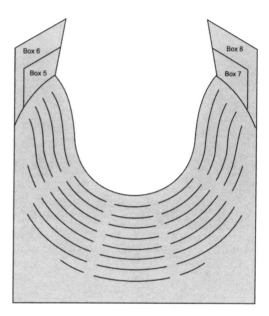

Dress circle (second floor)
of Ford's Theater

from his heavy responsibilities, often attended dramatic productions there.

Behind the theater was an alley, called "Baptist's Alley," which was approximately thirty feet wide. Two hundred yards away were some stables. According to later testimony, Mrs. Mary J. Anderson, a black woman who lived in a dwelling that fronted the alley, testified later that she watched Booth walk through the alley and down to the stables, where he kept a horse.

Booth entered the lobby of Ford's Theater to pick up his mail. Tom Raybold, a ticket salesman, handed the actor several letters and a package. As Booth was sifting through his letters, James Clifford, a stage carpenter, arrived in response to a summons from James Ford. Within earshot of Booth, the manager informed Clifford of the president's plans to attend the performance that evening and instructed him to make certain that the presidential box was in order.

After reading his mail, Booth walked to the stables on C Street operated by James W. Pumphrey, a friend of John Surratt's, and rented a small bay mare with a black mane and tail and a white spot on her forehead. Pumphrey warned Booth that the mare was high-strung and sometimes snapped her bridle when hitched. It was better, he explained, to have someone hold the reins, or she would break free.

Booth accepted the mare and told the stable owner he would return for her at 4:00 p.m.

While Booth was making arrangements to lease the horse, a theater employee was pasting up a poster containing the information that the president and his party would be attending that evening. He placed it in the box office, where it could be seen by passersby. This done, he hastily prepared newspaper ads and handbills that were distributed around town.

Around 1:00 p.m., Booth returned to Ford's Theater and spotted the poster and the information pertaining to the president's attendance. His rage and fury grew. He turned and hastened to Deery's Saloon in nearby Grover's Theater, where he ordered a bottle of whiskey and drafted a letter to James C. Welling, the editor of the *National Intelligencer*. The letter, a copy of which is located in a private collection belonging to Stanton's descendants, began with the sentence, "By the time you read this, I will either have accomplished my purpose or be myself beyond the reach of any man's hand." He also wrote of loving peace more than his own life. Toward the end of the letter, he wrote that Lincoln's acceptance of the blacks as citizens was preparing the way for "total annihilation" and that Lincoln's government "is the most corrupt in the nation's history."

Booth also provided the names of thirty-five men whom he identified as wishing to "exploit the now bloody, defeated Southern states." The names included Lamon, several major senators, military officers, the Speaker of the House, judges, bankers, and businessmen. After signing his own name, he added those of Atzerodt, Herold, and Powell. He folded the letter, placed it in a pocket, and departed the saloon.

Returning to the National Hotel, Booth went to his room, bathed, and then walked to the Kirkwood House, where Vice President Johnson was staying. There, he left a message for Johnson's secretary, Colonel Browning, and walked out. A few minutes later, Browning walked in, received the message, and went to his room. Learning that Browning had returned, Booth went back to the Kirkwood House and sent a bellhop to inform the secretary that he awaited an audience with him. The bellhop returned a few minutes later and informed Booth in a curt manner that Browning was not in.

Enraged at being refused an audience, Booth stormed out of the hotel. He went to a nearby saloon where he encountered an acquaintance named Ed Henson, who invited him to have a drink. Henson was a shadowy, rather elusive figure. Virtually all that is known of him prior to the assassination is that he was occasionally involved with Booth in smuggling contraband into the South.

As the two men drank whiskey, they lamented that, with the end of the war, they would no longer have an opportunity to earn money as smugglers. Henson, who closely resembled David Herold but was somewhat older, told Booth that he was going to miss the excitement. Booth told him that the excitement was just about to begin and invited Henson to participate.

Booth left the saloon and went to a room at the Herndon House, where he found Powell. He informed his compatriot that something was in the works and told him that it was important to meet back there that evening. He also told Powell that a horse would be tied in the stable behind Ford's Theater.

At Ford's Theater, workmen were preparing the presidential box. During the mid-1800s, theater boxes were much different from the somewhat more spacious lodges of playhouses that were constructed years later. The older boxes extended a bit over the stage and were separated from the rest of the auditorium not by curtains but by doors that could be locked.

The pine partition between the theater's box numbers 7 and 8 was removed, and a sofa and three extra chairs were brought in. A fourth chair—a black walnut rocker with seat, arms, and back upholstered in red damask—was placed in the box next to the wall screening it from the balcony audience and approximately four feet from the door. The rocker was reserved for Lincoln, who would sit close to the audience and about nine feet directly above the stage apron (some sources say twelve feet).

Access to the boxes could be had only via the south side of the second floor, and entry was through a single white door that led into a small antechamber. Next to this door, a cane-bottomed chair was placed for the White House guard. Anyone wishing to reach Lincoln would have to pass by the guard. A U.S. flag borrowed from the Treasury Department was draped across the front of the presidential box. Centered just above the flag hung a picture of George Washington.

Sometime during the day, Booth entered the president's box, from which he observed the actors in rehearsal. Using a knife, he carved a small niche in the plaster wall just inside the corridor. This was to accommodate a length of wood that would be used to secure the door. Using a gimlet—a small tool with a screw point, grooved shank, and

Presidential box, Ford's Theater
Library of Congress, Prints & Photographs Division, Civil War Glass Negatives and Related Prints Collection, LC-B811- 3404

crossed handle used for boring holes—Booth reamed a tiny opening at eye level in the upper wooden panel of the door to the box. Looking through this hole, Booth could see Lincoln's chair.

Around 2:30 p.m., Booth went to visit Mrs. Surratt once again at her boardinghouse. They conversed quietly for several minutes before she departed for church.

One hour later, Booth wrote several more letters. He eventually returned to Pumphrey's livery stable to obtain the bay horse he had selected earlier. Later, as he rode up Pennsylvania Avenue, Booth spotted John Matthews walking along the sidewalk. Matthews was a fellow actor whom Booth earlier had tried to enlist in one of his plots to kidnap the president. He handed Matthews the letter he wrote to the editor of the *National Intelligencer* and asked him to deliver it in the morning. Matthews expressed confusion but agreed to do so. The letter was never published.

For the rest of the afternoon, Booth visited some of his regular haunts. At one point, he rode the bay mare up and down Pennsylvania Avenue several times, getting used to her gait and bragging to anyone who would listen about the mare's speed. They all noticed that Booth was wearing spurs.

After riding, Booth entered Deery's and ordered more drinks. As he sipped a brandy, he stared out the window and observed the passage of a carriage that appeared to contain General Grant and his wife. Booth ran downstairs, untied his horse, mounted up, and galloped after the vehicle. Riding up to the carriage and peering in, Booth ascertained that it was, indeed, Grant. Booth rode along beside the conveyance for a short distance and realized that the general and his wife were leaving town. This meant, he determined, that Grant's usual military escort would not be present at Ford's Theater that evening.

Around 5:00 p.m., Booth was spotted in Taltavul's Tavern with James Maddox and Ned Spangler. A few minutes later, he met Atzerodt in the street in front of the tavern and spoke with him briefly. Atzerodt had also been drinking heavily and was already quite inebriated. After visiting with the German, Booth, accompanied by Spangler, rode his mare into the alley behind Ford's Theater. He told Spangler to summon John Burroughs to hold the reins of his mount while he tended to some business.

At 5:30 p.m., Booth entered Ford's Theater. Twenty minutes later, he was seen leaving the building and entering the National Hotel, where he took dinner. During his meal, Booth had several more drinks.

As Booth dined and drank, his fury was building, his hatred for Lincoln raging within. He was overcome with a sense of urgency to reach the president before anyone else. He wanted badly to beat the man who had replaced him as leader of the northern plot, the one whom Booth perceived as his rival for great and lasting fame.

FIVE

♦♦♦

The Assassination

As late afternoon transitioned into evening on April 14, an unusual quiet descended on Washington, D.C. As some later recalled, a perceptible change had taken place in the atmosphere, a darkening, curious, yet mostly unexplainable sensation, the kind that sometimes precedes disaster.

At 7:45 p.m. that night in 1865, the play *Our American Cousin* was scheduled to begin at Ford's Theater. Approximately half an hour before the curtain was to rise, John Wilkes Booth, now quite drunk, stood in front of the theater with Michael O'Laughlin. Waving his arms and behaving in an agitated manner, Booth exclaimed that things had gone awry and that the "major" was not coming, that he refused to go along with the plan.

When O'Laughlin asked Booth who the major was, the actor identified him only as the "major with the president." O'Laughlin still did not understand, and it was apparent to him that Booth was nearly incoherent. To this day, historians remain uncertain as to the identity of the major.

Booth raved on, telling O'Laughlin that his companions wanted to call the whole thing off. Raising his voice, the actor stated that he refused to quit now, that the deed must be accomplished this very night.

O'Laughlin finally realized that Booth was talking about assassinating the president. Fearing that his ravings would be overheard by others, he pulled the actor away from the gathering theatergoers and advised him to leave, to forget about the whole thing. Booth angrily refused, telling O'Laughlin that it had to be this night or never.

O'Laughlin, still concerned that passersby could overhear their conversation, convinced Booth that they should go inside the theater. They huddled in a quiet corner of the lobby, and Booth began to make hasty, revised arrangements. Once again, he brought up the "major" and stated that he would not wait for his advice. O'Laughlin, finally realizing he could not talk Booth out of his plans, excused himself and left the theater. For several minutes, Booth waited alone in the lobby, glancing at the clock every few seconds. The curtain was about to rise, but President Lincoln and his party had not arrived.

Growing impatient, Booth went outside and rode his mare to the Herndon House. He went directly to Powell's room, where he found the young man waiting. A moment later, Atzerodt arrived and asked where the others were. Booth replied that they were apparently not coming, and Atzerodt expressed relief that the mission would have to be aborted.

Angrily, Booth responded that nothing had been canceled, that there was a change of plans only because so many things had gone wrong. Too many of the original conspirators had quit, he explained, and there were growing, insurmountable difficulties to overcome with regard to kidnapping Vice President Johnson and Secretary of State Seward. Instead, Booth declared, we will kill them all.

As the two men listened, Booth gave instructions to Powell on how Seward should be killed. He then turned to Atzerodt and told him that he was to kill Johnson. The German was to knock on the door of his room at the Kirkwood House and shoot the vice president when he opened it. Following that, he was to escape via the Navy Yard Bridge and into Maryland, where he would rendezvous with the others.

Booth then informed both men that he would slay the president. Atzerodt, numb with shock, flatly refused involvement, stating he would not kill anyone. Powell considered his new mission for a few seconds and then agreed to participate. Atzerodt left the room.

At 8:00 p.m., Booth returned to his hotel. He rechecked the Derringer and placed a knife into a sheath at his belt. He placed a false beard and mustache, a makeup pencil, a wig, and a scarf into a small traveling bag. Atop these, he placed two large-caliber revolvers.

Booth departed the room, never to return. Left behind inside were keys for decoding top-secret Confederate messages that tied him to Rebel headquarters at Richmond. In addition, Booth left behind a briefcase containing evidence that implicated John and Mary Surratt in the kidnap and assassination plots.

Moments later, between 8:30 and 9:00 p.m., Booth mounted his bay horse and rode toward Ford's Theater. According to doorman John Buckingham, Booth, wearing tight black pants, a black coat, a black hat, and tan boots, entered and departed the theater at least five times between 9:00 and 10:00 p.m. Buckingham also related that the actor appeared highly agitated and very drunk.

In spite of several admonitions to refrain from attending the theater, Lincoln was insistent. Several who were originally invited to accompany him, including Stanton, made up excuses not to go.

For a time, Lincoln pondered the wisdom of attending the theater. Earlier in the week, he had related to Ward Lamon the essence of a strange dream he had. In the dream, Lincoln said, he was awakened by the sound of sobbing. He rose from his bed and went downstairs to the East Room of the White House, where he saw a body dressed in funeral garb and guarded by soldiers. He inquired about the identity of the body from one of the guards and was told that it was "the president. He was killed by an assassin."

Curiously, during the morning of April 14, residents of Manchester, New Hampshire, were informed that President Lincoln had been assassinated. Another mystery arose from the town of St. Joseph, Minnesota. During most of the afternoon of April 14, rumors spread throughout that community that the president had been assassinated. Around 2:00 p.m. of the same day, a newspaperman in Middletown, New York, received information from an anonymous source that Lincoln had been shot. Beginning approximately twelve hours before the president ever arrived at Ford's Theater, Lincoln's assassination had been reported in at least six newspapers throughout the region.

James Ford, the manager of Ford's Theater, had a message delivered to Mrs. Lincoln explaining that he was staging the popular *Our American Cousin* that evening featuring the well-known actress Laura Keene, who owned the worldwide rights to the production. Mary Lincoln informed the president that she wished to attend the production at Ford's Theater. The president, in turn, sent a message to the theater stating that he and his wife would attend with their guests, General and Mrs. Grant. The president's message arrived at the theater at 10:30 a.m.

General and Mrs. Grant were originally invited to attend the play with the president and his wife. The two women did not get along, and the general's wife was determined not to go. Grant offered the excuse that he had plans to visit his children in New Jersey. Some researchers are convinced that Grant was dissuaded from attending the play by Secretary of War Stanton in the hope that the president would cancel his own plans. Others who are committed to the notion of a wide-ranging conspiracy maintain that Stanton instructed Grant to stay away because he knew what was going to occur that night at the theater. Most, however, claim that Mrs. Grant simply refused to attend the evening's performance because she despised Mrs. Lincoln. Julia Grant, no shrinking violet, had previously expressed concern about Mary Lincoln's instability and made no secret of her dislike for the president's wife. Whatever the case, many have concluded that Grant's presence in the theater box would have encouraged a more efficient security procedure, particularly in the area of the door through which Booth eventually entered.

After being turned down by the Grants, Mrs. Lincoln invited Clara Harris and her fiancé (and stepbrother) Major Henry Reed Rathbone to accompany her and the president to the play. Clara was the daughter of New York Senator Ira Harris. Clara was one of the few women in Washington who got along well with Mary, and the president's wife had often expressed her fondness for the younger woman. Lincoln was not acquainted with either Clara or Rathbone.

The president, on the other hand, informed Stanton that he was going to invite Thomas Eckert to accompany him and his wife to the play. Lincoln was impressed with Eckert as a security man and believed that he would be quite safe in his presence. Stanton, however, told Lincoln that he had some important work for Eckert to finish and that he could not be spared. Ignoring Stanton, Lincoln personally invited Eckert, but the major refused, explaining he had some obligations to the secretary of war. In essence, both Stanton and Eckert refused Lincoln's request for protective escort.

Lincoln then invited Speaker of the House Schuyler Colfax. Colfax also declined the invitation, claiming that he was preparing to leave for the West Coast. With the play only a few short hours away, Lincoln was making preparations to attend and had no official protection arranged for him whatsoever.

The play was scheduled to begin at 8:00 p.m. At 8:15 p.m., President and Mrs. Lincoln left the White House and climbed into the carriage that was to take them to Ford's Theater. As the carriage pulled away, White House door guard Tom Pendel told night guard John Parker to proceed with haste to the theater and be prepared to escort Lincoln and his party to the box. A subsequent investigation into Parker's role revealed that he had been sponsored by Mrs. Lincoln, who specifically requested that he be assigned to the White House.

Thomas T. Eckert
Library of Congress, Prints
& Photographs Division,
Civil War Glass Negatives
and Related Prints
Collection, LC-B8172-
2057

A number of curious and unsolved mysteries surround John Parker. Parker was thirty-four years old and the father of three children. He had worked as a machinist in Frederick County, Virginia, then served in the Union army during the first three months of the war. In September 1861, he joined the Metropolitan Police Department, which in late 1864 began providing White House bodyguards.

In spite of Parker's constant run-ins with his superiors, all of them related to acts and behavior that would have gotten anyone else dismissed on the spot, Parker somehow remained on the payroll of the D.C. police force. Charges included sleeping on duty, insolence, insubordination, willful violation of rules, conduct unbecoming an officer, drunkenness, general inefficiency, and more. In each case, Parker was returned to duty with no punishment. Researchers have long wondered why Parker was allowed to remain on the force and concluded that someone was protecting him. Others have considered that someone was planning on Parker's participation in a special assignment in the future.

During the first week of April 1865, the Metropolitan Police Department received a request that John Parker be assigned to duty at the

White House as a guard. Of all of the officers on the force, Parker seemed the least likely candidate to be selected for such an important job. Even President Lincoln openly questioned Parker's reliability. Subsequent investigation has revealed that Parker was specifically requested for the duty by Mary Todd Lincoln, the wife of the president. Although it was not within her authority to do so, Mrs. Lincoln fired one of the special guards and filled the vacancy with Parker.

This appointment has mystified scholars for well over a century. Author Theodore Roscoe, however, offers a perspective that carries with it some troubling logic. Mary Todd Lincoln has been described as opinionated and volatile and intent on having her way. The rather short and hefty woman was prone to fits of temper and insisted that she be addressed as "Madame President." Roscoe suggests that Mary Todd Lincoln may have been involved with John Parker. It would not have been the first time the president's wife misbehaved. She was, according to Roscoe, guilty of several indiscretions, once with a White House gardener.

A few minutes after leaving the White House, the carriage containing Lincoln and his wife and driven by coachman Francis Burns and pulled by two highly groomed black horses traveled down G Street, turning on New Jersey Avenue. People on the streets and sidewalks waved, and the president tipped his hat to them. In a moment, the carriage pulled up to the Harris residence at H and Fifteenth streets and picked up Clara and Major Rathbone. At approximately 8:30 p.m., the carriage arrived at the front of the theater. The four occupants climbed from the vehicle and, waved on by doorman Buckingham, entered the theater. Lincoln carried an overcoat across one arm, and his aide carried the president's favorite shawl. Rathbone, who sported a wide mustache and muttonchops, was dressed in uniform but carried no weapon.

As the president and Mrs. Lincoln and guests walked through the door of the theater, White House guard John Parker greeted them. Parker informed the president that he had just come from inspecting the lobby, the stairs, and the presidential box. Since Parker left the White House a few minutes later than the president, he had hardly been in the theater long enough to conduct a thorough inspection.

As Lincoln and his party entered the hall, the actors onstage paused a moment to acknowledge him and applaud his presence. The orchestra, led by director William Withers Jr., played "Hail to the Chief," and the audience turned and watched as the group was escorted to the presidential box. Parker held the white door to the box open as the four passed through. He was dressed in civilian clothes and armed with a .38-caliber revolver. The guard had specific orders to remain outside the door and allow no one to enter. In short, John Parker was given the sole responsibility of protecting President Lincoln.

Once inside the box, Lincoln stepped up to the railing, where he could see and be seen by the audience. He bowed to a standing ovation and thunderous applause. After a moment, he mouthed "thank you" and motioned for everyone to be seated. When the last member of the audience had done so, Lincoln backed up to the rocker and sat down. Looking toward the stage, he motioned for the actors to continue.

Behind Lincoln and slightly to his left, a single door led from the presidential box to a short, narrow hallway. At the end of the hallway was another door, the white one. This white door was the only entrance to and egress from the box. It was outside this door that a chair was placed for John Parker.

As Lincoln settled into his chair, he was completely unprotected. There were no on-duty guards or policemen at the theater, neither outside in the front or rear nor backstage or in the audience. The only guard was John Parker, and he would leave his post within minutes. With Parker absent, there was nothing to stop anyone who wished to enter the president's theater box.

Lincoln's chair was four feet away from the door to box 7. Mrs. Lincoln sat to his immediate right. Miss Harris and Major Rathbone seated themselves on the sofa. Rathbone, by his own estimation, was eight feet from the president. Charles Forbes, Lincoln's footman who arrived in a separate carriage, sat in a straight-backed chair near the door to box 8. It was discovered later that neither of the locks on these doors to the two boxes worked properly.

Directly outside the two doors through which the party entered, John Parker stood next to the chair that had been provided for him. His responsibility was to intercept anyone coming through the white door and prevent them from reaching the president. Parker, however, decided that he wanted to watch the play, which could not be seen from his assigned position. He moved his chair through the white door and into the adjacent chamber but was still without an adequate view of the performance. Presently, he spotted an empty seat in the gallery and left his post to occupy it, leaving the presidential box unguarded.

Historians are in disagreement over whether Parker was merely an inept guard who did not take his duties seriously or was part of a plot to leave the president without a protector. The truth may never be known. The only protection for the president against disaster had left his assigned post. During the events that unfolded in the following weeks, Parker was never punished or even reprimanded.

After a few minutes, Parker appeared to grow bored with the performance and returned to stand outside the white door. A short time later, he went downstairs to the lobby, paused to look around, and stepped outside. He spotted the president's carriage and walked over to it. He woke the napping driver, Burns, and asked him if he wanted to go get a drink. The two men went next door to Taltavul's Star Saloon. On the way, they encountered Lincoln's footman, Forbes, who earlier had left his position near the president. Forbes accepted an invitation from the two men to join them, and they were all soon seated at the bar.

A few moments after Parker, Burns, and Forbes entered Taltavul's, Booth walked through the theater lobby and out into the street, where he untied the mare, mounted, and rode into the alley behind the theater. It was 9:30 p.m. Here, he dismounted and shouted for Ned Spangler. When the stagehand did not arrive, Booth told actor J. L. DeBonay, who was standing nearby, to summon Spangler to hold his horse. Moments later, Spangler, who knew nothing of the assassination plot, arrived and informed Booth that he was needed to help change scenes. Booth told Spangler to send out John Burroughs. When Burroughs arrived, Booth handed him the reins and instructed him to remain at that spot until he returned. Burroughs, who went by the nickname "Peanut John," was a lad who was employed part-time at the theater. Booth then entered the theater from the back door for the final time.

Booth walked behind the stage set and waved at the actors who remained there awaiting their cues. From where he stood, he looked into the presidential box but could discern very little.

Booth then entered the dark passageway that led beneath the stage, under the president's box, and into an access between the south wall of the theater and Taltavul's Saloon. At the same time in the president's box, Lincoln turned to his wife and told her he felt a chill. The president looked back to where Forbes was seated to ask him for his shawl but noticed that the aide was gone. He then stood to put on his black wool overcoat, one tailored specifically for him by Brooks Brothers. Lincoln's movement distracted Rathbone, who turned to watch him. When Lincoln sat down, Rathbone noticed that the door to box 7 was open. He thought little of it and returned his attention to the play. It was 10:07 p.m.

When Booth exited the passageway, he walked out to Tenth Street, entered Taltavul's, and spotted Parker, Burns, and Forbes drinking at the bar. Booth approached the bar and ordered a whiskey from the co-owner, Peter Taltavul. As he paid for his drink, he was approached once again by Ed Henson. Henson walked out of the gloom of one corner of the saloon and invited Booth to join him at his table.

The two men conversed in low tones as they drank, and presently Booth asked Henson if he was still in the mood for some excitement as he had indicated earlier in the day. Henson said he was. Booth told Henson to meet him later that night across the Potomac River in Maryland and the road to Upper Marlboro near Good Hope Hill. Henson agreed to do so.

A few minutes later, Booth drunkenly rose from his chair to leave. As he did so, a patron seated at the bar recognized him and said aloud that his acting would never equal that of his father. Incensed at the comment, Booth stomped out of the saloon, stating loud enough for all to hear that when he left the stage, he would soon be the most famous man in America.

Booth walked up to the doorman at Ford's Theater. He asked Buckingham what time it was. Later, Buckingham related how nervous Booth appeared, which was somewhat out of character. The doorman directed Booth to the lobby, where a clock hung from the wall. Booth stared at it for a full minute. It was 10:10 p.m. It was time, he decided.

While Booth stared at the clock, George Atzerodt, who decided to disentangle himself from the conspirators, was riding out of town. At about the same time, Lewis Powell, dressed in a heavy dark coat that concealed a revolver and a large Bowie knife, was riding toward the front door of the home of Secretary of State William Seward in the company of a man who historians believe was David Herold.

Booth walked behind the dress circle patrons and paused a short distance away from the president's box on the second level. He leaned casually against a wall near the door that led to the box and surveyed the theater. He saw the empty chair and remembered Parker drinking at Taltavul's. Actress Jennie Gourlay spotted Booth near the dress circle and later noted that he had a wild look in his eyes.

In silence and with deliberation, Booth moved among the patrons. He looked around the theater again. He pulled a card from his pocket and handed it to a messenger. The messenger looked at the card, nodded, and led Booth to the white door. The messenger departed immediately, leaving Booth standing alone just outside the door to the president's box.

Booth paused a few heartbeats, then pushed open the door and entered the dim inner corridor. After closing the door behind him, according to Roscoe, Booth wedged it shut with a wooden upright from a music stand, placing it in the cut he had made earlier in the day. This effectively kept the door from being opened from the outside. At this point, there was nothing to prevent Booth from his mission. Booth then stepped up to the inner door that provided entry into the theater box and placed an eye to the recently bored peephole. He saw the president seated in his rocking chair watching the play. He spotted Mary Todd Lincoln a few feet to the right of the president. Major Rathbone and Clara Harris were seated farther to the right closer to the wall.

As Lincoln and his party were intent on the play, Booth stood just outside in the anteroom. Looking around, he saw no guards anywhere. He reached into his coat pocket and withdrew his .44-caliber Derringer. The pistol, which he held in his right hand, contained only one bullet and had earlier been capped and readied for firing. In a belt scabbard he carried a knife. It was 10:15 p.m. For a few moments, Booth stood outside the door to the presidential box. His heart raced as the tension, fueled by alcohol, built inside him.

From the stage, Booth could hear the lines spoken by the mother to her daughter: "Go to your room. You may go to your room at once." As the two women walked off and disappeared stage left, the actor Harry Hawk, playing the character Asa Trenchard, was then highlighted at center stage. Glancing at the departing pair, he said, "Society, Eh? Well, I guess I know enough to turn you inside out, old gal—you sock-dologizing old man-trap!"

As the audience responded with laughter, Booth stepped through the door, strode the four feet to the president, and lifted the Derringer. As he advanced, Booth reportedly uttered, "Freedom."

Lincoln, sensing movement behind him, started to turn his head as Booth pointed the pistol and fired. The ball entered the president's skull midway between the left ear and the median line of the back of the head, inflicting a mortal wound. Dropping the pistol to the floor and raising the knife, Booth cried, "Revenge for the South!"

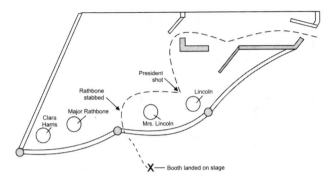

Booth's movements through boxes 7 and 8

This one mad act was to forever link the name "John Wilkes Booth" to "assassination." It was also the beginning of one of the greatest controversies and mysteries in American history.

SIX

✦✦✦

The Attack on Seward

As the drama within a drama was unfolding at Ford's Theater, a tall, well-built man was riding a one-eyed horse toward the three-story brick residence of Secretary of State William Seward. Lewis Powell was guided through the avenues of the capital by David Herold, the young man caught up in the plots and plans of John Wilkes Booth because he was so intimate with the roads, routes, shortcuts, and back alleys of Washington, D.C.

Powell's real name has presented a problem to those who have studied this case. He is often identified as Lewis Payne. Author Roy Z. Chamlee contends that "Lewis Paine" was not the man's real name, that it was taken from one Lewis Paine of Fauquier, Virginia, who eventually went on to become a U.S. attorney for Wyoming Territory.

The government, however, contended that Lewis Payne and Lewis Thornton Powell were the same man, but evidence exists that suggests otherwise. Civil War service records provide a convincing case that Paine and Powell were two different men and that they were, in fact, cousins. Paine and Powell were apparently so similar in appearance that each was often confused with the other.

Researchers Balsiger and Sellier obtained lost confession statements made by Michael O'Laughlin and George Atzerodt wherein they state that Payne and Powell were two separate individuals. In addition, O'Laughlin and Atzerodt suggested that Payne was arrested, tried, convicted, and executed for the attack on Secretary Seward when, in fact, it was Powell who committed the crime.

Author Vaughan Shelton has also expressed belief in Payne's innocence relative to the attack on Seward and even goes so far as to claim that the man known as Lewis Paine was not even known to Booth. Shelton's research, like that of others, also supports the notion that Paine and Powell were two different men.

62

Based on documents that Shelton uncovered, he was convinced that Powell was an agent for Stanton's War Department and that he reported directly to Lafayette Baker. Shelton also claims that Stanton's assistant, Thomas Eckert, made the contract with Powell to kill Seward. Major H. B. Smith, a Baltimore detective, was certain that Powell was a Union spy. After Payne was identified as Powell and subsequently hanged for his alleged role in the conspiracy, the real Lewis Powell was legally free to assume another identity.

On April 5, Seward, while riding in a carriage with his son, daughter, and another person, suffered a serious accident. The team of horses pulling the carriage bolted, and Seward was thrown out. His lower jaw and right arm were broken. In addition, he suffered a severe tearing of the ligaments in one foot. As a result, Seward was confined to bed during his recovery.

As Powell and Herold rode in darkness toward Seward's house near Lafayette Square, the secretary lay propped up in his bed, his arm in a sling and his chin secured by a tight leather and steel brace. The apparatus was uncomfortable, and it restricted his movements.

Secretary of State
William H. Seward
Library of Congress, Prints
& Photographs Division,
LC-USZ62-22180810633

Powell was wearing cavalry boots. Around his waist was belted a revolver and a knife. On arriving in front of the secretary's house, he dismounted and, leaving Herold on the street to hold the horse's reins, climbed the few steps to the porch and rang the bell.

Seward's butler, a young black man named William Bell, opened the door to find a tall, powerfully built man wearing black pants, a long overcoat, and a broad-brimmed hat. His jaw was slightly disfigured as though it had once been broken. He was carrying a small bottle in one hand. Once the door was opened, the stranger pushed his way inside and demanded to see Seward. Holding up the bottle and showing it to Bell, he stated that he had been sent by Dr. T. S. Verdi with medicine for the secretary.

Bell, maintaining his composure, told the newcomer that he could not be permitted to see Seward, and offered to take the medicine to him. Seward's physician had examined the secretary only one hour previously, and Bell thought this was odd since orders were left that Seward was not to receive visitors. The stranger then pushed past Bell and started climbing the stairs leading to the second floor and Seward's bedroom, with Bell behind him imploring him to tread quietly.

At that moment, Frederick Seward, the secretary's son and chief assistant, appeared at the top of the stairs in his nightclothes. Holding up a hand, he signaled for the stranger to stop, telling him that he was not allowed up there. Powell reached the top of the stairs and advanced toward Frederick. After two or three steps, he paused, held up the medicine, and then stated that he would leave. Frederick reached out a hand and told the stranger to give him the medicine. Powell handed the bottle over, then turned as if to descend the stairs and suddenly wheeled around, a navy Colt revolver in his hand. Pointing the weapon at Frederick's chest, he pulled the trigger, only to have it misfire. Cursing, he slammed the barrel of the gun across Frederick's head, knocking him to the floor unconscious. As Frederick lay motionless, Powell struck him again and again.

Witnessing the confrontation, Bell turned and ran down the stairs and out the front door of the residence screaming, "Murder! Murder!" Bell hastened to the next-door office of General Christopher C. Augur. Alarmed by the sudden appearance of Bell, Herold, who was still holding the two horses, tied his partner's mount to a nearby tree, quickly climbed atop his own, and fled down Fifteenth Street.

Powell, upset with the malfunctioning revolver, slammed it repeatedly against the banister until the weapon broke. Pulling the large

Bowie knife from inside his coat, he proceeded to search along the second-floor hallway for Seward's room. Finally locating it, he broke through the door and clumsily stumbled inside, where he was met by Sergeant George Robinson, who was attending the secretary, and Fanny Seward, the secretary's daughter, who was sitting with her father. Powell lunged at Robinson, slashing a long cut across his forehead. When Robinson fell, Powell, after punching Fanny in the face, leaped on Seward, who was lying in the bed, and began stabbing repeatedly at his head. The heavy splint on Seward's broken jaw served to deflect the knife from striking a major artery. The blade, however, sliced through Seward's right cheek and down the right side of his throat, causing blood to gush.

As Powell paused, Augustus Seward, another of the secretary's sons, ran into the room and attempted to pull the assailant from the bed. For his effort, he was stabbed several times. Robinson joined Augustus in the effort, and the two succeeded in throwing Powell to the floor. As Fanny watched in horror, the assailant slashed wildly with the knife and succeeded in plunging it into Robinson's chest and shoulder. One particularly vicious swipe sliced off a portion of Augustus's scalp.

Powell managed to stand and blurted out, "I am mad! I am mad!" Still clutching the knife, he turned and bolted from the bedroom. In the hallway, he encountered Emerick "Bud" Hansell, who had just arrived. Hansell, a State Department messenger, was stunned into immobility by what he had witnessed and merely stood and watched in confusion as Powell approached him. The messenger opened his mouth as if to say something, then turned to run just as Powell plunged the knife deep into his back.

As Hansell collapsed to the floor, Powell fled down the stairs and out the front door. Once in the street, Powell, now bareheaded and smeared with blood, threw the bloody knife into the gutter. At the same time, he discovered that he had been abandoned by Herold. A moment of panic set in because without Herold's knowledge of the streets of Washington, he would not be able to locate and follow the escape route. After untying his horse, Powell climbed into the saddle and rode down Fifteenth Street at a canter north toward H Street.

As the stranger rode away, William Bell was returning from the Augur house when he spotted him. He pointed at the rider and began screaming that it was the man who had invaded the Seward home. While a few soldiers and passersby were on the street at the time, no one came to Bell's aid. On foot, Bell attempted to pursue the intruder

but ran out of breath before he could cover a block. He watched as
the tall man disappeared up Vermont Avenue, where he turned east.

Around midnight, a horse was found near the capital. It was saddled
and bridled and sweating as though it had been ridden hard. It was
somehow determined to be the animal ridden by Seward's assailant.
Later, it was discovered that it was the same one-eyed horse that Booth
had earlier purchased from a neighbor of Dr. Samuel Mudd. The
saddle was subsequently identified as belonging to George Atzerodt,
which led to the initial belief that it was the German who tried to assassinate the secretary of state.

On the evening of Monday, April 17, it was announced by the U.S.
government that the man who tried to take the life of Seward was
Lewis Powell. According to investigators, it is believed that Powell,
after abandoning his horse, hid in the woods located north of Washington's Fort Lincoln.

Although military records showed that Powell and Payne were two
different men, the U.S. prosecutor, during the conspiracy trial of 1865,
maintained that they were the same person and saw that the record
stated this.

SEVEN

♦♦♦

Escape

The sudden sound of Booth's Derringer discharging against Abraham Lincoln's head caused Major Rathbone to jerk around. Gun smoke filled a portion of the tiny presidential box, but through the haze, Rathbone spotted a man standing seven feet away. As the major gazed in horror, the man dropped a pistol to the floor, shifted a knife from his left hand to his right, and quickly advanced toward the railing. Rathbone leaped for the assailant, but Booth turned, making a vicious slash at the major and inflicted a severe wound on the biceps of the left arm, a stab that cut clear to the bone.

Booth, after dropping the Derringer and switching the knife to his right hand, turned back to the railing and prepared to leap. Rathbone made another lunge at the actor and grasped unsuccessfully at his coat. The nimble though drunk actor placed a hand on the railing and vaulted it as he screamed, "The South is avenged!"

Booth was well known throughout the theater community and audiences for his leaping and gymnastic ability, sometimes rehearsed but often spontaneous. He had made leaps of this distance before without mishap. Booth's drunkenness, however, undoubtedly affected his timing and coordination. As he plummeted to the stage twelve feet below, the spur on the heel of his right boot caught on the flag and caused him to land off balance and in a kneeling position with his back toward the audience. Most researchers are convinced that, on impact, Booth's left fibula, the thinner of the two bones of the leg between the knee and the ankle, snapped two inches above the ankle. As he rose, Booth turned toward the audience and shouted, "Sic semper tyrannis!"—Thus always to tyrants.

The injury notwithstanding, Booth stood up and, brandishing the knife coated with Rathbone's blood, fled across the stage. He passed close to Harry Hawk, the only actor on the stage at the time, and disappeared into the curtains beyond. A blue shred of the flag that hung in front of the president's box had caught on his spur and fluttered from his heel as he ran. Hawk, perplexed, wondered why Booth had chosen to insert himself in the performance in such an odd manner. Hawk later testified that he was certain he heard Booth shout, "The South shall be free!"

James Ford, who was watching the play from the rear of the theater, assumed that the self-centered Booth was merely trying to get attention. At that moment, Rathbone, attempting to staunch the flow of blood from his wound, leaned out of the smoke-filled box and yelled, "Stop that man!" The audience, stunned, was now on its feet.

Former army officer Joseph B. Stewart was seated in the right front orchestra chair when he was startled by the vaulting man. Stewart immediately recognized Booth as the actor raced across the stage. At Rathbone's cry, Stewart rose from his chair and repeated the major's order.

As Booth entered the wings, he almost collided with actress Laura Keene. As he sought the passageway toward the door that opened into Baptist Alley, where John Burroughs held his horse, he encountered William Withers, the orchestra leader, standing between him and the exit. Booth slashed at him with the knife, the blade slicing through a layer of apparel and inflicting a slight wound on the neck. Booth then fled through the open back door and into the alley.

Subsequent testimony by Mary Jane Anderson, the black woman whose poor domicile fronted the alley, revealed that the door was open. She stated that she was looking through the open door and saw people moving about behind the scenes when all of a sudden Booth burst into the passage and ran to the back door. Inside the theater, people were now screaming that the president had been shot.

Stage carpenter Jacob Ritterspaugh was standing in the passageway and made a grab for Booth. The fleeing man raised his knife, and Ritterspaugh, seeing the blood-smeared weapon, backed away. The carpenter turned to see Spangler standing nearby and shouted, "That was Booth!" Spangler told Ritterspaugh to be quiet and not to tell anyone which direction he fled.

Stewart was only twenty feet behind Booth as the actor passed through the open back door. Oddly, when Stewart reached the exit, it was closed, and he experienced great difficulty opening it.

On entering the dark alley behind the theater, Booth spotted Burroughs tending to the bay mare. Snatching the reins from him, the assassin placed his left foot into the stirrup. Before mounting, he slammed the butt of his knife against the head of Burroughs, knocking him to the ground.

Once in the saddle, Booth had a difficult time controlling the skittish mare. Just as he wheeled the mount and spurred her hard, Stewart finally managed to open the back door and stepped out in to the alley in time to see Booth getting the horse under control. Stewart reached for the reins, but Booth swung the mare around and rode away down the alley. It has been estimated that only one minute passed between the murder of the president and Booth's escape from the theater.

From the presidential box, Rathbone dashed out into the antechamber and was surprised to find no guard. When he tried to open the white door, it failed to yield. From the box, audience members could hear the screaming and wailing of Mary Lincoln. Over and over she cried, "They've killed him! They've killed him!" As it became clear to the audience what had transpired, a growing murmur vibrated and echoed throughout the theater.

Booth, meanwhile, was riding away unimpeded. Although his exact escape route may never be known for certain, it is believed that he rode out of Baptist Alley onto F Street. From there, he likely turned and galloped hard until reaching Pennsylvania Avenue leading to Capitol Hill. Once on the other side of the capitol, Booth headed toward the Navy Yard Bridge, which spanned the Anacostia River.

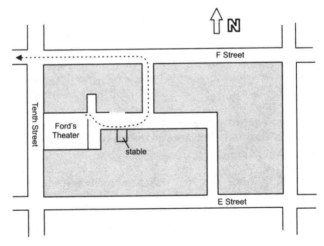

Booth's escape route after leaving Ford's Theater

Meanwhile, several men working together to open the white door to the presidential box were having no success. From the inside, Rathbone, despite bleeding profusely from his wound, was finally able to pull away the length of wood holding the door fast. As men tried to force their way into the box, the major blocked them and shouted for a doctor.

A young physician named Charles Leale arrived moments later and tended to the wounded president. Leale requested a lamp and ordered the door locked and no one allowed inside save for other physicians. Feeling in the dark with his fingers, Leale found the entry wound at the back of the president's head. There was no exit wound.

Distracted by Rathbone's request for medical help for his arm, Leale turned his attention to the major. He determined that the wound was not serious and returned his attention to the president. A moment later, Leale rose and announced to all present that the wound was mortal.

Under Leale's direction, the dying president was transported across the street from the theater to the home of William Peterson, 453 Tenth Street. Lincoln was carried into a bedroom and placed on a bed.

By now, theatergoers were rushing from the building shouting that the president had been shot. Inside Ford's Theater, Mrs. Lincoln's screams reverberated throughout. Other women were also screaming, theater seats were smashed, and cries of terror and sorrow resounded, creating a pandemonium, according to one observer, more terrible than that attending the assassination of Caesar. Two miles away, John Wilkes Booth lashed the bay mare through the deserted Washington streets toward the Potomac River.

During the seconds following the assassination, Booth was within ten feet of at least a dozen people who knew him well and recognized him immediately. In addition, a number of theatergoers in the audience knew him by sight. Less than fifteen minutes following the murder of President Lincoln, Booth's name was being shouted by throngs of witnesses. By 11:00 p.m., at least seventeen of them had been interviewed by the police, all of whom identified the actor as the killer. In spite of this, the War Department withheld Booth's name from official dispatches and, curiously, would not positively or publicly name the assassin or post his image on a reward notice for six days.

The perceived movements of John Wilkes Booth and a man identified as his coconspirator, David Herold, from the time of the assassination to the killing at Richard Garrett's barn in Virginia on April 26, 1865, have been pieced together from the minutes of trial testimony, from numerous public and military interviews, from government documents, and from dozens of standard references. The "official" version of Booth's flight and alleged death at the hands of the authorities as offered by the U.S. government and provided to most historians is summarized and represented in the next chapter. It is presented here for purposes of comparison with what follows.

EIGHT

‹♦♦♦›

Flight, Pursuit, and Death of John Wilkes Booth: The Traditional Version

After guiding the bay mare out of the alley behind Ford's Theater, John Wilkes Booth raced eastward toward the Anacostia River and the Navy Yard Bridge, a distance of three miles. At approximately 10:45 p.m., Booth rode down Eleventh Street and approached the bridge, reining in the lathered horse as he neared the sentry station. This end of the bridge was normally closed to travelers after 9:30 p.m. as a wartime precaution, but since the surrender, that order had been rescinded if one provided a good reason to pass.

Bridge guard Sergeant Silas T. Cobb confronted the approaching horseman, whom he later described as hatless, wearing a black suit and elegant black boots and having a pale face and a glossy black mustache. In response to Cobb's question, the rider gave his name as Booth and said he was heading home to Beantown, Maryland. He told Cobb that he had waited this late to travel so that the moonlight would help him find his way. Cobb allowed him to pass. Ignoring the stipulation that one must walk one's horse across the bridge, Booth set off at a gallop.

A few minutes later, a second horseman appeared, and Cobb likewise challenged him. The rider gave his name as Smith, but Cobb did not believe him. The rider then stated that his name was Thomas and said he was heading south to White Plains, where he claimed he lived. When Cobb asked him why he was traveling so late, the rider said he had been with a woman. Cobb waved him on.

Around 11:00 p.m., John Fletcher, the foreman at Nailor's Livery in Washington, rode up to Silas Cobb at the bridge and asked if a poorly dressed young man riding a roan had passed by recently. Earlier in the day, Herold, under instructions from Booth, rented a horse from

The Navy Yard Bridge
Library of Congress, Prints & Photographs Division, LC-B8184-40466

Nailor's Livery Stable on the promise that he would return it by sundown. As Herold rode through town after fleeing from his station in front of Stanton's house, he was spotted by Nailor employee Fletcher. When Fletcher hollered at Herold, the young man galloped away. Fletcher ran to the nearby stable, saddled up, and went in pursuit.

Cobb told Fletcher that one such man had crossed only minutes earlier. Fletcher told him that the roan had been stolen and that he wanted to pursue the rider. Cobb informed Fletcher that if he crossed over, he would not be able to return until morning. Without a word, Fletcher turned his mount and rode back into town.

Fletcher rode to the Washington Metropolitan Police station and reported the stolen horse. After explaining his pursuit of the thief as far as the bridge, he was taken to Military Police Headquarters to relate his experience to General C. C. Augur. Fletcher's story, along with those of a number of other witnesses, convinced Augur and police superintendent A. C. Richards that the killer of the president was John Wilkes Booth and that the assassin, along with David Herold, had escaped into southern Maryland.

According to the majority of historians, Herold caught up with Booth at Good Hope Hill, about a mile and a half southeast of the Navy Yard Bridge. From there, the pair rode to Surrattsville. Booth's leg was now causing him severe pain.

Back in Washington, Michael O'Laughlin was in the bar at Rullman's Hotel on Pennsylvania Avenue. He had been drinking for most of the evening and was now quite drunk. During his stupor, he heard the bartender announce that the president had been shot. Despite his degree of inebriation, it became clear to O'Laughlin that Booth was responsible. He also realized that he must leave town immediately before someone connected him to the plot.

Surrattsville was located eleven miles south of Washington. The Surratt family owned and operated a tavern where the Port Tobacco, Chapel Point, and Leonardtown roads intersected. Once a popular stagecoach stop, Surrattsville had seen business drop off significantly during the war, and the place had been neglected and become run-down.

Years earlier, Mary Surratt had acquired permission to use the tavern as a post office. Her son John was named postmaster. It was believed by many that the Surrattsville Post Office became an important letter drop for the Confederate underground route that ran from Richmond, Virginia, to Montreal, Quebec, Canada.

When Booth and Herold arrived at the tavern, they encountered hired innkeeper John Lloyd. They instructed Lloyd to fetch some supplies that had been stashed in the building earlier by Herold. Lloyd returned with pistols, rifles, field glasses, and some tack. During the exchange, Herold dismounted, but Booth remained on his horse. He asked Lloyd for some liquor to relieve his pain.

After asking about a doctor, Lloyd told the men that there was no longer one living in Surrattsville. Booth recalled that Dr. Samuel Mudd lived northeast of Bryantown. Herold mounted up, and they rode away into the night. Just before Booth and Herold departed, according to Lloyd's subsequent testimony, Booth exclaimed, "I have murdered the president."

At 2:00 a.m., Booth and Herold rode into the town of TB and left the main route to take a back road toward Bryantown. It was nearly 4:30 a.m. when the two men arrived at Mudd's house. Herold dismounted, stepped up onto the porch, and knocked on the door. When Mudd answered, Herold stated that his friend, whom he identified as "Mr. Tyler," had been injured in a fall and needed treatment. (Some sources give the name as Mr. Tyson.) Mudd admitted the two men, both of whom smelled of whiskey. According to Mudd's later testimony, Herold identified himself as Mr. Henson.

Mudd later claimed to investigators that the injured man kept his face hidden in a scarf, his chin tucked well into it, and acted very suspicious. After placing him on a living room sofa, Mudd cut the boot from his swollen foot and lower leg. On examination, the physician discovered a transverse fracture of the fibula of the left leg. Mudd set the bone as well as possible under the circumstances and bound it with a splint he fashioned from pieces of a bandbox (a hatbox made from stiff cardboard). This done, Booth was helped up the stairs, led to a second-floor bedroom, and placed on a bed. Herold went outside and slept in the barn.

In Washington, George Atzerodt, drunk as usual, walked the streets of the capital. He was beginning to suspect that he would soon be identified as being part of the conspiracy to kill the president, the vice president, and the secretary of state. He decided not to return to his room at the Kirkwood House. Around 3:00 a.m., he checked into a room at the Pennsylvania House, where he was assigned a roommate—police lieutenant W. R. Keim. Keim wanted to talk about the killing of the president, but Atzerodt told him he needed to get some sleep.

As Atzerodt slept, detectives were already examining the belongings he left at his room in the Kirkwood House, including a ledger from a Montreal bank with the name John Wilkes Booth on the inside cover as well as other items that implicated both Atzerodt and Booth.

Around the same time, investigators received an anonymous tip relating to the involvement of Mary Surratt. They arrived at her boardinghouse but found nothing of importance. Surratt, however, did mention that the actor John Wilkes Booth had visited twelve hours prior to the assassination. She also mentioned that her son John left Washington two weeks earlier. The police departed.

At almost the same hour, another tip led police to Booth's room 228 at the National Hotel. Here they found a business card bearing John Surratt's name; a letter from one of the original conspirators, Samuel Arnold; and more. It was now becoming clear that Booth had several accomplices.

At 7:22 a.m., President Abraham Lincoln was pronounced dead
from the bullet wound inflicted by John Wilkes Booth.

Secretary of War Stanton oversaw the search for the assassin Booth.
Soldiers, cavalry, police, and every other available manifestation of
law enforcement were ordered into the pursuit. In an odd move, Stanton summoned Lafayette Baker, who was in New York City.

Baker had been reassigned as a result of being caught tapping Stanton's telegraph lines, so he was somewhat surprised at the order. Having earlier learned of the president's assassination, Baker wondered if
he was being enlisted for a legitimate search for the murderer or if he
would be instructed to locate and kill Booth before the actor revealed
Stanton's role in the conspiracy. After meeting with Stanton, Baker
realized he had been placed in complete charge of the investigation.

George Atzerodt woke up at the Pennsylvania House hotel, unaware
that he was at that moment the object of a search, but he realized that
he needed to get far away from Washington, the sooner the better.
The original plan provided for him to meet up with Booth, Herold,
and Powell at some location in Maryland, but he had no interest in
doing so.

Atzerodt walked from the hotel to Georgetown, where he knocked
on the door of a former girlfriend, Lucinda Metz, and told her he was
leaving town for a while. Minutes later, he walked into a pawnshop
and accepted ten dollars for his revolver. With the money, Atzerodt
purchased a ticket for a stagecoach into Maryland. Shortly after
the coach crossed into the state from the capital, it was stopped
and searched by a contingent of federal soldiers. No one suspected
Atzerodt, and the coach was waved on. Even with a severe hangover,
Atzerodt was convinced he would easily elude pursuit.

Around noon, Mudd reexamined the injured man's leg. During the
examination, Booth kept his face turned and remained silent. He appeared to be suffering not only from pain but also from fatigue and
lack of sleep. Mudd ordered his hired man to make a pair of home-
made crutches for his injured guest. He let the visitor sleep throughout
the remainder of the afternoon. Mudd was paid twenty-five dollars for
his service.

Herold asked Mudd if the pair could borrow his buggy to transport
the injured man to Port Tobacco. Mudd refused but suggested that a

buggy might be found in Bryantown, a short distance to the south. Herold, riding Booth's mare, set out for Bryantown. On nearing the small town, Herold realized it was surrounded by federal troops. The soldiers were questioning the citizens and not allowing anyone to leave. Herold raced back to Mudd's house.

Some time later, Herold asked Mudd for directions to the home of Colonel Samuel Cox's Wicomico-Potomac plantation. Cox's farm, like Surratt's tavern, also served the Confederate underground. Late in the afternoon, Dr. Mudd left his house on an errand. Not long after, Herold assisted Booth down the stairs, out into the yard, and onto the saddle of the roan. Herold rode the bay mare because the pain in Booth's leg made the skittish and hard-to-control animal too much to handle. The two men rode away into Zekiah Swamp, which extended southward from Mudd's house. Along the way, they bypassed Bryantown.

Following a trail that wound through the swamp, Booth and Herold became lost several times. They finally arrived at Cox's farm around midnight. Here, they asked about a boat to take them across the Potomac River but were told that none were available and that the Union soldiers were patrolling the roads and river.

Booth and Herold were led to a hiding place in the woods by Cox's foster brother, Thomas A. Jones, another Rebel sympathizer. Each evening for the next six nights, Jones carried food, liquor, and newspapers to the fugitives.

During their time of hiding out in the woods near Cox's farm, Booth suffered terribly from the pain in his leg. It rained constantly, and the temperature dropped, making the setting quite uncomfortable. The two men were unable to construct any kind of a shelter for fear that the noise would attract attention from passing patrols. Jones continued to bring Booth brandy to help ease the suffering. On reading the reports of the assassination and its aftermath, Booth realized he was not the hero that he expected to be proclaimed. Rather, he was condemned and labeled a coward. In his frustration, he ranted at Herold.

From their secluded campsite, Booth and Herold could hear cavalry patrols passing along the nearby trails. Booth told Jones that remaining in the cold and wet hideout was unbearable and that they needed to leave as soon as possible. Jones explained to Booth that the soldiers were thick throughout that part of the country. In fact, he suggested they kill the horses lest they give away the position. Booth argued against this at first and then relented. He told Jones to take the horses.

During this miserable time in the swamp, Booth wrote in his diary, maintaining an abbreviated account of their time on the run and his killing of the president. Several of the entries were self-congratulatory.

Police detectives returned to Mary Surratt's boardinghouse in response to another tip, this one from Louis Weichmann, who met with the investigators and reported the frequent visits to the address from Booth and the other conspirators. He suggested that Mary Surratt was a part of the plots to kidnap or kill the president. Surratt and her twenty-two-year-old daughter, Anna, were arrested. As they were preparing to escort the two women out, the officers were surprised by a knock. When the policemen open the door, they found a tall man carrying a pickax. His boots were muddy, and there appeared to be blood on his coat.

On seeing the policemen, the newcomer said he made a mistake and turned to leave but was restrained by the officers. As the two women were taken to a police vehicle parked outside, other detectives questioned the man. He identified himself as Lewis Payne and said he came in response to a summons from Mrs. Surratt, who wanted him to excavate a ditch. Following a few more questions, the man was placed under arrest. When he was delivered to the station, they found in his pockets a newspaper article devoted to Lincoln's second inaugural address.

In time, it became clear that Payne resembled the man who attacked Secretary of State Seward. William Bell, Seward's butler, was brought to the station to identify Payne. Bell claimed it was the same man. Payne was handcuffed and shackled, a seventy-five-pound kelso attached to his leg chain. A heavy canvas hood containing only a breathing hole was fastened over his head. Lewis Payne would never experience freedom again.

By Tuesday, April 18, the search for Booth in southern Maryland was growing in intensity. It included 700 members of the Illinois cavalry, 600 men from the Twenty-Second Colored Troops, 100 from the Sixteenth New York Cavalry Regiment, as well as whatever local law enforcement personnel could be spared. Most of the searchers were concentrated in the area of Zekiah Swamp, Scrub Swamp, Atchall's Swamp, Allen's Creek, and the adjacent wilderness. On foot, they assumed a line starting at one end of a swamp and slogged through the muck and mire until they reached the opposite bank. The searches were long and tedious, and the weather was cold and biting. In addition, all of the area towns and villages were filled with soldiers and policemen interrogating as many people as they could. Hundreds of suspects were arrested, but Booth and Herold remained elusive.

A cavalry contingent of twenty-four riders arrived at the house of Dr. Mudd. Among them was Mudd's cousin, George, a passionate Union sympathizer. Mudd informed George at Sunday services that two men stopped at his house early Saturday morning, one of them seeking medical treatment for a broken leg.

Mudd was questioned. The nervous physician did not respond well to the interrogation, fumbling his words and contradicting himself. Lieutenant Alexander Lovett, the leader of the unit, concluded Mudd was not telling the truth. Lovett decided to ride on but informed Mudd he would return.

On April 20, Stanton issued a proclamation offering a total of $100,000 in reward money. The capture of the president's assassin would fetch $50,000. Rewards in the amount of $25,000 each were offered for John H. Surratt and David C. Herold, both of whom were listed as Booth's accomplices.

The proclamation also stated that "all persons harboring or secreting the fugitives, or aiding or assisting in their concealment and escape . . . will be treated as accomplices in the murder of the president and the attempted murder of the Secretary of State, and shall be subject to trial before a military commission and the punishment of death."

George Atzerodt was traveling northeast. On the fourth day of his flight, he arrived at the home of a cousin in Germantown, Maryland, only twenty miles from Washington, D.C. At a tavern earlier in the day, Atzerodt, while dining at a table of men he did not know, expressed his satisfaction that the president had been killed. When Atzerodt left the tavern, one of his companions alerted a U.S. marshal. That evening, a cavalry detachment rode up to the cousin's house and arrested the conspirator. Just like Lewis Payne, Atzerodt was chained, shackled, and covered with a hood. In a short time, he was charged with conspiracy to kill the president.

The funeral for President Lincoln was held on Wednesday, April 19, at the White House. It was attended by 600 mourners who were admitted to the East Room. Following the funeral, the casket containing the body was transported through the streets of Washington to the Capitol Building. It was estimated that 100,000 mourners lined the streets.

On Friday, April 21, Lieutenant Lovett and his cavalry force returned to the home of Dr. Mudd. Mudd was absent, but Lovett ordered his hired man, Thomas Davis, to go find him. Mudd, who was having lunch with a neighbor, returned within the hour.

Mudd was aware that Lieutenant Lovett had been searching and observing the farm for the past three days. This time, he informed the physician, he wanted to search the inside of the house. Mudd acquiesced, and as the officer was addressing his troops, the doctor whispered something to his wife, Mary. Mary hurried into the house. She climbed the stairs to the second floor, and as the soldiers massed in the downstairs living room, she returned carrying a boot and a razor. She handed the items to Lovett, stating she encountered them while cleaning the room a few days earlier.

Mudd told Lovett that one of the men used the razor to shave off his mustache. The boot was cut from his broken leg. Lovett asked the doctor if he knew who the owner of the boot was. Mudd replied that he did not. Lovett separated the cut halves of the boot, exposing the name "J. Wilkes." Mudd was placed under arrest.

Jones persuaded a fisherman, later identified by government investigators as Henry Rowland, to secret a rowboat into a Potomac River backwater near Dent's Meadow. That evening, Jones arrived and told the fugitives it was time. Because he had difficulty walking, Jones and Herold helped Booth mount a horse, and the three men made their way toward the river. Booth was helped into the stern, and Herold took a position in the bow. After handing Jones some money and a bottle of whiskey, Herold rowed away.

Most researchers believe that Herold rowed four miles upstream to Nanjemoy Creek west of the Port Tobacco River. A few are convinced that he traveled in this direction in search of a Confederate blockade-runner. Whatever the case, no such boat was available. As Booth and Herold hid in Nanjemoy Cove all the next day, Union boats patrolled the Potomac channel while troops searched the banks. At sundown, Herold rowed out of the cove toward Mathias Point downstream and on the Virginia side of the river.

When Baker learned of the discovery of Booth's riding boot and the circumstances surrounding it, he determined that the assassin would likely forgo traveling by horseback and take to the rivers. He was also convinced that Booth was heading for Kentucky by way of Virginia. Using military maps, Baker examined various routes and concluded that Booth would attempt to cross the Potomac River at or near Port Tobacco.

Early Sunday morning, April 23, Herold landed the boat at Mathias Point. Booth and Herold walked a short distance to the home of a Mrs. Queensbury. Following a short discussion, the woman directed the two men to the residence of Dr. Richard Stewart, yet another Confederate sympathizer. By this time, Stewart had learned of the assassination of the president, the search for the fugitives, and the threat to hang anyone aiding them. Nervously, Stewart provided a meal for the two men and then sent them to stay at the poor cabin of his black slave, William Lucas.

At sunrise on Monday morning, Lucas transported Booth and Herold southwest to Port Conway on the Rappahannock River in a spring wagon. Herold gave Lucas ten dollars for his help and sent him away. After climbing out of the wagon, Herold spotted three Confederate cavalrymen and requested an escort for some specified distance to the south. The riders agreed to carry the fugitives to the home of Richard Garrett a few miles away. Garrett had a reputation for helping southerners in need. A short time later, a ferry arrived and carried Booth and Herold and the three troopers across the river to Port Royal on the opposite shore.

At the Garrett farm, Booth was introduced as John W. Boyd, a Confederate soldier whose leg was wounded at Richmond. Booth remained at the farm while Herold rode into Bowling Green with the cavalrymen.

On Tuesday morning, Herold returned to the Garrett farm. He and Booth spent most of the day sitting on the front porch and visiting with Garrett's sons. At sundown, horsemen dressed in Confederate uniforms rode up to the porch and informed all present that Union soldiers were spotted crossing the Rappahannock River and were heading toward that location.

At Port Conway, a twenty-five man cavalry detail led by Luther Baker Jr., Lieutenant Edward P. Doherty, and Lieutenant Colonel

Conger learned from ferryman William Rollins that a crippled man hobbling on crutches and accompanied by a younger man had crossed the river to Port Royal. Luther Baker was a cousin to Colonel Lafayette Baker. On arriving in Port Royal, Baker learned that a Confederate trooper named Willie Jett had led the two men down the road toward Bowling Green.

One hour later, Booth and Herold spotted a squadron of Union cavalry approaching along the road leading to the town of Bowling Green. They left Garrett's front porch and fled into the woods behind the tobacco barn. John Garrett, one of Garrett's sons who had just returned home from the war, watched as the two men fled, and their hasty departure at spotting the cavalry caused him to grow suspicious.

Concerned that the Federal troopers were seeking their guests, John Garrett approached the two men hiding in the woods and suggested that they be on their way in the morning so as not to create any problems for his father.

Later that evening when the two men came out of hiding, the injured man told the oldest son that he did not want to sleep in the house. The strangers were led to the tobacco barn and told they were welcome to spend the night there. Convinced that the two were fugitives and concerned that they might try to steal some of the horses on leaving, the son locked them in the barn.

In Bowling Green, Lieutenant Baker located Jett at the home of his fiancée. The Rebel was immediately taken prisoner and questioned at the point of a gun. On learning that Jett's passengers had stopped at Garrett's farm, Baker, Conger, Doherty, and the troop, along with Willie Jett, raced back up the road.

Around 3:00 a.m., the cavalry contingent arrived at a position approximately 100 yards southwest of Garrett's home. After dismounting and tying the horses, the troopers crept up to the residence. Conger reminded the troops that Booth was to be taken alive. Baker deployed them around the house. Baker and Doherty then stepped up to the front door and knocked loudly. When Garrett opened the door, he was grabbed by Baker, pulled outside, and questioned.

Baker asked Garrett where he was hiding Booth. The farmer replied that a man named Boyd had stopped the previous day but fled into the woods with his companion when the Union soldiers were spotted. Baker and Conger were convinced that Garrett was lying. They pulled him out into the yard and threatened to hang him from a nearby locust tree unless he told them the truth.

At this point, Garrett's sons, John and William, who had been keeping watch over the horses, arrived. As soon as the oldest son discerned the reason for the appearance of the soldiers, he told Conger that the men he was looking for were sleeping in the tobacco barn. When the location of the barn was pointed out, Doherty ordered several troopers to surround the forty-eight-by-fifty-foot wooden structure. Baker and Conger walked up to the closed door of the structure and hailed the men inside, ordering them to lay down their weapons and come out.

For the next twenty minutes, Baker and Conger conversed with Booth, who remained in the barn, which was littered with hay and corn husks as well as tobacco-drying equipment. The two officers urged the fugitive to surrender, but Booth refused to give himself up.

Herold told Booth that he wished to surrender, that he was tired of running and hiding and wanted more than anything else to go home. His entreaties were almost tearful. Herold's pleas drew curses and recriminations from Booth.

As Booth berated the young man, Herold walked toward the door, which was now unlocked and slightly open. Baker told Herold to extend his arms through the open door. As soon as he did, the lieutenant grabbed his wrists and pulled him roughly outside. Several cavalrymen seized Herold, dragged him some distance away, and tied him to a tree. Herold cried and whimpered, begging for mercy and claiming that he had no role in the assassination of the president of the United States.

Baker and Doherty continued their discussion with the man inside the barn. As they did so, Conger walked around to the rear of the building, struck a match to a wad of straw or corn husks, and thrust the burning mass through a gap in the planks. Almost immediately, a great blaze took hold of the dry material inside the barn. Flames illuminated the interior, and the men standing outside could look through gaps in the planking and see a figure standing inside, a man propped up on a crutch and facing the door, a rifle held close to his chest.

As the troopers watched in fascination, the figure suddenly dropped the rifle, picked up a small table, and turned to strike at the approaching flames. Seeing that this effort was useless in stopping the blaze, the figure threw the table to the ground and turned back toward the front door, drawing a pistol from his belt as he did so. Suddenly, a shot was heard above the din of the inferno, and the man in the burning barn pitched forward, falling face down onto the ground.

Reacting quickly, Baker leaped into the open doorway, snatched the revolver from the dying man's hand, and pulled the spastic body

outside. After dragging it several yards from the burning barn, Baker
was approached by Conger, who asked why the lieutenant had shot
the fugitive. Stunned, Baker looked at his fellow officer and told him
that he thought he, Conger, had shot him. Doherty joined the two men
and asked if Booth had committed suicide.

Confusion as to who shot the man reigned for several minutes until
a trooper, Sergeant Boston Corbett, came forward and admitted firing
the shot, stating that God had told him to do so. Other troopers standing nearby laughed and jeered on hearing the admission. Not one of
them believed that Corbett, a former inmate of an insane asylum, was
capable of doing such a thing.

Meanwhile, Booth was carried to Garrett's front porch and laid gen-
tly onto the boards. He had been struck by a pistol ball in the nape of
the neck, the shot having severed the spinal column. He was in intense
pain and begged for water, his voice a mere whispering gasp. Baker
sent one of the troopers to fetch a doctor.

A short time later, Dr. Urquhart arrived from Port Royal and attempted to get Booth to drink, but he was not able to swallow. Urquhart told Baker that the man would not live much longer.

Minutes later, Booth looked up at the faces hovering over him and
begged them to kill him. No one moved. Behind them, the barn collapsed. Garrett's roosters began to crow.

Finally, around 7:00 a.m., the wounded man died. It was announced
late that day that John Wilkes Booth, the assassin of President Abraham Lincoln, had met his fate.

Continuing and concentrated research and investigation into the traditional version of the flight, pursuit, and alleged killing of John Wilkes
Booth have yielded a number of pertinent and troubling inconsistencies. With the passage of time, many aspects of the long-accepted
history associated with the assassination of President Abraham
Lincoln have come into question as a result of close examination of
government documents as well as the discovery of new information.
Following a critical analysis of the long-accepted and so-called historical traditional version as well as utilizing some knowledge that
has become available throughout the years following the assassination, along with recently discovered documents, a revised sequence of
events that provide for alternative interpretations is presented in the
following chapters, events that contradict the established accounts.
The evidence presented herein points to the likelihood that the con-

spiracies to kidnap and kill President Abraham Lincoln extended to the higher echelons of public office and implicates some of Lincoln's close associates, including a cabinet member. Prominent among these interpretations is the revelation that the assassin, John Wilkes Booth, did not die at the hands of the federal soldiers at Garrett's farm but rather went on to live another forty-three years.

NINE
◆◆◆

Flight from Washington

Moments after shooting the president of the United States, John Wilkes Booth whipped his tired mare beyond the outskirts of Washington toward the Navy Yard Bridge. The Navy Yard was located near the end of Eighth Street. The bridge, a wooden structure, spanned the Anacostia River (sometimes referred to as Eastern Branch), a tributary of the Potomac River.

Around 10:30 p.m. on the night of the assassination, Booth rode up to the small guardhouse positioned at the Washington end of the bridge. As he approached, the sentry, Sergeant of the Guard Silas T. Cobb, stepped out to greet him. Cobb had been given orders to deny the passage of anyone across the bridge after 9:00 p.m. unless they had written permission from someone in authority.

Cobb stepped up to the hatless rider and asked him to identify himself. Booth provided his name. When Cobb asked Booth where he was going, the actor replied that he was on his way home to Charles. Charles was the county immediately south and west of the adjacent Prince Georges County. Booth told Cobb he lived near Beantown.

According to chronicler Benn Pitman, Booth told Cobb that he was unaware of the restriction and said, "I had business in the city and thought if I waited I'd have the moon to ride home by."

The sergeant, believing the rider to be an innocent reveler in Washington who merely lost track of the time, stepped aside to let him pass. Booth rode across the bridge and a short time later crossed the border into Maryland. During his testimony at the subsequent trial of the conspirators, Cobb stated that Booth was riding a small bay mare. The horse had been ridden hard, and both mount and rider seemed uneasy.

Fifteen minutes following the shooting of President Lincoln, all of the telegraph wires in the city of Washington had been severed. Researchers are convinced that the only person who knew enough about the telegraph system to render it inoperable was Major Thomas Eckert. When this catastrophe was reported to Eckert, he replied that he was too busy to look into it. Sabotage was immediately suspected, but investigations into the matter were never forthcoming.

Less than ten minutes after Booth crossed the Navy Yard Bridge, Sergeant Cobb stopped a second rider who arrived and asked him his name. The newcomer identified himself as "Smith" and told the guard he was heading to his home in White Plains a few miles to the south. When Cobb expressed his opinion that Smith was not his real name, the rider changed it to "Thomas." When Cobb asked "Thomas" why he was out so late, the man, who was riding a roan, replied that he had been in bad company. Cobb invited the rider to come closer. After examining him and his roan in the lamplight emanating from the guardhouse door, he waved him on.

Most historians have written that the second rider was David Herold. Recently uncovered information, along with Cobb's own testimony, cast serious doubt on this identification. Furthermore, encounters with documents long made unavailable provide evidence suggesting that the rider was Ed Henson.

During Cobb's time on the witness stand at the trial of the conspirators, the prosecution ordered David Herold to stand up so he could be identified. Cobb stated that Herold was "very near the size of the second horseman; but I should think, taller, although I cannot be sure, as he was on horseback." Cobb also stated, under oath, that the man who crossed the bridge that night had a lighter complexion than Herold. In short, Cobb was not at all certain who crossed the Navy Yard Bridge after Booth.

Within a few minutes after "Thomas" crossed the bridge, yet a third rider arrived, pulling his mount right up to Cobb. Before the guard could say anything, the rider identified himself as John Fletcher, an employee of Nailor's Livery Stable. He said he was chasing a stolen horse, a roan. Cobb, according to his testimony, decided that the newcomer "did not seem to have any business on the other side of the bridge," so he turned him away. Fletcher reined his mount around and rode back into the city.

As Fletcher returned to town, he was relatively certain that the man who entered the stable in the dark and stole the horse was David Herold because Herold had visited Nailor's establishment several times during the previous week. Fletcher returned to the stable and was putting away his horse when he learned from passersby that the president had been shot.

Fletcher walked out to Fourteenth Street, encountered a cavalry sergeant, and asked him if any stray horses had been rounded up. The sergeant replied in the affirmative and suggested that Fletcher proceed to Metropolitan Police headquarters on Tenth Street to inquire. Fletcher did so and while he was there reported the theft of the roan and provided a name and description of the man he believed stole the animal. Thus, it is only on Fletcher's say-so that most of the world believes it was David Herold who crossed the Navy Yard Bridge minutes after Booth.

TEN

❖❖❖

Surrattsville

After crossing the Navy Yard Bridge, Ed Henson rode to Good Hope Hill, located approximately one and a half miles southeast from the Anacostia River. This rendezvous remains controversial in that evidence suggests that it was at or near this location that Booth broke the fibula of his left leg as a result of his horse falling on him shortly after arriving.

The most commonly held belief that Booth broke his leg as a result of his leap from the presidential box to the stage immediately following the killing of the president is derived entirely from the actor's own diary. A close examination of the diary reveals that Booth attempted to create a daring and heroic image of himself during what he regarded as one of the most important events in the history of the United States. In the diary, he says, "I shouted Sic Semper before I fired. In jumping I broke my leg."

Not a single witness to the assassination heard Booth shout "sic semper" before shooting the president. No one heard him say anything until he landed on the stage. Once on the stage, over a dozen people described Booth as either running or rushing for the exit. Not a single person stated that Booth limped or favored one leg or another after jumping. A. M. S. Crawford stated, "I saw him as he ran across the stage." Harry Hawk referred to Booth "rushing" toward him. Edwin Bates said Booth "rushed rapidly across the stage." Frederick A. Sawyer was quoted as saying that Booth "ran with lightning speed across the stage." Julie Adeline Shepherd said, "[Booth] rushes through the scenery." Spencer Bronson states that the actor "rapidly left the stage." Major General Butler said that Booth "ran to the opposite side of the stage." Charles Sabin Taft stated that Booth was "springing quickly to his feet with the suppleness of an athlete." G. B. Todd noted that Booth "fled behind the scenes." Mary Jane Anderson, whose poor apartment's front door opened onto Baptist Alley opposite the back of the theater, said that Booth "ran out the back door." A man with a broken fibula is not likely to respond in the manner described by these (and more) witnesses.

Furthermore, when Cobb testified about his meeting Booth at the Navy Yard Bridge, he described the actor in detail but never once mentioned that he was in pain or distress. When John Lloyd, the tavern proprietor at Surrattsville, was questioned, he swore that Booth complained of a broken leg that was the result of his horse falling on him. Dr. Samuel Mudd swore in a statement to interrogators that the man he treated told him one of their horses had fallen on him, causing the break in his leg.

Mike Kauffman, author of *American Brutus*, says that the National Library of Medicine maintains statistics on equestrian-related injuries. According to the library, the second most common injury is when a horse trips and rolls on its side. The rider, unable to remove his or her foot from the stirrup, suffers the weight of the horse on the lower leg, snapping the fibula straight across, usually a couple of inches above the ankle. This is exactly the type of injury Booth suffered. According to physicians, the clean break experienced by Booth cannot occur as the result of a leap. The pressure from such an action would cause the fracture to be oblique, not transverse.

On approaching the summit of the low prominence, Henson heard his name called. Bringing his horse to a halt, he looked around, spotted Booth, and returned the greeting. Booth, still breathing heavily from his ride and grimacing from the pain in his broken leg, told Henson that he had killed the president. He asked his companion if he was going to accompany him. Henson said he was.

The plan, according to Booth, was to ride toward Upper Marlboro ten miles to the east. After stopping there, they would turn south and ride twenty miles to Benedict's Landing on the Patuxent River. There, they would board a ship registered to England but flying the Canadian flag.

As Booth and Henson rode in a southeasterly direction toward Surrattsville, the actor explained that they needed to stop at the old Surratt house, seven miles to the southeast. Around this time, Secretary of War Stanton ordered all routes out of Washington closed. Curiously, all exits were covered save for the Navy Yard Bridge, the most logical route for the assassin (or anyone else for that matter) to travel into the

Maryland countryside. Documents in the War Department archives prove conclusively that it was well known at the time that this route was part of the so-called Underground Railway traveled by Confederate messengers, smugglers, and spies. A search of War Department files, however, has failed to yield any information whatsoever that this avenue of escape was ever considered or mentioned by Stanton.

According to historians, Stanton knew a great deal about Booth and his planned escape route, but his decision relative to pursuit apparently took none of this information into consideration. A number of conspiracy theorists claimed that Stanton wanted Booth to get away. Others maintain that Stanton needed to confuse and divert federal and police patrols so that his own men would have the time and opportunity to capture and kill Booth.

On the way to Surrattsville, Booth told Henson that some arms, ammunition, and other things they needed were stored inside the tavern. They arrived around midnight, and while Booth remained on his horse nursing his broken leg, Henson dismounted and knocked on the tavern door, waking a drunk John Lloyd, the proprietor.

Following a short discussion with Lloyd, Henson went inside and returned a few minutes later with a drink for Booth along with a carbine and a package containing several items. He also carried two bottles of brandy. Booth inquired about a doctor, but Lloyd said there was no longer one practicing in the vicinity. The closest, he said, was Doctor Mudd, who lived three and a half miles north of Bryantown and near the head of Zekiah Swamp. As the two men rode off, Lloyd later testified that he heard them talking about having killed the president.

Around 2:00 a.m., and after riding three and a half-miles, Booth and Henson passed through the small community of TB and continued along the road to where it crossed the Mattawoman Swamp three miles farther south and then onto the road that led past St. Peter's Church and to the home of Dr. Samuel Mudd.

By the time Booth and Henson were on their way to Dr. Mudd's house, Stanton's press releases relative to the pursuit of the president's assassin did not even mention Booth's name, even though the killer was already known to dozens of people. It was not until 4:45 a.m. on Saturday morning, April 15, that Booth was formally identified by Stanton as the murderer, and even then the information was kept quiet.

Most Lincoln-era historians agree that if Stanton wanted Booth captured, he would have made certain the actor's name and likeness were broadcast far and wide as soon as his role in the assassination was determined. Stanton, however, was apparently in no hurry to capture Booth or to inform the country of the identity of the murderer. The War Department effectively withheld the assassin's name until the afternoon papers of the following day were already out. Could it be, as some have suggested, that Booth knew enough to incriminate Stanton and others in the assassination?

Cavalry troops were already patrolling roads paralleling the Potomac River, roads leading to Barnesville, Darnestown, and Tenlytown. Soldiers had orders to intercept all vessels on the Potomac River from Washington, D.C., to Point Lookout, where the river entered the Chesapeake Bay. Stanton also had all roads leading to Virginia blocked, but by the time the order was carried out, Booth had ridden twenty-five miles. By Easter Sunday morning, the mouth of the Patuxent River was closed, and the entire western shore of the Chesapeake Bay east of the capital was thick with army and navy patrols.

Booth managed to evade the roadblocks for several reasons: he had a good head start, the blockings were haphazardly undertaken, and the earliest roadblocks had been established in the least likely direction Booth would have traveled.

Furthermore, the only road Stanton had not closed was the one that ran from Washington to Port Tobacco, precisely the one taken by Booth. Even more bizarre, it was later learned that Stanton had earlier been informed by Louis Weichmann that the Port Tobacco road was the one Booth had planned on using.

When Captain James William Boyd heard the news of the Lincoln assassination, he was stunned, disappointed, and frightened. Booth, he realized, had completely destroyed his plan to kidnap the president. Boyd was now concerned that the subsequent investigation into the assassination would eventually lead to him and that he would be in great danger. The Confederate spy was convinced that he would be set up to take the blame and would receive no protection whatsoever from the Union speculators or from Stanton, the man who initially enlisted his services. He also feared that, once captured, he would be tried for his earlier killing of Thomas Watkins. In a hurry, he packed a change of clothes into a small bag and rode into Maryland. Boyd decided that the only sensible thing for him to do was to run. He sent a message to a son in Tennessee, telling him that he was leaving the United States for Mexico. Boyd asked his son to meet him in Brownsville, Texas. Boyd would never arrive.

The superintendent of Washington's Metropolitan Police, Major A. C. Richards, reviewed John Fletcher's description of the events involving the stolen horse. Richards, in fact, had been enjoying the play at Ford's Theater at the time of the assassination and had just returned to his office. Acting on his own initiative, Richards deduced the sequence of events from the theater to the Navy Yard Bridge. He wanted to send out a posse of policemen immediately in pursuit of the assassin, but as researcher Roscoe has explained, law enforcement protocol limited his authority in the matter and kept him "chained to his desk."

Richards ordered Detective John Carvoe to summon twelve policemen and go in pursuit of the suspected assassins. Richards, however, was confronted with a major problem—the Metropolitan Police did not have any horses. The military, on the other hand, had hundreds of available mounts, so he requested some from them. At first, the military did not want to provide horses to Richards. It is believed that members of the federal army were more concerned about earning rewards than in actually assisting Richards in the capture of Booth. Finally, after laboring through a dense network of government red tape, Richards was able to obtain enough horses for his policemen. By the time the horses were delivered and ready to go, however, the escapees had a ten-hour head start.

ELEVEN

❖❖❖

Dr. Samuel Mudd

Booth's fractured fibula was causing him great pain as he and Henson neared the home of Dr. Samuel Mudd. Although Mudd's residence was well off the route to the rendezvous on the Patuxent River, Booth determined a stop was necessary. In addition, he told Henson, there was a second British ship anchored at Port Tobacco, located a dozen miles southwest of Mudd's farm. Booth explained that the ship would take them out of the bay, into the Atlantic Ocean, and then on to England.

At around 4:00 a.m. on Saturday, Booth and Henson rode into the yard in front of Dr. Mudd's home. Prior to arriving, Booth donned the false whiskers he was carrying in his bag in the hope that the physician would not recognize him.

As the two men guided their mounts toward the house, they spotted Mudd watching them from a second-floor bedroom window. Henson dismounted and called out that his friend had a broken leg and needed attention.

When Mudd opened the front door, Henson introduced himself using his own name and, nodding toward Booth, said his name was Tyler (not Tyson or Tysen as has been reported). "Tyler," Mudd related to authorities later, had a heavy beard and kept a shawl wrapped around the lower part of his face. With help from Henson, Mudd helped Tyler off his horse.

Mudd invited the men into the house and led Tyler to a bed in the front room. The left ankle was swollen badly, forcing the doctor to cut away the leather riding boot. After examining the leg, Mudd discerned a slight fracture of the fibula about two inches above the ankle. Mudd told Tyler it was not a particularly dangerous injury. While Tyler complained of back pains, Mudd splinted the leg with pieces of a bandbox and bandaged it. With help from Henson, he carried the injured man to the second floor and placed him in a bed to rest. Mudd also provided him with an odd shoe for the left foot.

At 7:00 a.m., two hours after treating Tyler, Mudd sat down to breakfast with Henson and engaged in small talk during the meal. A tray of food was sent upstairs to Tyler.

At 7:22 a.m. on April 15, President Abraham Lincoln died from the wound inflicted by John Wilkes Booth. Surgeon General Dr. Ezra W. Abbott folded Lincoln's arms over his chest. The Reverend Phineas Gurley, who was standing nearby, whispered, "Our Father and our God," and began to pray. Following the prayer, Stanton is reputed to have said, "Now he belongs to the ages."

At 8:00 a.m., Police superintendent Richards dispatched a posse to Surrattsville. On arriving, the policemen banged on the door of the tavern, awakening John Lloyd. When he came out, the lawmen asked him if he knew anything of the whereabouts of Booth and Herold. Lloyd replied that he did not. Lloyd then sent the policemen away on a false lead.

Ford's Theater on the day following the assassination of President Lincoln
Library of Congress, Prints & Photographs Division, Civil War Glass Negatives and Related Prints Collection, LC-B8171-7765

Under orders from Stanton, Lieutenant David D. Dana, brother to Assistant Secretary of War Charles A. Dana, was busily establishing a command post at Piscataway, less than ten miles northwest of Dr. Mudd's house. From this location, Dana wired Assistant Adjutant General Chandler that he had arrived and posted his troops, thus making it impossible for fugitives to cross the Potomac River in this direction. In the same message, Dana included a strange statement: he told Chandler that he had reliable information that the person who attempted to murder Secretary Seward was a man named Boyd and related that he was the same man who had killed Thomas Watkins in Maryland. The source of this erroneous information is unknown.

While in Piscataway, Dana sent a message to a small command at Chapel Point near Port Tobacco. He informed them that the president had been assassinated and directed them to scatter out along the shores of the Patuxent River to the east. This order was rather odd in that instead of leaving the troops on the route that Booth was presumed to have taken, a well-known and often-used Confederate route, he dispersed them to a region where there was no chance at all of finding the fugitive. Historians have long pondered this odd and illogical order. No one knows for certain if it was at the initiative of Dana or if it came directly from Stanton. Whatever the case, Dana's patrol, according to Roscoe, was "hobbled."

In New York, Colonel Lafayette C. Baker, chief of the National Detective Police, received a telegram from Stanton requesting that he come to Washington and assist in finding the president's assassin. Only five days earlier, Stanton had accused Baker of aspiring to do the same thing. When Baker arrived, Stanton told him that "they" have now performed what they have long threatened to do and told Baker that it was time for him to go to work.

According to author Dewitt, Baker quickly determined that the aim of Booth had been to cross the Potomac River and land on the Virginia shore as close as possible to the Rappahannock River, cross it, and then turn west and flee into the mountains of Kentucky or Tennessee. Virtually all of Virginia was placed under military control.

The trail was growing cold, and the men in the field seemed somehow reluctant to share with Baker all they learned about the fugitives. During his career, Baker had stepped on many toes and was not a popular officer among the soldiers.

Following breakfast, Henson asked Dr. Mudd for directions, specifically the quickest route to the Potomac River. Mudd pointed toward Zekiah Swamp, which began just beyond the boundary of his farm. The shortest route was through the swamp, he explained, but one had to be wary of quicksand. On the south side of the swamp, he continued, was the Wicomico River, a tributary of the Potomac.

After learning the directions, Henson asked Mudd if he could borrow a razor so that Tyler could shave. While Mudd rummaged through a drawer for one, Henson inquired about the possibility of renting a carriage for a couple of days. Mudd said that he would ride into Bryantown and look into the matter.

Washington blacksmith James Booth (no relation to the actor) was a neighbor to the Herold family on Eighth Street. On the afternoon of the assassination, James's sixteen-year-old son, Johnny, left with David Herold for a horseback ride into Maryland. Herold claimed that he had an opportunity to sell a horse and had made an appointment with a prospective buyer. When the pair had not returned by Friday evening, James grew concerned. He hitched up a buggy and rode off to look for them. His search took him down the road that led past Dr. Mudd's house and into Bryantown.

It was early Saturday morning when James finally found his son at the home of Walter Edeline. The youth and Herold had gotten drunk and fallen asleep on Edeline's front porch. The father woke his son, helped him into the buggy, and returned to Washington. David Herold was left sleeping on the porch.

Mid-afternoon on Saturday, Henson received word from Mudd that no carriages were available at Bryantown; all of them been rented out to farmers to transport their families to Easter services the following morning. While in town, Mudd conducted some business.

Mrs. Mudd determined that Tyler would not be able to walk without crutches. Since there were none in the house, she asked the gardener to fashion a pair from whatever materials were available. Henson took the crutches upstairs to Tyler. An hour later, he was assisting his companion down the stairs to the first floor. As the two struggled with the descent, Mary Mudd noticed that Tyler had shaved off his mustache and that his whiskers, clearly a false beard, had become detached.

Henson informed Mrs. Mudd that they would be leaving shortly. Noting that Tyler was in great pain, she cautioned them not to travel.

Before another hour passed, however, the two men had mounted their horses and rode away into the swamp. Mary Mudd later recalled that it was between 4:00 and 5:00 p.m. when the men departed. Later, when Dr. Mudd returned, he informed his wife that he learned the president had been assassinated. He told his wife that the roads were crowded with military patrols.

Later that evening, Mary told her husband about the fake beard worn by the injured man named Tyler. She commented that there seemed to be something suspicious about the two visitors. She encouraged her husband to ride back to Bryantown and report the incident.

TWELVE

◆◆◆

The Swamp

Booth and Henson traveled along a cart road that wound throughout the upper section of Zekiah Swamp. The swamp, fifteen miles long and one mile wide, wound in a southerly direction from near Mudd's house to Allen's Fresh, a small settlement where the Wicomico River broadens into a wide backwater of the Potomac River. Save for a few squatters and woodcutters, no one lived in the isolated location of the lower part of the swamp, particularly along Allen's Creek. Trappers occasionally entered the area in search of raccoon, muskrat, and opossum. Dense foliage blotted out most of the sunlight, and deep pools of dark water often forced travelers to leave the dim trail and hack their way through the undergrowth.

Presently, the two riders came on a crude residence. A short distance from the ramshackle cabin and in the inky darkness of the thick woods stood a black man who quietly and without moving watched the newcomers approach. The two rode toward him and asked for directions to the farm of Samuel Cox. The black man, Oswald Swann, remained in the shadows and pointed down the trail and provided directions.

Having difficulty understanding him, the strangers told Swann to get a horse and lead them to the Cox farm. Swann climbed atop a swaybacked mare and rode up to the two men. Looking them over, he noticed that one was carrying crutches. Swann indicated the direction they were to travel and, placing his horse in the lead, rode down the path. The strangers followed single file.

Sometime between midnight and 4:00 a.m. Easter Sunday, the three men arrived at Rich Hill, the formal name of the Cox farm. Samuel Cox, the owner, heard the approaching riders and came out to greet them. Several minutes passed in conversation between the white men while Swann sat his horse some distance away.

Cox, like many landowners in this part of Maryland, was a southern sympathizer and known to offer help to Confederates from time to time. By way of identification, Booth showed Cox the initials tattooed on his hand. It appeared to Swann that Cox then explained some directions to the two. A few minutes later, the men rode away with Cox's overseer, Franklin Robey. After Cox reentered his house, Swann turned his horse and rode back to his home in the swamp.

Early the following morning, Cox rode down the path taken by the two strangers. After traveling about half a mile, he encountered them lying in a ditch. The man who identified himself as John Wilkes Booth was obviously in great pain from a broken leg. With help from Cox and Henson, Booth was lifted onto his horse, and the trio rode another mile to the south until reaching a dense, nearly impenetrable pine thicket located not far from a tributary of the Potomac River.

On returning to his farm later that morning, Cox sent word to his foster brother Thomas A. Jones that he needed to see him immediately. Jones was originally from Port Tobacco and owned a small farm four miles south and slightly west of Cox's. Jones was also a well-known southern sympathizer, had once been arrested and detained in a federal prison, and despised Lincoln. During the war, he transported people and goods across the Potomac River into Virginia in his boat.

When Jones arrived at Cox's farm at 9:00 a.m., he was told that Lincoln's assassin and a companion were hiding in the swamp and that they needed transportation across the river. Jones said that such a trip would be risky with all of the military on the lookout for Booth. He told Cox that he needed to talk to the two men. Cox gave Jones the directions to the pine thicket two miles west of the house and instructed him to carry food and drink to the fugitives.

The pine thicket in which Booth and Henson lay in hiding was dark, cold, and uncomfortable. From this location, the two fugitives could hear the passage of cavalrymen along the road a short distance away. They were to remain here for six days and six nights.

When Jones was fifty yards away from the pine thicket, he spotted Booth's bay mare. The horse was still saddled and bridled and was grazing in a small clearing. Jones caught the horse and tied it to a tree. As he approached the hiding place, Jones gave a whistle, a signal previously agreed on by Cox and Booth. Presently, Henson stepped from behind cover, pointing a carbine at the newcomer. Jones identified himself, showed Henson the food and drink he was carrying, and was taken to Booth. The actor was lying on the ground and partially covered by a blanket. Next to him were a rifle, two pistols, a knife, and his crutches. In his book published in 1893, Jones relates that Booth was dressed in travel-stained black clothes but that otherwise his appearance was "respectable."

Realizing that Booth was in intense pain, Jones told him he would take him across the river as soon as the patrols thinned out somewhat. To do it now, he explained, would be foolhardy. He told the two men he would bring them food and liquor every day until such time as they could cross.

During his visit, Jones told the men that he could see the bay mare grazing nearby. He suggested that the presence of the animal might betray their hiding place. Some time later, Henson moved the horses a significant distance away from the thicket and shot them. It is believed that the animals were led into quicksand before being shot, for they were never found.

When Jones reached his home that evening, he summoned Henry Woodland (identified in government documents as Rowland), a free black and his employee. He told Woodland to go fishing every morning in the boat that was kept at Dent's Meadow on the Potomac. If any federal officers were watching, explained Jones, they would soon be used to the presence of that boat in the nearby waters.

At church on Easter Sunday, Mudd told his cousin George about the visit from the two men. He stated that he provided medical assistance to one of them and admitted that he was rather suspicious of the pair. Later that day, George, a Union soldier, passed this information on to Lieutenant Alexander Lovett. The two men rode to the Mudds' house with a contingent of cavalry and questioned the physician. Mudd told Lovett that he never got a good look at the injured man's face and that the fellow complained often of back pain, likely brought on by spending a great deal of time on horseback. Every time he approached his patient, explained Mudd, he would cover his head with his shawl. Mudd told Lovett that he splinted the man's broken leg.

By the time Lovett finished questioning Mudd, he was convinced that the injured man was John Wilkes Booth and said so. Appearing startled, Mudd admitted that he had met Booth months earlier but insisted that the man who stopped at his house could not have been the actor. Lovett bade Mudd good-bye and rode away.

Lovett assigned three detectives—Bernard Adamson, Aquilla Allen, and Wallace Kirby—to hide in the trees near the Mudd house and keep watch on the chance that Booth might reappear. Lovett was convinced that Booth was hiding somewhere near Zekiah Swamp and might soon return to Mudd's house seeking medical aid for his broken leg. The three men were left with instructions to shoot anyone who appeared. Outwardly, the War Department was saying that Booth should be brought back alive to stand trail, but historians are convinced that Stanton secretly wanted him dead.

Mid-morning on Easter Sunday, detectives William Bernard and Ernest Dooley found David Herold sleeping along the side of the road leading to Hughesville, Maryland. Bernard recognized Herold as an accomplice of Booth's and placed him under arrest. Herold was taken back to the capital for questioning.

When Lafayette Baker arrived in Washington in response to the official request, he was taken directly to the offices of the secretary of war. Here, he found a panicked Stanton begging for help and explaining that Booth had to be found and quickly. If allowed to escape, said Stanton, the actor could identify a number of highly placed people as plotters and traitors, and many would be ruined. If Booth could be found before such a thing happened, however, everyone involved in the capture would receive hefty rewards.

Baker quickly organized a team of investigators. He informed his charges that Stanton had put up $200,000 in reward money to be split among the team should Booth be captured.

Baker ordered one group of troopers to Benedict's Landing to see what they could find out. He sent three men to Port Tobacco to search for Booth. Baker also arranged for a boat, the *Jenny B.*, to cruise up and down the Potomac River and intercept any suspicious craft. During one such patrol, the officers on board encountered an elderly black man who said that he saw two men resembling Booth and Herold entering a small boat to cross the river. One of the men, he said, was lame.

Meanwhile, David Herold was delivered to National Detective Police (NDP) headquarters for questioning. While Herold was held in confinement, Baker was meeting with NDP operatives Luther and Andrew Potter along with an Indian tracker named Whippet Nilgai. Nilgai had earlier worked with the government on several occasions. Baker unrolled some maps and showed Nilgai a number of suspected routes that Booth might have taken after crossing into Virginia. Baker explained that secret operatives had already infiltrated most of southern Maryland searching for clues to Booth's whereabouts.

Nilgai was to accompany the Potter brothers. Baker ordered the three men to find Booth before he was captured by civilian authorities and said that he was to be taken dead or alive. After the Potters and Nilgai departed, Colonel Everton J. Conger entered Baker's office with a rough sketch of a reward poster. The two men briefly discussed the pursuit efforts and the reward money. Baker confided in Conger that he wanted Booth dead. If the actor were to tell everything he knew to the wrong people, said Baker, a lot of high-placed officials would hang. The conversation between the two men was interrupted by a soldier who entered the room and informed Baker that David Herold had been captured and was waiting outside.

Herold was brought into Baker's quarters and seated in a chair. Threatening the young man with hanging, Baker got Herold to admit that he was involved in the kidnapping plans but not with the assassination. When it became clear that Herold knew about Booth's planned escape route, Baker told him pointedly that if he led authorities to the assassin, his life would be spared. If he refused, he would be killed. Herold agreed to cooperate.

During the time that Herold was in custody, authorities, acting on information they found in Booth's trunk, arrested Sam Arnold in Fort Monroe, Virginia. Under interrogation, Arnold implicated Michael O'Laughlin and Ned Spangler, both of whom were arrested shortly thereafter.

Around 10:30 p.m., Major H. W. Smith led several soldiers to the Surratt boardinghouse, where they arrested Mary Surratt, her daughter Anna, and a young boarder named Honora Fitzpatrick. As the women were taken into custody, a tall man dressed in filthy garb appeared at the front door. He was wearing mud-caked workman's clothes and was carrying a pickax. When asked his business, he glared at the officers and told them that he had been hired by Mrs. Surratt to dig a trench. He was there, he claimed, to find out when he could begin work in the morning.

Mary Surratt was called back into the house to identify the newcomer. When she saw him, she became alarmed, threw up her hands, and denied ever having seen him before. She told the officers she did not hire him. The man was relieved of his pickax and arrested. When

The boardinghouse of Mary Surratt
Library of Congress, Prints & Photographs Division, LC-USZ62-22438

asked his identity, he withdrew an oath of allegiance from a pocket and handed it to them. The name on the oath was Lewis Payne.

Payne was taken to General Augur's headquarters and interrogated but continued to maintain that he was just a ditchdigger. William Bell, Seward's butler, was brought in. Without hesitating, he identified Payne as the man who assaulted Secretary of State Seward. Payne was placed in shackles and imprisoned aboard the navy monitor *Saugus*. There, more interrogation continued with Major Thomas Eckert. Later, when questioned by Baker, Payne denied any knowledge of the attack on Seward. Additionally, he denied any involvement with Booth's plans to kidnap or kill President Lincoln.

After Payne was led away, Baker summoned an NDP detective and instructed him to have a reward poster made up, one that contained an image of Booth. The poster was to declare a $30,000 reward for the assassin. At the bottom of the poster, continued Baker, was to be a description of and reward for Lewis Payne. When the detective asked Baker why a reward was being offered for a man already in custody, Baker refused to respond and dismissed him.

Authorities now had under arrest six people who they were convinced played significant roles in the kidnap and assassination plots—Samuel Arnold, Michael O'Laughlin, Lewis Payne, Mary Surratt, Ned Spangler, and a man named Benjamin Ficklin. All were in custody aboard the *Saugus* and the *Monitor*. Herold was still in the custody of the NDP. It was determined a few days later that Ficklin had nothing to do with the plot and was released. Only John Surratt and John Wilkes Booth remained at large.

At noon on Monday, a contingent of soldiers led by Lieutenant Lovett and aided by tracker William Williams rode to Surrattsville and arrested John Lloyd. For two days, Lloyd was questioned while hanging by his thumbs from a tree. A notorious alcoholic, Lloyd was also denied alcohol. Eventually, the tavern keeper caved in and talked, stating that he had turned over guns and liquor to two men who had come to the tavern, men who could have fit the descriptions of Booth and Herold. Lloyd's information sent Lovett hurrying toward Bryantown.

In addition to being chained and shackled, each of the prisoners had a canvas bag fitted over their heads and tied around the neck. They were separated so that they could not speak with one another. Before being transferred from the ship to the Washington Penitentiary to await trial, the hoods, under orders from Stanton, were replaced with tight-fitting bags that, according to author Roscoe, fit the heads of the prisoners like the gas masks used during World War II and the Korean War. The new hoods were eyeless and possessed only slits for the nose and mouth. The prisoners also had their ears stuffed with cotton. The intention of these procedures was to keep each of them from seeing, hearing, or speaking. Each prisoner was chained to a seventy-five-pound kelso.

A number of the soldiers expressed shock and disgust at the cruel and brutal treatment of the prisoners. Prison surgeon Dr. George Loring Porter protested the methods to Stanton, claiming that the tight-fitting hoods would cause the prisoners to suffocate or lose their minds. Only Mary Surratt's hood was removed. Years later, Samuel Arnold wrote that the headpieces were actually tightened on the rest of the prisoners.

During the incarceration, Lewis Payne reportedly confessed to attacking Secretary Seward. Some are convinced that he confessed so that he would be relieved of the torture of the hood. It was for naught.

THIRTEEN

✦ ✦ ✦

Reenter Boyd

On Wednesday morning, April 19, David Herold led detectives Andrew and Luther Potter, along with Whippet Nilgai and four other agents into southern Maryland. The previous evening, Baker had coached the terrified Herold to claim that they were all friends of Booth and were trying to find him so that they could help him escape.

The ruse was ineffective. The first time it was used, the man being questioned was so insulted and infuriated at the suggestion that he might be hiding the assassin of the president of the United States that he exploded in a rage and threatened the party of lawmen with a rifle.

After riding away, Andrew Potter decided to try another approach. He knew that James William Boyd had been working undercover for the National Detective Police (NDP) and believed that the secret operative could help them find Booth. Potter also knew that Boyd, after fleeing Washington, was hiding at the Maryland farm of Colonel Frank Beale. Boyd worked for a short time at the Beale farm as part of his recent undercover operations in the area. On arriving at the Beale residence, Potter located Boyd and explained their mission to him. Boyd was fearful of more involvement with the federals and refused to participate. Potter told Boyd that if he did not agree to his terms, he would be arrested for the murder of Watkins and would likely be sent to prison for the rest of his life. Boyd eventually relented and agreed to cooperate. One hour later, Boyd secured his gear behind his saddle and rode off with the detectives.

One mile away, Andrew Potter spotted a farmhouse fifty yards off the main road. Boyd told Potter that the farmer was a Confederate sympathizer and might be worth questioning. While the detectives waited, Boyd and Herold rode up to the farmhouse. As they made their way slowly along the tree-lined lane, the two men engaged in conversation and learned that both of them were southerners and were being shamelessly used by the Yankees. Before much distance was covered, Boyd and Herold agreed to attempt an escape at the first opportunity.

Thirty minutes later, the two men returned to the point in the road where the detectives waited, stating that no one was home at the farmhouse. The group continued down the road toward Port Tobacco.

In the pine thicket near the Cox farm, Booth continued to nurse his wounded leg. From time to time, he wrote in his journal. During one spate of writing, the actor rationalized his role in the assassination and blamed others for weakness. Painting himself as a hero, Booth wrote that all of the troubles in the country could be attributed to Lincoln and that God simply assigned him, Booth, to be the instrument of punishment.

Throughout Washington and parts of Maryland, wanted posters engineered by Lafayette Baker were being tacked up. Oddly, the description of Booth contained little substantive information and no mention of his mustache, a principal indentifying feature:

> Height 5 feet 8 inches; weight 160 pounds, compact build; hair jet black, inclined to curl, medium length, parted behind; eyes black, and heavy dark eyebrows; wears a large seal ring on little finger; when talking inclines his head forward; looks down.

To this day, no one has been able to explain why, when more complete details of Booth's appearance were available, the circular provided information that was of little use and partly misleading; Booth's eyes were hazel. Why the contrived description was placed on the poster remains a mystery unless Baker simply did not want Booth found by anyone until his officers could catch up with him. By contrast, the description of Lewis Payne, who was already incarcerated at the time, was incredibly detailed and totaled 160 words as compared to the forty-two words of Booth's specifications.

Late Tuesday afternoon, the NDP detectives, along with Boyd and Herold, set up camp just off the road they were traveling. Following a late dinner, the men wrapped up in their bedrolls and fell asleep near the campfire.

Boyd awoke around 2:00 a.m. After looking around the camp and determining that the detectives were asleep, he awakened Herold and cautioned him to silence. Slipping noiselessly from the blankets, the two men managed to take one Spencer carbine and three pouches containing full magazines. Without disturbing anyone, they crept away in the darkness. When the detectives awoke the next morning, they discovered Boyd and Herold gone. Without pausing for breakfast, they mounted up and rode to the nearest headquarters to report the loss of the prisoners.

After sending a message to Washington informing Baker of the escape, the detectives continued on with their assignment. Luther and Andrew Potter followed the trail left by Boyd and Herold. The others rode to Bryantown to try to find Booth.

Within a short time, the Potters, along with ten other detectives, were assigned to the *Jenny B.* as it patrolled the Potomac River. At one point, the vessel was called in to the nearest port where a message from Baker was delivered to the operatives. The message stated that Booth was traveling with a male companion and that the two were likely hiding somewhere near the shore waiting to board a ship. The vessel, however, was unable to wait any longer and finally departed.

Andrew Potter decided that both pairs of men—Booth and Henson as well as Boyd and Herold—had already crossed the Potomac River and were in Virginia. After studying maps, the Potters decided that the only logical route that Booth and his companion could take to cross the river would be from Chapel Point near Port Tobacco to Lower Cedar Point on the Virginia side, a distance of ten miles. The Virginia site was between Mathias Point and the mouth of Machodac Creek four miles to the south.

Detectives Bernard and Dooley were provided with Spencer carbines, pistols, and plenty of ammunition. They were dropped off from the *Jenny B.* at Mathias Point and told to patrol the roads. Andrew Potter and several other detectives were taken farther downstream to St. Mary's City, where they leased riding mounts. From there, they undertook a concentrated search for the fugitives.

While all of these preparations were being made, the truth was that none of the men they were searching for had yet to cross the Potomac. Boyd and Herold were hiding in the southern Maryland woods not far from the point where Booth and Henson had taken refuge near the Cox farm. Unknown to one another, each pair had decided to cross the river, go to Gambo Creek, and proceed on to Port Conway on the bank of the Rappahannock River. From there, they would cross to Port Royal on the other side.

While Booth and Henson waited in the pine thicket, Thomas Jones continued to bring them food, liquor, and newspapers. During the evening of Tuesday, April 18, Jones stopped at the Brawner Hotel in Port Tobacco for a drink. While there, he was approached by a federal officer who identified himself as Captain Williams. After asking Jones a few questions, Williams informed him that the government was offering a reward of $100,000 for information leading to the capture of John Wilkes Booth. Jones was tempted, but his loyalty to the South was unswerving.

When Jones left the hotel, he noted that he was being followed. Everywhere he turned in Port Tobacco, he encountered detectives and cavalrymen, all searching and making inquiries. Jones's own house had been entered and searched. Fearing that he was being observed, Jones did not carry supplies to the pine thicket that night.

Meanwhile, Booth was growing more and more uncomfortable in his hiding place. The cold and dampness aggravated his wound, which was becoming more painful by the hour. When Jones finally arrived the following day, Booth insisted that he take him across the river. Jones told the actor that the river was being patrolled and that all access points were closely watched.

On Thursday, April 20, another reward poster was released, this one offering $50,000 for the murderer of the president. Booth's name was not mentioned, no picture of him appeared on the poster, and only a brief description of the actor was included, part of which stated that he wore a heavy, black mustache. On the same poster were $25,000 rewards for John Surratt and David Herold. Herold, whose name was misspelled as "Harold," was described as a chunky, little man; very young; and wearing a thin mustache. Herold, in fact, had been in NDP custody since April 16.

Yet another poster featured what were supposed to be photographs of Booth, Surratt, and Herold. The photograph of Herold, according to Roscoe, was "a schoolboy portrait that bore little resemblance to the way he looked in 1865." The photo had reportedly been obtained from Herold's mother, who removed it from a family album. The image of Surratt was clearly a picture of someone else. It was later identified as being a photograph of his older brother, Isaac, who was serving in the Confederate army in Texas at the time. Both Herold's and Surratt's names were misspelled.

A short time later, a revised wanted circular was produced under orders from Baker. One would like to believe that the NDP chief

SURRAT.   BOOTH.   HAROLD.

War Department, Washington, April 20, 1865,

$100,000 REWARD!

THE MURDERER

Of our late beloved President, Abraham Lincoln,

IS STILL AT LARGE.

$50,000 REWARD

Will be paid by this Department for his apprehension, in addition to any reward offered by Municipal Authorities or State Executives.

$25,000 REWARD

Will be paid for the apprehension of JOHN H. SURRATT, one of Booth's Accomplices.

$25,000 REWARD

Will be paid for the apprehension of David C. Harold, another of Booth's accomplices.

LIBERAL REWARDS will be paid for any information that shall conduce to the arrest of either of the above-named criminals, or their accomplices.

All persons harboring or secreting the said persons, or either of them, or aiding or assisting their concealment or escape, will be treated as accomplices in the murder of the President and the attempted assassination of the Secretary of State, and shall be subject to trial before a Military Commission and the punishment of DEATH.

Let the stain of innocent blood be removed from the land by the arrest and punishment of the murderers.

All good citizens are exhorted to aid public justice on this occasion. Every man should consider his own conscience charged with this solemn duty, and rest neither night nor day until it be accomplished.

EDWIN M. STANTON, Secretary of War.

DESCRIPTIONS.—BOOTH is Five Feet 7 or 8 inches high, slender build, high forehead, black hair, black eyes, and wears a heavy black moustache.

JOHN H. SURRAT is about 5 feet, 9 inches. Hair rather thin and dark; eyes rather light; no beard. Would weigh 145 or 150 pounds. Complexion rather pale and clear, with color in his cheeks. Wore light clothes of fine quality. Shoulders square; cheek bones rather prominent; chin narrow; ears projecting at the top; forehead rather low and square, but broad. Parts his hair on the right side; neck rather long. His lips are firmly set. A slim man.

DAVID C. HAROLD is five feet six inches high, hair dark, eyes dark, eyebrows rather heavy, full face, nose short, hand short and fleshy, feet small, instep high, round bodied, naturally quick and active, slightly closes his eyes when looking at a person.

NOTICE.—In addition to the above, State and other authorities have offered rewards amounting to almost one hundred thousand dollars, making an aggregate of about TWO HUNDRED THOUSAND DOLLARS.

Reward poster issued by Secretary of War Stanton six days after the assassination

Library of Congress, Prints & Photographs Division, LC-USZ62-11193 hastened to correct the mistakes manifested by the earlier poster, but the revised version was never seen by the public until after the trials of Atzerodt, Herold, Payne, and Mary Surratt. Inexplicably, the new poster contained a photograph of David Herold that was taken after he was captured by the NDP on April 16. The new photograph of John Surratt was made well after April 20, 1865, the date indicated on the poster.

One week following the assassination, Thomas Jones was purchasing supplies at a store in Allen's Fresh, located two and a half miles east of his farm, where Zekiah Swamp ends and the Wicomico River begins. While he was selecting goods, half a dozen cavalrymen rode into town, entered the store, bought drinks, and gathered around a table in conversation. A few moments later, a scout rode up and approached the soldiers. He told them that he had just learned that their quarry had been spotted in St. Mary's County twelve miles east of where they sat.

The troopers guzzled their drinks, mounted their horses, and rode away. Looking around, Jones determined that there were no soldiers left in the town. He decided that it was time to get Booth and Henson across the river.

FOURTEEN

◆◆◆

The Crossing

On Friday evening, it was dark when Jones entered the pine thicket and signaled the fugitives. When he was allowed to approach, he informed Booth of what had transpired in Allen's Fresh and told him that the time to make a break for freedom was now.

Jones and Henson helped Booth onto a horse, and together the three men left the thicket. For two hours, they traveled through the darkness, stopping once to eat. It had been cloudy and foggy the entire day, and as the night progressed, Jones later wrote that "clouds seemed to grow denser and the dampness more intense." Finally, they arrived at Dent's Meadow near the Potomac River. The meadow was a secluded spot located behind Jones's farm and a mile and a half north of Pope's Creek. The meadow was, in fact, a narrow valley located between relatively high and thickly wooded cliffs. A stream flowed through the center, widening gradually as it neared the Potomac River. In some tall marsh grass near a grove of trees, Jones retrieved the twelve-foot-long flat-bottomed boat hidden earlier by Henry Woodland. Jones pulled the boat to the shoreline.

Booth was helped into the stern, given an oar, and told to use it as a rudder. Next to him were placed two seven-shot revolvers. In his belt, Booth carried a large knife. He still clung to his crutches. Henson was directed toward the bow, where he seated himself and grabbed two oars. By candlelight and using a compass, Jones conferred for a moment with Booth, directing him to a point far across the wide river. He cautioned Booth to stay with the compass direction, and they would eventually arrive at the mouth of Machodoc Creek. Once there, they would see a house nearby. Jones told Booth to introduce himself to the woman who lived there, a Mrs. Queensbury. He was to tell her that he was sent by "the farmer," and she would hide him. Booth thanked Jones and handed him a wad of money. Jones took only eighteen

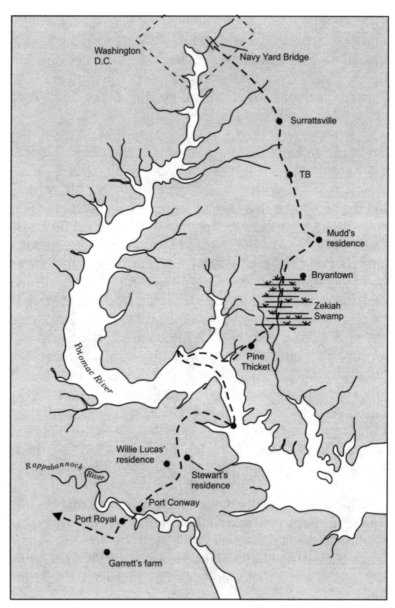

John Wilkes Booth's escape route

dollars—the cost of the boat—and handed the rest back to Booth. A
moment later, with Henson rowing, the boat disappeared into the inky
blackness that descended on the Potomac River.

While Booth and Henson were attempting to cross the Potomac River
in the darkness, Boyd and Herold were picking their way through the

woods and swamp in an attempt to reach a location on the Maryland side just west of Mathias Point, Virginia. On arriving, they located a boat that they intended to use in crossing the river.

For the first few minutes, Henson found the rowing relatively easy. After crossing one-third of the river, however, the boat was pulled along by the strong tide. Henson fought the current with all his strength, but ninety minutes later the boat was carried four miles back upstream to the Maryland shore in Nanjemoy Cove. Here, Henson helped Booth out of the boat and pulled the craft into a grove of trees. This done, they located a suitable place to camp for the night nearby.

That evening, Booth sat in the dampness next to Henson and wrote in his journal,

> After being hunted like a dog through the swamps, woods, last night chased by gunboats till I was forced to turn wet, cold and starving, with every man's hand against me, I am here in despair. And why? For doing what Brutus was honored for—what made Tell a hero. . . . I have only heard of what has been done (except what I did myself) and it fills me with horror. . . . To-night I will once more try the river with the intention to cross; though I have a greater desire and almost a mind to return to Washington, and in a measure clear my name, which I feel I can do. Tonight I try to escape these bloodhounds once more. . . . I have too great a soul to die like a criminal. . . . I do not wish to shed a drop of blood, but I must fight the course. 'Tis all that's left me.

This portion of the diary has long puzzled researchers. Why did Booth think it possible to clear his name? It is believed that the only way he could have avoided the gallows was to implicate men in high office in the conspiracies to kidnap and kill the president. Some historians are convinced that Booth intended the passage as a hint and that he intended to leave his diary where it might be found.

Boyd and Herold successfully crossed the Potomac River on the evening of Thursday, April 20, landing on the west side of Mathias Point. They moved quietly through the woods, passed Owen's store before the detectives arrived, and made their way toward the farm of Dan Green. By this time, it is estimated that as many as 10,000 men—soldiers, naval brigades, detectives, and volunteers—were involved in the hunt for Lincoln's assassin.

Two hours later, Boyd and Herold approached Green as he was cutting timber on the farm of William Spellman. The farmer immediately recognized Boyd, who was walking with the aid of a crutch.

The two men, old friends, embraced one another. Without bothering to introduce Herold, Boyd told Green that his leg had been bothering him, causing him severe pain. Green led the newcomers to the shade of a nearby barn.

Boyd explained to Green that he wanted to get to Tennessee and from there flee to Mexico. Until such time as they could arrange transportation, he asked if Green would hide them at his place. Boyd offered the farmer twenty dollars for his efforts. Green excused himself to tell Spellman that he needed to go home. He returned to Boyd and Herold a few minutes later and led them to his house.

On the evening of April 21, Lieutenant Lovett, accompanied by a squad of cavalry, returned to the home of Dr. Mudd. He asked the physician to turn over the razor used by the visitor. Mudd did so and informed Lovett of the boot he cut from the injured party. Lovett examined the boot. It was from the left foot, and on the inside he found a portion of an inscription: "J. Wilkes ———." The last name appeared to have been worn away.

Lovett showed Mudd a photograph and asked him if it was the man who visited his home. Mudd stated that there was a resemblance about the eyes and hair but added that it did not look much like Booth. The photograph was of Edwin Booth. It is unlikely that Lovett knew this. Why would he be provided with a photo of the assassin's brother? And who provided it? His superior was Stanton.

Lovett held up another photograph, this one of David Herold. The officer asked Mudd if it was the man who accompanied Booth. Mudd replied that it was not, that the photograph bore no resemblance to Booth's companion. In response to another question, Mudd described the horse ridden by Booth. His description matched that of the bay mare that Booth leased from the Washington livery stable.

Toward the end of the visit, Mudd stated that he had grown convinced that the injured man he treated was, in fact, John Wilkes Booth. Lovett arrested Mudd and sent him under guard to the outpost at Bryantown. The boot with Booth's name inscribed in it was sent by courier to Washington, where it was forwarded to the manufacturer in New York. The maker telegraphed the Washington operative that the boot had indeed been made for John Wilkes Booth.

During the afternoon of Friday, April 21, Dan Green left Boyd and Herold at his home and returned to the Spellman farm to undertake more work. When he returned Saturday evening, he found his wife visibly upset and complaining that the two strangers had been drinking and growing abusive. She pleaded with her husband to get them to leave.

When Green informed the two men that they were making his wife uncomfortable, Boyd begged his friend that they be allowed to remain hidden on the premises for just one more night. Boyd offered Green an additional twenty dollars. Besides, claimed Boyd, his leg was paining him badly, and he found it difficult to move. Green took the money and agreed to let the two stay if they promised not to upset his wife.

Late that evening, Booth and Henson made another attempt at crossing the Potomac River. The crossing was uneventful, and they finally landed the boat on the east side of Mathias Point near the mouth of Machodoc Creek early Saturday morning. From there, the two fugitives made their way a short distance inland and, one hour later, arrived at the home of Mrs. Queensbury. Here, they were introduced to Thomas H. Harbin, Thomas Jones's brother-in-law, and Joseph Badden. Harbin had been one of the original members of the planters group involved in the plot to kidnap the president.

While Booth and Henson were meeting with Harbin and Badden, Andrew Potter ordered the *Jenny B.* pulled to the shore at Mathias Point a short distance north of Gambo Creek. Here, Potter learned that some of his operatives were based at Owen's Store and had apparently arrived shortly after Boyd and Herold passed it in the early morning.

Potter listened to rumors that the fugitives might be in the area. He determined that if Boyd and Herold made a successful crossing, then it was likely that Booth and Henson did also. Potter selected four detectives, including William Bernard and Ernest Dooley, along with the scout Whippet Nilgai, to accompany him on a search toward the south. After acquiring the necessary supplies and armament, the group set off toward Port Conway by way of Gambo Creek.

FIFTEEN

The Diary

Harbin and Badden provided Booth and Henson with directions to the home of Dr. Stewart, reportedly a man who might provide refuge and supplies. By sundown, the two fugitives reached Gambo Creek, a tributary to the Potomac located north of Stewart's home. Needing to stop and rest, they hid in the dense woods alongside the creek. When finally ready to leave, the two men proceeded toward the physician's home, leaving behind them in the woods a number of articles, including Booth's diary.

Booth and Henson reached Stewart's house around 7:00 p.m. on April 22. They were disappointed to find the doctor somewhat unsympathetic to their plight. Stewart was aware of the government's death sentence promised to any and all who harbored or aided the assassins. He provided the two men supper but refused to allow them to remain at his house. Instead, he directed them to the hut of Willie Lucas, a free black man, where they spent the night. During the evening, Booth, upset at the treatment they received from Stewart, wrote a terse note to the physician from loose pages earlier torn from his diary:

Dear Sir: Forgive me, but I have some little pride. I hate to blame you for your want of hospitality: you know your own affairs. I was sick and tired with a broken leg, in need of medical advice. I would not have turned a dog from my door in such a condition. However, you were kind enough to give me something to eat, for which I not only thank you, but on account of the reluctant manner in which it was bestowed, I feel bound to pay for it. It is not the substance, but the manner in which a kindness is extended, that makes one happy in the acceptance thereof. The sauce in meat is ceremony; meeting were bare without it. Be kind enough to

accept the two dollars and a half (though hard to spare) for what we
have received.
Yours respectfully,
Stranger

On Saturday, April 22, Andrew Potter and his party arrived at Port
Conway. There had been no sign of the fugitives. Potter assigned Nilgai to scout the countryside and see if he could learn anything of the
whereabouts of his quarry.

One hour after sunrise the following day, Nilgai returned to the temporary headquarters established by Potter. During his search, he said,
he found a place in the woods near Gambo Creek that had apparently
served as a temporary campsite. At the location, Nilgai found a pistol,
a compass, two empty brandy bottles, a wallet, and a diary. Andrew
Potter examined the diary for a moment and gasped in astonishment.
It was Booth's.

Together, Andrew and another brother, James, also a National Detective Police (NDP) detective, read the entries. As they examined the
book, they were startled to read of Booth's secret meetings with influential politicians, businessmen, and military leaders, including Jay
and Henry Cooke, Thurlow Weed, John Conness, Everton Conger, and
even Lafayette Baker. Tucked inside the pages of the diary, according
to Potter's notes, were six photographs of women.

Andrew Potter, accompanied by Bernard and Dooley, hurried back
to the *Jenny B.*, where they encountered Luther Potter. They showed
him the diary. Luther informed Andrew that it had been learned that
Booth stopped at Dr. Mudd's house to have his broken leg treated and
while there shaved off his mustache. He also told Andrew that Booth
and another man fled into Zekiah Swamp. Luther said that the man
could not have been David Herold since he had been in custody at the
time, escaping only Tuesday night with Boyd. Andrew deduced that
Booth's traveling companion was Ed Henson.

Andrew and Luther discussed their findings. In the end, they decided not to return to Washington immediately, believing that it was
important to remain on the trail of Booth, whom they believed was
heading south. Andrew entrusted Booth's diary to Bernard and Dooley
and gave them instructions to deliver it personally to Lafayette Baker.
They did so on the evening of Saturday, April 22.

Long before daybreak on Sunday morning, April 23, Booth and
Henson packed their few possessions and loaded them into Lucas's

wagon. Lucas agreed to transport the two men through the woods to Port Conway, two hours away to the southwest. He was to be paid ten dollars.

By now, the reward money for Booth, Surratt, and Herold totaled almost $300,000 and had lured a number of bounty hunters who swarmed into the Maryland and Virginia countryside where the suspects were believed to be located. General Ewing, Dr. Mudd's attorney, observed that frenzy and madness ruled with excitement both intense and feverish and that reason was swallowed up in patriotic passion. Reports of Booth having been seen from as far away as Ohio, Illinois, Pennsylvania, Massachusetts, New York, Michigan, and Ontario, Canada, began arriving at NDP headquarters.

Frank Boyle and William Watson, two civilians each of whom bore a strong resemblance to Booth, were shot and killed. Boyle's body was taken to the Armory Square Hospital, where an autopsy was conducted. Subsequently, the body was buried in an unmarked grave at the Fort Lincoln Cemetery. Watson's body was taken to St. Mary's City, placed aboard the *Jenny B.*, and delivered to the Old Arsenal Penitentiary. Following an autopsy, the corpse was sewn into a canvas bag weighted with cannonballs and dumped into the Anacostia River where it meets the Potomac.

Sunday morning found Boyd and Herold aggravating Mrs. Green once again with their cursing and drinking. This time, she told them that they would have to leave. When Green arrived home, Boyd asked him if he would take them to Port Royal on the Rappahannock River. Green said that he was not able to leave, but a neighbor, a freedman named Willie Lucas, might be able to carry them to the riverbank town.

Following directions from Green, Boyd and Herold walked to Lucas's home, a squalid cabin in the woods. Lucas had some chores to do and was unable to drive the two men to Port Royal. Maybe in the morning, he offered. If they did not want to wait that long, he said, his son Charlie could do it on the condition that Green accompany them. Boyd and Herold returned to the Green home and asked Green to go along, offering him another twenty dollars. Green agreed, saying that he would arrive the next morning. Boyd and Herold walked back to the Lucas cabin, where they spent the night in the nearby woods, one night after Booth and Henson had slept in the cabin.

One hour before dawn, Willie Lucas drove the wagon into his yard, having just returned from delivering Booth and Henson to Port Conway. Since daylight was approaching, he decided to get busy on some chores. When it was full light, Boyd and Herold approached Lucas and asked about transportation to Port Royal. Lucas told them that he had work to do but that his son, Charlie, would take them. A short time later, Green arrived at the cabin, spotted Boyd and Herold sitting in the back of the wagon with Charlie Lucas at the reins, and climbed in behind them.

Young Charlie Lucas was confused. He could swear that the two men riding in the back of the wagon were the same ones his father carried to the river earlier that same morning.

Major O'Bierne picked up the trail of Booth and Henson after learning that they had crossed the Potomac into Virginia. He sent a wire to the War Department requesting additional forces to pursue the fugitives. Oddly, Lafayette Baker refused permission. Soon afterward, O'Bierne received strict orders to remain on the Maryland side of the river. Some historians claim that Baker neutralized O'Bierne so that he would not be able to share in the reward.

By 9:30 a.m., Monday, April 24, Booth and Henson were searching for a way across the 300-yard wide Rappahannock River near Port Conway. They walked along the north bank until they encountered the home of ferryman William Rollins. They told Rollins that they needed to cross over to Port Royal on the southern shore. Rollins explained that the ferry was at that moment on the other side of the river waiting for the tide to come in so that it could cross back. Booth explained that they were in a hurry. Rollins responded by telling him that he was going fishing.

An hour later, Rollins returned from fishing and found Booth and Henson still hanging around the shore. Rollins told them that he would row them across, but at that moment they spotted the ferry making its way back. Booth and Henson boarded the ferry shortly after it struck the north bank. Moments later, the craft, poled by Peyton Washington, was crossing back to the south side. After landing at Port Royal, Booth and Henson found a southwesterly trending road and took it.

One mile from Port Royal, Booth and Henson rendezvoused with a black man leading two horses. Henry Johnson, one of Booth's accomplices, former valet, and sometime dresser during his performances, handed the reins of the two animals to the fugitives. Johnson's mother, called Aunt Sarah, had worked for the Booth family for many years. Henry, likewise, had enjoyed a long employment with the Booth family.

Johnson and Henson helped Booth into the saddle. Johnson climbed up behind Henson and pointed the way to Fredericksburg, twenty miles to the northwest. Now on horseback, the men followed the route that paralleled the Rappahannock River toward that city.

On that same Monday morning, Andrew and Luther Potter, along with their contingent of detectives, had breakfast in Belle Plain on the Virginia shore. After dining, they saddled fresh horses and rode toward Fredericksburg. Luther was convinced that Booth left his diary behind on purpose in order to lead pursuers to believe that he was escaping in a southerly direction. Luther Potter reasoned that Booth's original intention was to escape to Canada. He decided that the road west from Fredericksburg was a logical route to depart into the Shenandoah Valley and thence northward and across the international border.

The Potters reached Fredericksburg round 9:00 a.m. and began making inquiries. By this time, however, Booth and Henson had not yet crossed the Rappahannock River twenty miles downstream. In Fredericksburg, a liveryman told the detectives that he had rented a wagon late the previous night to a man matching Booth's description. He stated that the man was using crutches and appeared to be in pain. He said that the stranger had a full beard but no mustache. After negotiating for the wagon, the stranger called to a black man who was waiting in the shadows. The liveryman said that he thought the black man was drunk. After climbing into the wagon, the pair drove northwest toward the town of Culpepper, thirty-two miles away. The Shenandoah River, considered Luther Potter, was only another forty miles beyond Culpepper. The road taken by the presumed fugitive matched the escape route suspected by the NDP detectives. They rode toward Culpepper in the hope of overtaking what they believed was their quarry.

On receiving Booth's diary on the evening of Sunday, April 23, Colonel Lafayette Baker examined it closely before handing it over to Stanton. As he read, he grew more and more concerned about certain entries in the little book that tied him to the kidnap plots, entries that could implicate him and possibly get him hanged for treason. Baker did not trust Stanton to afford him any protection. Around dawn, Baker turned the diary over to the secretary of war.

Stanton, Representative George Julian of Indiana, Major Eckert, Senator Zachariah Chandler, and Senator John Conness gathered in Stanton's quarters to review Booth's diary. They were reeling at the implications of the information contained therein.

When all had examined the diary, Stanton placed it in an envelope and sealed it. He handed the envelope to Thomas Eckert and instructed him to place it in the safe and that it was not to be released to anyone under any circumstances without his, Stanton's, personal endorsement.

Representative Julian remarked that it was one thing to hide the diary, but it was not likely that they could silence Booth when he appeared at his trial. Stanton replied that Booth would never be tried in an open court.

SIXTEEN

◆◆◆

Closing In

When Stanton, Eckert, Conness, Julian, and Chandler were examining Booth's diary, Lafayette Baker summoned his cousin, Lieutenant Luther B. Baker, Lieutenant Colonel Everton Conger, and Lieutenant Edward P. Doherty. He assigned the men to track and capture Booth. Lieutenant Baker was to lead the expedition, which included twenty-six mounted troops of the Sixteenth New York Cavalry. Luther Baker and Conger were officers in Colonel Baker's "Mounted Rangers," a battalion based in the nation's capital. Doherty was an officer with the Sixteenth.

Because Conger was the senior officer, he would be the leader of record of the patrol, a courtesy command. Colonel Baker, however, advised Doherty that he would actually be in charge of the pursuit and the acknowledged commander but that his troops would also be at the disposal of Lieutenant Baker. He instructed Doherty that he was to find Booth, capture him, and return him to Washington alive. Colonel Baker showed the lieutenant a photograph of Booth and asked him if he recognized him. Doherty replied that he recognized the actor's image but stated that he had never seen him in person. Colonel Baker handed the photograph to the lieutenant and told him to show it to his men so that they would be familiar with their quarry.

Leading Doherty to a large map hanging on a nearby wall, Baker traced Booth's presumed escape route and stopped at Port Royal. Drawing a fifteen-mile-diameter circle around Port Royal, Baker told Doherty that Booth would likely be found within that area. Doherty, Baker, and Conger, accompanied by the troopers, rode to the Sixth Street docks, where they boarded the streamer *John S. Ide*. Around 4:00 p.m., the boat headed downriver toward Belle Plain.

On Tuesday, April 25, O'Bierne received information that a crippled man hobbling on a crutch and accompanied by a younger man had been spotted near the edge of a swamp two miles north of Bryantown. Accompanied by Captain Beckwith, O'Bierne raced to Bryantown, picked up the trail, but lost it in a dense pine thicket. The two men, according to witnesses, resembled Booth and Herold. It was subsequently determined that this was a diversionary tactic to throw pursuers off the trail.

Shortly after noon, young Charlie Lucas pulled the wagon carrying Boyd, Herold, and Green up to the ferry at Port Conway. While Boyd struggled out of the wagon, Herold passed some money to Green and the driver. As Lucas and Green pulled away, Herold walked up to the ferry operator Rollins and made arrangements to cross the river. Rollins helped Boyd into the boat, Herold followed, and the trip across the Rappahannock was made without incident.

On reaching the south bank, Rollins assisted Boyd out of the boat. As the crippled man and Herold made their way up the bank, they were met by three mounted men in Confederate uniforms—A. B. Bainbridge, Mortimer B. Ruggles, and W. S. Jett. There remains some confusion with regard to the actual military ranks of these three soldiers. At various times, ranks ranging from private to major have been attached to them by various researchers. According to some documents, Jett, only eighteen years old, once served as a captain in the Confederate army but relinquished the rank when he joined Mosby's irregulars. Ruggles and Bainbridge appeared to be not much older than Jett. It is believed that Ruggles, who joined the Confederate army at a very young age, rose to the rank of lieutenant but like Jett gave it up when he joined Mosby. War Department records indicate Bainbridge and Ruggles as having once served as privates. At least one researcher claims that there is no record that Jett ever served in the regular army.

Herold approached the soldiers and introduced himself as David E. Boyd. Pointing to his partner, he identified him as James W. Boyd. He told the three Confederates that James was wounded in action at Petersburg and asked if they could help get him through the lines and deeper into the South.

Ruggles stated later that the crippled man was dressed in dark clothes and wore a black, soft hat. Bainbridge subsequently described the older man as wearing a dark suit of clothes, striding about on a crutch, and having a long mustache. He also stated that the man had the initials "JWB" tattooed on his right hand.

Jett told Herold that the only place in the region where a Confederate soldier might hide would be at Garrett's farm three miles to the south. The three agreed to take them there. Ruggles climbed off his mount and helped the injured Boyd into the saddle. Ruggles then doubled up with Bainbridge, and Herold climbed onto the back of Jett's horse. The five men arrived at the Garrett farm, six miles from the Rappahannock River, around 4:00 p.m. They were met by Richard Garrett.

Jett introduced his fellow soldiers, as well as John W. and "David" Boyd, to Garrett. He explained that the crippled man had been wounded at Petersburg and asked if he could remain at the farm to recuperate while the soldiers rode south to Richmond on a scout.

Garrett, who was known to aid wounded and hungry travelers, told Boyd he was welcome. As the soldiers started to ride away, Herold showed them one of his boots with a sole almost completely detached. He asked if he could go along to purchase a new pair at the next town. The troopers said they would ride back this way on Wednesday. Herold told Garrett he would return earlier.

Garrett introduced Boyd to his wife; his sons Jack, William, and Richard Jr.; his sister-in-law Lucinda Holloway; and his daughters Kate, Lily, and Cora. Following the introductions, Garrett encouraged Boyd to get some rest on the porch chair while he prepared something to drink for him.

In Culpepper, the Potters' search party was informed that a man resembling Booth and accompanied by another man had arrived by wagon earlier in the day, a wagon driven by a black man. The pair continued on toward Sperryville. The description matched the same one they had heard in Fredericksburg, so the National Detective Police party took off in pursuit. They caught up to the two strangers a few miles out of Sperryville, but the suspects turned out to be two innocent travelers. As the Potters were interrogating the two men in the wagon, Booth, Henson, and Henry Johnson were approaching Fredericksburg from the southeast.

SEVENTEEN

···◆◆◆···

The Killing at Garrett's Farm

Late Monday afternoon, April 24, Captain James William Boyd sat on the front porch of the Garrett home. He was visiting with Garrett's daughters Cora and Lily, likely the only pleasurable moments he had experienced in recent weeks. The little girls were delighted when he pulled out his gold watch chain and showed them the gold ring that hung on it, telling them that it was a gift from his late wife but too small for his finger. He also showed the little girls his initials, "JWB," tattooed on his right hand.

Boyd also showed the little girls his watch, explaining how it was wound and how the key was attached to the eighteen-carat cover. He said that when the hour struck, it was so hard that it vibrated the watch.

On Tuesday morning, Boyd's ankle pain lessened somewhat. He wound his watch and placed it in the pocket of his vest. Around mid-morning, Jack Garrett returned from an errand with the news of Lincoln's assassination and information about the rewards for John Wilkes Booth and David Herold. During dinner that evening, Jack asked Boyd if he had ever seen Booth, and the officer stated that he once saw him in Richmond during the John Brown raid.

As Jack Garrett and Boyd were discussing John Wilkes Booth, the contingent of the Sixteenth New York Cavalry led by Baker, Conger, and Doherty were riding toward Port Conway from the north. Among the riders was Sergeant Thomas P. Corbett, nicknamed "Boston" and soon to go down in history. Corbett was regarded as a bit odd by his fellow soldiers, and they referred to him as the "Glory to God man" because of his constant evangelizing. Corbett was regarded by most who knew him as being mentally unstable.

Corbett was thirty-three years old and five feet five inches tall and possessed an unlikely background for a cavalryman. Born Thomas H. Corbett in London, England, in 1832, he moved with his family to New York when he was seven years old. The family moved often, and Corbett's childhood was characterized as troubled.

As a youth, Corbett entered the hat-making trade. It has been contended that working around nitrate of mercury, the principal chemical used in treating felt, had an adverse effect on Corbett, causing hallucinations, twitches, and psychosis. He married when he was very young, but his wife and child died in childbirth. Corbett took to drinking heavily and became homeless. In Boston, Massachusetts, he was taken in by a Methodist-run mission and baptized. Corbett changed his name to "Boston" at the christening.

Thomas P. "Boston" Corbett
Library of Congress, Prints & Photographs Division, reproduction number unavailable

In a short time, Corbett became a street preacher. He often spoke of hearing voices and seeing angels and other signs in the sky. He grew his hair down to his waist because, as he told his listeners on New York City's Fulton Street, that was the way Jesus wore his. During his street-preaching days, Corbett was approached by two prostitutes. The experience unnerved him to the degree that he cut off his testicles with a pair of scissors. He said that the act was necessary for him to remain a holy man. His scrotum was mangled so badly that he spent a month recovering in a hospital.

During the Civil War, Corbett joined the Union army, where he acquired a reputation as a religious zealot. He carried a Bible everywhere and pulled it out and read it whenever the mood struck. Sometimes he read it aloud in ranks, occasionally condemning his commanding officers for what he perceived to be violations of God's word. Because of his bizarre behavior and refusal to follow most orders, he was court-martialed and sentenced to be shot. His sentence was later reduced, and he was discharged from the army. Somehow Corbett was allowed to reenlist in 1863. He was assigned to the Sixteenth Cavalry and, incredibly, rose to the rank of sergeant. In June 1864, Corbett was captured by the enemy and sent to Andersonville Prison. He was freed a few months later in a prisoner exchange.

During the early afternoon of Tuesday, April 25, Luther Baker found William Rollins, the ferryman, and asked him if he had seen a man fitting Booth's description. Rollins admitted that he had and that he had ferried him and another man across the river the previous day.

Rollins also told Baker that, after landing on the south side of the river, the two men visited briefly with a Confederate soldier named Jett and then departed. In response to more questioning, Rollins told Baker that Jett often went to Bowling Green to visit a lady he was courting. Baker asked Rollins to lead the troops to Bowling Green, but the ferryman refused, claiming that it would go poorly for him if it were known that he was aiding the Union. Baker then placed Rollins under arrest and ordered him to serve as a guide. During the next hour and a half, the ferryman transported Baker, Conger, Doherty, and the entire cavalry contingent across the river. It took three trips.

Around 3:00 p.m., a pair of horsemen approached the Garrett farm from the southwest. As they neared the house, it became apparent that one of the mounts was carrying two riders. When the newcomers rode up, David Herold slid off the rear of one of the horses, thanked Bainbridge and Ruggles, and joined Boyd on the front porch. The two Confederates proceeded on up the road toward Port Royal.

Boyd introduced Herold to the Garretts as his cousin David Boyd. After Herold showed Boyd the new shoes he purchased in Bowling Green, the two men began discussing plans for leaving the next morning and traveling to Mexico.

Two hours later, Bainbridge and Ruggles were spotted riding at full gallop from the northeast. They pulled up in front of the house just as Garrett walked out onto the porch. The two men informed the farmer that a contingent of Yankees had landed at Port Royal and were heading in this direction. With that, the two soldiers rode away toward Bowling Green.

Boyd and Herold heard the warning. After the riders had passed, they hurried across the yard and into the woods behind the tobacco barn. Garrett was taken by surprise at their sudden reaction to the news.

One hour later, the troop of Union soldiers rode past the Garrett house on their way toward the south and Bowling Green. When the last of them had disappeared around a bend in the road, Boyd and Herold crept out of hiding and made their way back to the house. Concerned about the mysterious behavior of his two guests, Garrett and his son Jack approached the pair and asked them why they ran when the soldiers approached. Boyd tried to pass it off as a minor problem stemming from some difficulties he had had with Union soldiers in Maryland. Both of the Garretts, however, were growing suspicious.

Later in the day, Jack Garrett was visiting a neighbor when he learned that the cavalrymen were hunting a crippled man accompanied by a young companion. He hurried home, rode directly up to Boyd and Herold, and told them that they needed to leave before they caused problems for his father. Boyd asked Garrett if he could purchase a horse, but Jack refused.

Boyd agreed that they should leave, but as it was growing dark, he promised that they would depart in the morning. Jack insisted that the men be gone at once, but he finally relented and agreed to allow them to spend the night in the tobacco barn on the condition they go at first light. Boyd handed Jack ten dollars for his help. Jack Garrett led Boyd and Herold to the barn, pointed out a place they could sleep in the hay, and left them around 9:00 p.m. Once outside, Jack closed the barn door and locked it.

The planks of the barn were of milled timber and nailed up such that four-inch-wide spaces remained between them. The spaces allowed for air to move freely throughout the structure to dry the tobacco. There was loose hay scattered throughout the interior along with a few pieces of unused furniture. In addition to the main door, there were two smaller ones that were fastened on the inside.

After locking the barn, Jack walked into the house and handed the key to his aunt, Mrs. Holloway, explaining what he had done. Recalling the other doors, he told her that he feared the two men would try to steal some of the horses. He told her not to give the key to anyone but him. With that, Jack left the house and fetched his brother William, and together the two went to the corncrib, where they spent the night standing guard over the barn and corral.

Around midnight, Baker located Willie Jett at Bowling Green's Goldman Hotel. Baker, accompanied by Conger, told Jett that they knew of his role in aiding Booth and demanded to know the whereabouts of the president's assassin and his companion. At first, Jett denied the charge, but Conger placed a revolver to his head, and several cavalrymen filled the hotel room. Visibly frightened and intimidated, Jett explained that he dropped two men off at Garrett's farm but that he had no idea one of the men was Booth. Aware that they must have ridden past the location, Conger ordered Jett to guide them back to the farm. Conger threatened to kill Jett if the information turned out to be false.

The cavalrymen, accompanied by Jett and Rollins, rode up to the Garrett farm around 4:00 a.m. on Wednesday, April 26. After deploying the tired soldiers around the house, Baker stepped onto the porch and knocked loudly on the front door. Garrett leaned out an adjacent window to see what was going on. Baker laid the end of his revolver against the farmer's temple and commanded him to open the door. Seconds later, Garrett unlocked and opened the door and, wearing only a nightshirt and pants and holding a candle, stood facing the soldiers.

Conger stepped up to the farmer and inquired about the two men who they knew to be on the premises. Garrett told Conger that they left, that they ran away into the woods. Baker did not believe Garrett and had him led out into the yard. Garrett's hands were tied behind his back, and he was forced to stand on a chopping block near a tree. A rope was thrown across an overhanging limb and a noose looped around the farmer's neck.

At this point, Mrs. Holloway came out of the house and took in the situation. When she spotted Jett, she screamed at him for bringing Union troops to the farm. Baker, placing the point of his revolver into Garrett's throat, asked him once again to reveal the whereabouts of the two men. Garrett, terrified, stammered out a response that the federal troops scared the men into the nearby woods when they passed the house the previous day.

Jack Garrett, alerted by the noise near the front of the house, left his post in the corncrib and, followed by his brother, hurried to the scene and shouted for Baker to wait. Pointing to the tobacco barn, Jack told him that the men he wanted were inside.

Conger ordered several of the nearby troopers to seize the brothers. While the elder Garrett was still standing on the chopping block with the noose around his neck, they were pushed toward the tobacco barn.

Jack Garrett told Conger that the two men were locked inside the barn and that his aunt had the only key. A trooper was sent to the house to retrieve it. Several soldiers were ordered to surround the barn and informed them that under no circumstances were they to shoot the suspects and that the fugitives were to be taken alive. When Conger received the key, he handed it to Jack and ordered him to open the door.

Baker stepped up to the barn door with Jack and knocked on it with the end of his revolver. Receiving no answer, he told Jack to go into the barn, collect whatever guns were in there, and bring the two men out. Jack demurred, telling Baker that the strangers were armed and that he was afraid of getting shot. Baker shoved Jack roughly toward the door. As he unlocked it, the chief of the National Detective Police called out to the two men inside to hand their weapons over to the man coming in. Following that, he commanded that they surrender and step outside.

All was silence outside the barn as Jack stepped into the dim interior. Seconds later, muffled conversations could be heard, then someone shouted, "Damn you! You have betrayed me! Get out of here or I'll shoot!" With that, Jack turned to leave, but Baker told him that he could not come out until he secured all of the weapons. Jack replied that they would not turn them over and, sounding anxious and frightened, asked to be let out. After pausing a moment, Baker opened the door, and Jack hurried out of the barn.

Baker called again to the men inside the barn to surrender, that they were surrounded by fifty soldiers, and that the structure would be set afire if they did not accede to the demands. From inside the barn, a voice called out, asking who it was making these demands and what they wanted. Baker answered that he knew their identity and that he was placing them under arrest. He insisted that they throw down their weapons and come out. The voice from inside called out again, repeating the questions.

Conger stepped up to the door and yelled that it did not matter who they were. The voice inside said, "This is a hard case. It may be that I am taken by my friends." After a few seconds of silence, the man in the barn said that if the soldiers would be led away, he would come out and fight the leaders one at a time. "Give me a chance for my life," he said.

Baker repeated his command to throw down any weapons and surrender. The voice responded, "Well, then, my brave boys. Prepare a stretcher for me." This was followed by silence.

During the exchange between the man in the barn and the officers, the cavalrymen dismounted and led their horses away from the structure should it be set afire. The soldiers, exhausted from not having slept for at least two days and nights, dropped to the ground under the nearby trees for some needed rest. Conger prevailed on six of the tired men to sit on some rails thirty feet from the front of the barn, rifles at the ready.

Conger then ordered Jack Garrett to pile some dry sticks against one wall of the barn, that they were going to set it on fire. Hesitantly, Jack carried an armload of kindling and stacked it against one wall. A minute later, he returned to Conger and told him that the men inside the barn threatened to shoot if any more sticks were set down.

At that moment, the voice inside called out, stating that there was a man in the barn wanting very much to surrender. A few seconds later, Herold cried that he was coming out, that he was willing to cooperate. He said he was unarmed.

Baker told Herold to come ahead. The young man stepped toward the partially opened door and, according to Baker, said, "Let me out quick. I do not know anything about this man." With caution, Herold extended his arms through the door. Baker stepped forward, grabbed one of the exposed wrists, and jerked Herold out and onto the ground. The fugitive was immediately grabbed by Doherty and several troopers. As he begged for mercy, Herold was led away.

From the moment he was seized and pulled from the barn, Herold maintained that he was unacquainted with the man inside. Later, Doherty questioned Herold and stated that he insisted that the man in the barn was named Boyd. When told it was Booth, Herold, according to Doherty, said, "I did not know it. I did not know it was Booth."

Baker turned back toward the doorway and called once again to the man inside to surrender and come out. From within, the fugitive repeated his offer to fight, this time stating that he would take on the entire cavalry troop. Baker replied that such a proposal was out of the question and repeated his command to surrender. The voice asked for some time to consider the proposition. Baker told him he would give him two minutes.

A few seconds later the voice said, "Captain, I've had half a dozen chances to shoot you. I have a bead drawn on you now, but I don't wish to do it. Withdraw your men from the door and I'll come out. Give me a chance for my life, for I won't be taken alive."

Baker, maintaining his position, said, "Your time is up. We will wait no longer. We will fire the barn."

The voice responded, "Don't destroy the gentleman's property. He is entirely innocent. He doesn't know who I am."

As Baker spoke to the man in the barn, Conger instructed his charges not to approach the structure and reminded them that under no circumstances was anyone to fire a shot. Following this, Conger crept to the side of the building where the kindling had been piled. After placing an armful of hay atop the loose sticks, he struck a match and started a blaze. The dry hay and wood caught instantly and began to spread to the dry barn timbers.

The dim light from the flames slightly illuminated the man inside. Conger saw him rise from a bed of straw and balance himself precariously with the aid of a crutch. He was wearing the uniform of a Confederate officer. With his right hand, the man raised a carbine and pointed it toward the growing fire. Anticipating that the fugitive might shoot, Conger reached for his pistol, prepared to return fire if necessary.

The man in the barn took a step toward the fire. He peered through the cracks of the siding as though attempting to catch sight of a target. He reached down, grabbed a small table, and appeared as if he intended to throw it at the blaze. After a moment, he dropped it, then his crutch, and moved the carbine from his right hand to his left. With the right, he drew a revolver from his belt and, noticing that the main door of the barn was still partially open, turned and began limping toward it.

A pistol shot was heard, and the man fell forward in a heap, rolling partly over. Reacting quickly, Baker, followed by Jack Garrett, ran into the barn, twisted the revolver out of the man's hand, and began dragging him outside.

According to Doherty, when he heard the shot, he pulled Herold over to where the wounded man lay just outside the barn, presumably so that the captive could identify him. Herold asked Doherty who the man was. The lieutenant replied that he, Herold, knew who it was. Herold stated that he did not and was aware only that the man's name was Boyd.

As Jack Garrett was calling for help to put out the fire, Conger ran around to the front of the barn as the wounded man was pulled outside. Baker asked Conger why he had shot him. Looking down at the wounded man, Conger replied that he did not shoot, that the man must have committed suicide. Baker said no, that one of the other soldiers must have shot him through an opening in the barn planking. Conger continued to insist that the man shot himself.

In subsequent testimony, Baker stated that he believed Conger had fired the fatal shot, an action he considered odd since Conger himself gave orders that the suspects were to be taken alive. Baker said, "If Conger shot Booth, it better not be known."

Baker and Conger, with help from Jack Garrett, carried the wounded man from the growing heat of the burning barn and laid him on the grass under some trees. As Baker examined the man, Conger and Doherty went among the troops trying to find out who fired the shot.

Boston Corbett stepped forward and claimed that he shot the man in the barn. When asked why he disobeyed orders, Corbett stated, "Providence directed me." At this statement, he was scoffed at and derided by his fellow troopers. There were soldiers near Corbett during the incident, but no one saw him fire a shot. Lieutenant Ruggles stated that no one saw Corbett fire and that one chamber of the wounded man's revolver was empty. Ruggles also insisted that the man shot himself. For reasons unexplained, Corbett's weapon was never examined.

When Corbett later testified about the shooting at Garrett's barn, he claimed that he accomplished the deed with a pistol, that he determined that the man was going to shoot his way out of the barn and that he simply aimed and shot him. Richard Garrett said that this was not true and that the man in the barn made no move whatsoever to fire on anybody.

According to Conger, an officer experienced in firearms, the shot came from a revolver. The man in the barn carried a revolver. According to all available research, Corbett carried only a rifle. In the end, Corbett was legally credited by the government with killing John Wilkes Booth.

William Hanchett, in his book *The Lincoln Murder Conspiracies*, stated, "One thing is certain: The shot that killed [the man in the barn] had not been fired by the emotionally unbalanced trooper." Author Otto Eisenschiml states that Corbett was standing thirty feet away from the tobacco barn when the shot was fired, a position ordered by Conger. Some maintain that Corbett might have crawled up to a position adjacent to the barn. If true, he would have been plainly seen by his fellow troopers, but not a single one confirmed that is what happened.

If Corbett indeed shot and killed the man in the barn, then he was in direct violation of specific orders. Although he was charged with breach of military discipline, he was never punished for his disobedience. Later, the original complaint was dismissed by Secretary of War Stanton.

Corbett ultimately received a total of $1,653.85 reward for his participation in the capture and killing of John Wilkes Booth. For years afterward, Corbett toured the country as "The Man Who Killed Booth" and delivered lectures on his self-described role in the killing.

In 1878, Corbett moved to Kansas, where he homesteaded eighty acres near Concordia. Friends eventually secured him a position as a doorkeeper in January 1887 for the state House of Representatives. He worked for only one month when, according to some accounts, he fired on and attempted to kill several members of the legislature. A short time later, he was judged insane and confined in an asylum in Topeka.

In May 1888, Corbett escaped from the asylum. Accounts vary of his life afterward. Some believe that he went to Mexico. Others claimed that he sold patent medicines from a wagon in Oklahoma. A few maintain that he became a revivalist preacher in Texas.

In the end, and in truth, no one actually knows Boston Corbett's role with regard to how the man in the burning barn met his death. The determination that Corbett was solely responsible for the killing was an easy and expeditious way to put an end to the case. To this day, however, contemporary historians who have examined the incident in detail maintain serious doubts that Corbett fired the fatal shot.

Blood was streaming from the wounded man's neck. The bullet had entered the right side below the ear and followed an oblique downward course at an angle of twenty degrees, penetrating three vertebrae, exiting on the left side, and leaving a noticeable hole. The ball had nearly severed the spinal column. From where he still stood on the chopping block with the noose still around his neck, farmer

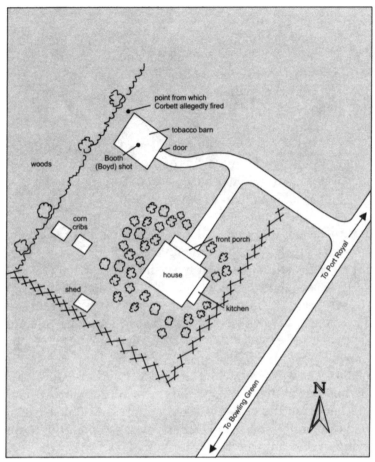

Map showing Richard Garrett's yard, farmhouse, and outbuildings

Garrett looked down on the wounded man, who was wearing a Confederate uniform. Nervously, Garrett asked Lieutenant Baker who the man was, stating that he heard someone say it was John Wilkes Booth. Garrett explained to Baker that the man gave his name as Boyd when he had arrived the previous day.

On the grass, the victim was having trouble breathing, and his body appeared to be completely paralyzed. In a halting, choking voice, he gasped out the words, "Tell mother . . . tell mother . . . I die for my country."

A mattress was dragged out of the house and onto the front porch. The wounded man was lifted from the ground and placed on it. A trooper was dispatched to Port Royal to locate a physician and return with him.

As the man lay on the mattress, he caught sight of Jett. He turned slightly toward Conger and asked, "Did that man betray me?"

As he bled from the neck, the dying man's clouding eyes watched as Conger went through his coat pockets, removing a pocket knife, two pistols, a compass, an ammunition box, a handkerchief, a pipe, keys, some tobacco, a bill of exchange drawn on a Montreal bank, a small amount of money, a file, and a leather-bound memorandum book. The signet ring, always worn by John Wilkes Booth, was not found.

Clearly in pain, the wounded man muttered, "Kill me . . . kill me." Baker looked at him and said, "No, Booth." In later testimony, Baker stated, "When I said 'Booth,' the dying man seemed surprised, opened his eyes wide, and looked about."

The physician, Dr. Urquhart, arrived some time later and, after examining the wound in the neck, told Baker that the ball had passed though the bones of the neck. He said that the victim could not live another hour.

With that pronouncement, Conger scooped up some of the belongings of the wounded man, including the memo book, compass, and bill of exchange, and stated that he was going to ride back to Washington and file a report with Lafayette Baker.

From the mattress, the wounded man was having difficulty breathing. He hissed, "Kill me. Kill me."

Around 7:00 a.m., the suspect died where he lay. History has long recorded that it was John Wilkes Booth, but from the time the man was dragged out of the burning barn, a great deal of confusion reigned, and doubt was expressed regarding his actual identity. Prevailing evidence suggests that it was not John Wilkes Booth at all but rather James William Boyd.

One of the first to observe the dying man who was not the assassin was Wilson D. Kenzie, one of the enlisted troopers with the Sixteenth New York Cavalry present at the Garrett farm. Kenzie had known Booth previously when the actor was smuggling medicines to Confederate troops. Kenzie was not one of the troopers who surrounded the barn but had remained some distance away. After the wounded man was placed on the Garrett porch, a private named Joseph Ziegen ran up to Kenzie and told him that the officer in charge claimed that the man who had been shot was John Wilkes Booth, Lincoln's assassin. Later, when he heard that "Booth" had been declared dead, Kenzie wanted to get a look at the man who murdered the president. When no one was around, he approached the body, lifted one edge of the blanket that covered it, and stared down at the victim.

During an interview published by the Beloit, Wisconsin, *Daily News* on April 20, 1898, Kenzie stated, "It was not Booth, nor did it resemble him." He said that the corpse he gazed on had red hair and was wearing a Confederate uniform. Booth, it was well known, had black hair and was wearing the same black suit he wore when he shot the president. Confederate Captain James William Boyd had red hair.

On March 31, 1922, Kenzie and trooper Ziegen both signed affidavits stating that the man dragged from the barn had red hair, was dressed in a Confederate officer's uniform, and wore heavy, mud-caked, yellow brogans similar to those supplied to Rebel officers. By this time, it was already a matter of record that John Wilkes Booth wore one tall riding boot on his right foot and a shoe provided by Dr. Mudd on his left. Kenzie told several people at the scene that the dead man was not Booth, but he was told to keep his mouth shut by a Lieutenant Norris.

The events that took place at the Garrett farm have been characterized by scholars as confusing and contradictory. Exhaustive research into the role of the government in the event reveals stunning evidence of secrecy, lying, conspiracy, and cover-up. Eisenschiml wrote, "Due to strange gaps and contradictory hedging in formal subsequent testimony, no senatorial inquest or ultimate historical inquiry could determine exactly what happened that night at the Garrett barn."

Perhaps not, but as more information has become available, as the recorded events of the assassin's flight and ultimate death have been opened for inspection, and as the subsequent events surrounding the body are examined in detail, it becomes shockingly apparent that John Wilkes Booth escaped and that James William Boyd was mistaken for the actor.

EIGHTEEN

The Body

Luther Baker was given charge of disposing of the body of the man killed at the Garrett farm. Still dressed in a Confederate uniform, the corpse was sewn securely into the horse blanket that covered him.

Baker needed a wagon to transport the body and asked Garrett if he had one. Garrett, who had been standing on the chopping block for over three hours, explained that he did not own a serviceable one. He told the lieutenant that a neighbor, a black man named Ned Freeman, had one. Baker sent two troopers to the Freeman cabin to secure the wagon.

About half an hour later, the wagon, an old army ambulance in poor condition, was guided into the Garrett yard driven by Freeman himself. The body was tied to a board and placed on the wagon bed. The saddle blanket was too short to cover the entire body, and the corpse's booted feet stuck out from one end.

Baker told Freeman that the body was to be delivered to Belle Plain, Virginia, twenty miles northwest of Port Conway, where it would be loaded onto the awaiting streamer *John S. Ide*. Lieutenant Baker, accompanied by one trooper along with the prisoner Willie Jett, was to serve as escort. When Baker had at least twenty-six soldiers at his disposal, the decision to have such a light escort for the body of the man whom they believed killed the president was an odd one. Even odder was the selection of Willie Jett to accompany the wagons since Jett was technically a prisoner. The decision by Baker to include him makes no sense and was never explained.

At 8:30 a.m., the wagon and escort pulled out of the Garrett yard and proceeded toward the Rappahannock River crossing at Port Royal. The remaining troopers, led by Doherty, followed several minutes behind Baker. David Herold, now a prisoner, was forced to run alongside a mounted trooper, a rope fastened tightly around his neck.

Even as he struggled to keep up with the column, Herold continued to maintain his innocence, claiming that he was only an accidental traveling companion to the dead man. He insisted on referring to the deceased as Boyd. After covering three miles, Herold, after much complaining, was allowed to ride a horse that was procured for the purpose.

On reaching Port Royal, Baker, seemingly in a hurry, did not wait for Doherty and the troops to catch up. Instead, he hastened to have the wagon, the trooper, and Willie Jett loaded onto the ferry. The river was crossed, and the ferry landed at Port Conway on the north shore without incident.

One mile out of Port Conway, the road forked. The right fork went directly to Mathias Point. The left fork wound across a seldom-traveled portion of King George County, eventually terminating at Belle Plain near the Potomac River. Baker, Conger, Doherty, and the twenty-six troopers had ridden down the Belle Plain road on the way to Bowling Green the previous day, so the lieutenant was aware that it was muddy from recent spring rains and replete with deep ruts and potholes. Furthermore, the road snaked through a densely wooded wilderness, and there were no towns between the fork in the road and Belle Plain.

Baker was inclined to travel the better route to Mathias Point and arrange to rendezvous with the *Ide* there, but Freeman turned off the main road onto the narrower lane. When the lieutenant inquired, the former slave replied that he had taken this route to Belle Plain many times. Baker, feeling a need to inform Lieutenant Doherty and the rest of the unit of the route selected, sent the trooper back down the road to relate the information. Baker, Jett, and Freeman continued on. Why Baker did not insist that Freeman travel the more acceptable road is beyond comprehension.

Around early afternoon, the day grew warm and uncomfortable. The Belle Plain road was in bad repair and wound around and among steep hills. The wagon, already old and in need of maintenance, strained in the deep ruts and groaned on the inclines. According to historian Osborne H. Oldroyd, the wagon broke down nine miles out of Belle Plain in a region known as Skinker's Neck, an isolated wooded spot adjacent to a pronounced meander of the Rappahannock River. A kingbolt, the vertical bolt that fastened the body of the wagon to the forward axle, broke, and the front wheels slipped out from under the vehicle. The body in the back almost slid out.

Somehow, Baker found another wagon and, as Oldroyd described, "pressed it into service." According to subsequent reports and publications, the time that elapsed between the breakdown and the procurement of another wagon was three to four hours. During that time, the prisoner, Willie Jett, escaped.

Sometime in the late afternoon, Freeman steered the newly procured wagon toward an old steamer landing he knew of, and the small party finally arrived at the shore of the Potomac River. Unfortunately, this landing had been abandoned for a least one year and was over half a mile downstream from the *Ide*.

Baker decided to ride upstream along the bank of the river to the steamer and arrange for some help. Concerned that roving forces of Confederate soldiers might still be in the area, he and Freeman hid the body in a nearby copse of willows. While Freeman waited with the body, Baker rode to the *Ide* and returned in two hours with a pair of sailors. The body was loaded back onto the wagon and transported to the ship, finally arriving around 6:00 p.m. The body was unloaded from the wagon, laid on the deck of the *Ide*, and placed under guard.

This segment of the journey represents another odd decision by Baker. Since he rode directly to the *Ide*, it was clear that he was not in need of a guide. Further, since he and Freeman unloaded the body and hid it in the woods, it is only logical to presume that they could have loaded it back onto the wagon by themselves. If Baker was worried about running into a contingent of Confederate soldiers, the two sailors whose help he enlisted would have served no useful purpose whatsoever. In addition, it is difficult to determine why he was concerned with such a thing at this point when they had just traveled well over thirty miles through similar country without it being an issue.

One hour later, the cavalry led by Doherty and Conger arrived and delivered Herold. The prisoner was immediately placed in irons and his head covered with a burlap sack. He was locked in the hold of the ship.

Sometime during the following day, Herold made a statement to Judge Advocate General Holt and Special Judge Advocate John A. Bingham. The statement, for reasons unknown, was never released. Herold, in fact, was never allowed to be interviewed or even given a chance to speak in court. The conclusion arrived at by a number of researchers was that Herold possessed information that the authorities did not want released. Educated speculation believes that it had to do with the true identity of the man who was killed at the Garrett farm.

During subsequent questioning by Holt and Bingham, according to author Otto Eisenschiml, Herold maintained that he crossed the Navy Yard Bridge in the afternoon of April 14, not the evening. Herold also insisted he was not with Booth when the assassin stopped at Dr. Mudd's residence.

Later, say the interrogators, Herold admitted that the man in the barn was Booth. Some are convinced this statement was either coerced or falsified. Eisenschiml contends that if Herold did indeed say that the man shot dead in the barn was Booth, it might have been because he believed that the real Booth now had a better chance for escape. Eisenschiml also believed that for Herold to continue to insist that the man was Boyd would cause him to be ridiculed. Ultimately, claims Eisenschiml, Herold realized that the authorities needed a dead Booth, so he gave them one.

Herold was isolated from the other prisoners and not permitted to talk to anyone. He was convinced that if he remained silent about the identity of the body and did what the authorities wanted him to do, he would eventually be given his freedom. The naive young man trusted Baker and Stanton, unaware that they could not let him live.

As the *Ide*'s boilers were stoked for imminent departure, Andrew and Luther Potter arrived at the Belle Plain landing and came aboard. While searching for Booth near Fredericksburg, the two officers received word that the assassin had been shot at Garrett's farm. The report convinced them that they had been following a false trail, so they packed up and returned to the ship.

On boarding the vessel, the Potters asked to see the body. Lieutenant Baker led the brothers along the deck to where the corpse lay. As two guards stood nearby, Baker pulled the blanket away from the corpse's face. The Potter brothers leaned over to stare. The two men looked down on a face that sported a long, shaggy red mustache. Straightening up, the brothers expressed shock and surprise and informed Baker that Booth's mustache was black and that he had shaved it off at Mudd's home only eleven days earlier.

According to Balsiger and Sellier, who quoted from Andrew Potter's personal papers, Baker was staggered by the news. "My God!" he exclaimed, "we got the wrong man!" The lieutenant then ran down the deck and off the boat, yelling for a fresh mount. He told the Potters that he was going back to the Garrett farm, and the two detectives decided to ride along with him.

The three men arrived at Garrett's late in the evening and awoke the family once again by pounding on the front door. When Garrett answered, Baker told him that they were looking for clues as to the identity of the man killed that morning. Garrett once again insisted that the visitor introduced himself as Captain James W. Boyd of the Confederate army. While Baker was interviewing Garrett, Luther Potter pulled his brother aside and told him that it was plain to see that Baker, Conger, and Doherty had caught up with Boyd and Herold and mistook the former for Booth. Andrew concurred.

Lieutenant Baker searched throughout Garrett's house but found nothing to assist him with the identity of the dead man. He bade the Garretts good night and, with the Potter brothers, returned to Washington.

Meanwhile, Colonel Lafayette Baker, in the company of Lieutenant Colonel Conger, took a carriage to Stanton's residence. Baker was shown to the secretary's bedroom. When he entered, he announced, "We've got Booth!"

Stanton, according to Baker in his 1868 book, placed his hands over his eyes and lay quietly for several seconds without saying a word. Then he rose and very slowly pulled on his coat. Stanton, described as a man normally given to frenzy, explosive behavior, shouting, and even hysteria, one who was characterized as impetuous and would have been expected to respond excitedly, demonstrated an uncharacteristic reaction to the information.

Stanton, in fact, reacted like a man who had just received some troubling news. He appeared very concerned, and his eyes reflected fear and worry. Baker later stated that Stanton "exhibited all the symptoms of a person who dreaded a deadly blow" and implied that he was concerned, perhaps afraid, that Booth had been taken alive. Stanton's apparent fear did not subside until Baker finally told him that Booth was dead.

When the Potter brothers arrived in Washington, the capital was rejoicing in the news of the capture of Herold and the death of John Wilkes Booth. They decided that it was imperative that they find Colonel Lafayette Baker and inform him of the true identity of the man killed at Garrett's barn. Baker was stunned at the revelation, refusing at first to believe it. Luther Potter explained to Baker that Herold would be able to testify that the man who was killed was Boyd, not Booth. Baker, clearly worried, stated that Herold must never testify.

The Potters reminded Baker that Herold would surely be tried and that the information would come forth at the time. Baker repeated his promise that he must never testify. A number of researchers believe that up until the time David Herold was hanged on the gallows, the troubled young man was convinced that the government had an agreement with him to let him go free if he kept quiet about the body that was being passed off as Booth's.

The ship bearing the corpse that was being identified as that of John Wilkes Booth sailed from Belle Plain up the Potomac River to the Alexandria. There it was transferred to a government tugboat (some sources say steamboat) named *Burnside*, which carried the remains to the Washington Navy Yard and anchored in the Anacostia River around midnight on the evening of April 26. At 3:00 a.m. the next morning, according to Doherty, the body was transferred to the *Montauk*, anchored nearby. Other sources state that the body was transferred at 1:45 a.m. The blanket was removed from the body, and the corpse was laid on the open deck on a carpenter's bench and covered with a tarpaulin. A single guard at a time was assigned to keep watch on the body.

One of the guards was Marine serviceman Henry Washington Landes. In his diary, as well as in a letter he penned to his sister Emma on April 28, Landes wrote that he saw the body, as well as Herold, transferred to the *Montauk* at 1:45 a.m. At 2:00 a.m., he wrote, they removed Booth's head. Landes guarded the corpse from 6:00 to 8:00 a.m.

David Herold was placed aboard the *Montauk* along with Jack and William Garrett, both of whom had been arrested and charged with harboring an assassin. At the time, Payne, Atzerodt, O'Laughlin, and Spangler were also imprisoned aboard the same vessel.

Commandant J. B. Montgomery of the *Montauk* sent a telegram to Secretary of War Stanton informing him that the corpse was deteriorating rapidly and requested instruction as to what to do with it. There was no ice on the vessel with which to preserve the body. Stanton replied only that Montgomery was to allow no one on board the *Montauk* unless they possessed a joint pass issued by the secretary of war and the secretary of the navy.

Several historical references indicate that Thomas Eckert, Stanton's aide, was appointed by the secretary of war to head an Identification Committee. Other sources say that Surgeon General J. K. Barnes was in charge. The committee, which gathered mid-morning on April 27 aboard the *Montauk*, consisted of Barnes, his assistant Dr. Joseph Janvier Woodward, Judge Advocate Joseph Holt, Special Judge Advocate John A. Bingham, Stanton's personal secretary William G. Moore, chief of the National Detective Police Colonel Lafayette Baker, Lieutenant Luther Baker, and Lieutenant Colonel Everton Conger.

Alexander Gardner, noted Washington photographer, was called aboard to take photographs. A number of witnesses were produced, including William W. Crowningshield, Charles M. Collins, Timothy O'Sullivan (Gardner's assistant), Charles Dawson (a clerk at the National Hotel), Dr. John Franklin May (a prominent Washington physician), Dr. Merrill (a dentist), and a lawyer named Seaton Munroe. The charge given to the committee was to formally identify the body as that of Lincoln's assassin, John Wilkes Booth. Technically, it was an inquest.

There was no autopsy performed in the manner they are performed today. There was, however, what has been called a postmortem examination. It was conducted by Surgeon General Barnes and Woodward on April 27. In the report, Woodward mentions the fractured fibula of the left leg and the mortal gunshot wound in the neck. Woodward stated that the wound was the result of a pistol ball fired from a cavalry revolver from a distance of "a few yards." Since the ball passed through the body and was never recovered, it must be presumed that Woodward was acting on information that had been fed to him. Woodward also proclaimed that death from asphyxia occurred two hours after receiving the wound. How would he have known this unless someone informed him or told him what to write?

Curiously, there are several extant lists of the members of the Identification Committee, and witnesses vary from list to list. The truth is that there is no clarity on the actual members of the committee, all of which adds to the growing evidence of confusion associated with the circumstances surrounding the body.

The only thing that the members of the committee had in common was that none of them had been personally acquainted with Booth. None of Booth's relatives were asked to participate in the identification, and neither were his friends, fellow actors, or any of the kidnap and killing conspirators, most of who were in custody only a few feet away on the ship. The identification witnesses were clearly hand-picked by the government. Regarding the corpse that the witnesses were picked to identify, writer Roscoe states that it "bore little resemblance to the photographic portraits of John Wilkes Booth."

The first witness interviewed by the committee was Crowningshield, a naval officer. During questioning, he stated explicitly that he knew Booth to be five feet nine and three-quarter inches tall. How he arrived at this figure is unknown. Booth was, in truth, slightly less than five feet eight inches. Crowningshield, however, expressed confidence that the body that lay before him was that of Booth.

Another witness, Charles M. Collins, the signal officer of the *Montauk*, identified the corpse at 2:00 a.m. in the light of flickering torches. In spite of the dramatic changes that had taken place in the face and body in the previous hours, Collins, who did not know Booth, provided a positive identification in that dim light.

History does not record lawyer Seaton Munroe's qualifications for identifying Booth, and not a single researcher believes that he had any. Munroe, however, stated that he was confident that the body was that of the president's assassin. When Munroe was asked by Judge Advocate Holt if he recognized any special marks on the body, Munroe replied that he recognized it "only from its general appearance." The fact is that the real Booth had several identifying marks, including a number of facial scars as well as scars on his arms and body, along with the initials "JWB" tattooed on one of his hands, that could have easily been identified by family members and friends. Furthermore, the signet ring that bore the initials "JWB" that Booth always wore was not among the possessions.

According to the report, witness Dawson, questioned by Judge Advocate Holt, identified the body solely on the basis of the tattooed initials "JWB" on the "left wrist." Dawson was a clerk at the National Hotel, where Booth sometimes stayed. Other official reports state that Dawson identified the initials on the "right hand." Regarding initials, Thomas A. Jones (who brought food and drink to Booth and Henson in the pine thicket) wrote that he saw initials tattooed on Booth's right arm. Booth's initials, according to his sister Asia, were located on the soft part of the hand between the thumb and forefinger. She could not remember for certain which hand they were on.

The tattooed initials should have proven to be an unmistakable mark of identification. Rather than settle the identity of the corpse once and for all, the various reported locations and descriptions of the initials merely added to the confusing accumulation of evidence. Earlier on April 26, Maryland Provost Marshal General J. L. McPhail told Secretary Stanton in a dispatch that Booth could be recognized by initials tattooed on his right arm as well as a small cross on his left hand between the forefinger and thumb. Dr. G. L. Porter, an army surgeon who viewed the body, wrote that he saw the initials "JWB" tattooed on the right hand.

Booth biographer Francis Wilson wrote that the assassin possessed the "distinctive mark of identification . . . the initials JWB which were pricked in India ink on the right hand." Bainbridge, one of the soldiers who accompanied Boyd and Herold, stated some years later that he had noticed the initials "JWB" tattooed on the man's right hand. It was known for certain that James W. Boyd had his initials tattooed on his right hand. Booth was right-handed. It seems logical to assume that, using his most dexterous hand, he would have self-tattooed the initials on his opposite, or left, hand.

Dr. John Frederick May was summoned to provide testimony. Eighteen months earlier, the Washington physician removed a fibroid tumor from the neck of a man who he believed was John Wilkes Booth. May treated and stitched the resultant opening. One week following the surgery, the patient returned. The wound, he claimed, had torn open during a play. May had to restitch the wound and told the patient that it would leave a scar.

May ignored several requests to appear. He was finally escorted to the deck of the *Montauk* by Lafayette Baker, who asked the physician to identify the corpse. Within seconds after Surgeon General Barnes removed the covering from the face, May, looking down on the corpse, stated that the body bore no resemblance to Booth whatsoever and said that he could not believe it was him.

Barnes asked May to describe the scar that was left on the back of Booth's neck. Without hesitation and without looking at the neck of the corpse, May did so. Official documents state that Barnes replied that May had described the scar on the body as well as if he were looking at it. Barnes said that May described the scar as being much like the cicatrix of a burn than that made by a surgical instrument.

During his subsequent testimony at the conspiracy trial, Barnes stated that the body had a scar "upon the large muscle of the left side of the neck three inches below the ear." He stated that it looked like result of a burn instead of an incision.

May later recalled that he was eventually allowed to examine the back of the neck and found the mark. He stated again that it resembled a burn. May made no mention of the bullet wound on the neck, which must have been very close to the scar. Subsequently, Dr. May provided a written statement relative to examination of the body on the *Montauk*. In it, there was no mention that he examined the neck of the corpse at all. It must be pointed out here that the bullet that struck the neck of the deceased had torn it up significantly, causing many to believe that a simple sutured wound may have been completely obscured or obliterated. A few researchers suggest that the "burn," as the mark was identified by Barnes, could have resulted from a weapon being fired close to the neck. Such a burn would be consistent with a suicide.

To add to the confusion, though May and Barnes initially identified the location of the "burn" as being on the left side of the neck, Barnes stated during subsequent testimony that it was on the right side. Several other witnesses also mentioned that the scar was on the right side of the neck. According to witnesses who were present at Garrett's farm when the deceased was shot, the man was struck on the right side of the neck.

May stated that the body possessed some of Booth's features but appeared to be altered and much older in appearance. Booth was twenty-six years of age, Boyd forty-three. The physician commented that he did not recall Booth's body being freckled, as was that of the corpse. May also pointed out that the corpse had a mustache. Several days following his testimony, May stated in a letter to a friend that the mustache he observed on the corpse was so long and untrimmed that the hair curled into the nose.

In his formal statement, May observed that he had never seen a greater change in a human being than that between the healthy and vigorous Booth he knew and the haggard corpse with its yellow and discolored skin, its unkempt and matted hair, and its facial expression, sunken and chapped with exposure and starvation.

The statement by May is puzzling. It is a fact that Booth was well fed by Thomas A. Jones while hiding in the pine thicket. The man who was killed at the Garrett farm was provided meals for two days. Furthermore, it can be safely presumed that while a guest of the Garrett's and in the presence of ladies, he had ample opportunity for personal grooming. Yet the corpse lying on the deck of the *Montauk* was "haggard," "unkempt," and starved and had a red bushy mustache. This certainly could not have been the body of John Wilkes Booth, and some have suggested that it may not have even been the body of James W. Boyd.

Even more bizarre and in direct conflict with the physician's observations, Seaton Munroe was quoted as describing the corpse's countenance as handsome and unmarked by any agony of lingering death. Munroe also pointed out that the corpse he examined had no mustache. It is not possible that Munroe and May examined the same body.

Continuing with his report, May stated that the right leg of the corpse was greatly contused and black from a fracture of one of the long bones of the leg. Booth had broken his left leg. Boyd's injury was to his right leg. Significantly, there is no consensus that the man shot in the barn possessed a splint as was provided to Booth by Dr. Mudd.

In spite of these dramatic differences and contradictions, May's testimony was concluded with the statement, "I have no doubt that it is [Booth's] body." On close inspection, however, it is clear that Dr. May's statement had been altered. In an apparent attempt at modifying the physician's testimony, several of his original words and sentences were crossed out and others inserted above. In addition, May originally used the term "scar." His statement was altered and the term "wound" substituted. Following the "identification" of the body by the committee, Surgeon General Barnes removed the perforated section of the dead man's neck to keep as a memento.

The question of suicide was never addressed by the committee or anyone else. Ultimately, the inquest amounted to little more than having as its objective the identification of the corpse as being John Wilkes Booth regardless of the conflicting testimony. Not a single witness who had known the actor well was ever called on to identify the body.

Following the work of the Identification Committee, the body was photographed by Alexander Gardner. Gardner conducted his work in the presence of War Department detective James A. Wardell. Gardner was allowed to take only one photograph and was immediately escorted to a darkroom to develop it. Wardell stood by his side the entire time, and when the photograph was ready, he took possession of it, along with the plate. According to Wardell, the photograph resembled Booth except that the hair was longer, the mustache was shaggy, and there was a bit of growth on the chin.

Moments later, Lafayette Baker received the photograph and the plate from Wardell. In response to subsequent inquiries, the government denied that any photographs were ever taken of the body. Sometime later, according to information uncovered by Balsiger and Sellier, the photograph became the personal property of Secretary of

War Stanton. To this day, no one knows what became of the photograph or the plate.

On the afternoon of April 27, Clarence E. Cobb, a former schoolmate of John Wilkes Booth and who had remained a friend for years, was asked by General G. W. Brice to go to the *Montauk* and identify the corpse. On his way to the vessel, Cobb was stopped by Surgeon General Barnes, who told him that his statement was unnecessary. He stated that the body had already been identified. Barnes also told Cobb that Dr. William Merrill, a Washington dentist, filled two teeth for Booth during the first week of April and that the committee noticed the new fillings in the corpse's mouth. The truth is that Booth was not in Washington during the first week of April. It has been documented that he was out of the city from April 1 to April 8. Furthermore, no testimony from Dr. Merrill has ever been found among the records.

During the identification process, a number of people were shown what was purportedly a photograph of John Wilkes Booth. They included Navy Yard Bridge guard Silas T. Cobb, ferryman William Rollins, and several soldiers who were present at the Garrett barn. In each case, they identified the photograph as being an image of John Wilkes Booth. The photo was placed in an envelope marked with the name of U.S. District Attorney Dawson and included in the archives of the judge advocate general. Years later when someone examined the photograph, it turned out to be one of Edwin Booth.

While the corpse was on the *Montauk*, a lock of hair was cut from the head by Dr. J. M. Peddicord. These same hairs were analyzed years later by a Dr. Muehlenberger, who declared that they were entirely unlike Booth's hair.

One can only ponder the significance of all the secrecy and deception and not a little incompetence on the part of the government. The inquest was clearly a mock (perhaps fraudulent) affair, without a doubt biased, and ineptly conducted, and it lacked the necessary honesty and thoroughness expected of such an undertaking.

Stanton gave the responsibility of disposing of the body to Lafayette Baker, telling him to hide it where it would never be found. Enlisting the help of his cousin Luther and an enlisted man named Edwin H. Sampson (some sources say Stebbins), Stanton ordered the body removed from the *Montauk* late in the evening and placed into a rowboat. A moment later, according to many witnesses who observed from the shore, a heavy ball and chain were also lowered into the boat.

The body was removed without the knowledge of *Montauk* Commander Montgomery, a highly irregular procedure. Montgomery learned that the body had been suddenly and unexpectedly taken from the ship from one of his officers.

The news of the removal of the body from the vessel immediately spread throughout Washington, and a large crowd gathered along the shore almost as soon as the off-loading had been completed. As hundreds of spectators watched, Sampson rowed the boat downstream and away from the *Montauk* past Buzzard Point and Greenleaf Point and into the Potomac River. Observers watched the progress of the craft until it disappeared a few hundred yards away into the gathering darkness of the evening.

Night fell as the rowboat neared Giesboro Point on the Maryland shore. Here, the boat was steered close to the bank among the brush and reeds, a location where sick and aged military horses were brought to be killed. The air hovering above this location was putrid and rank. The boat moved along the river toward the location of the Arsenal Penitentiary, eventually reaching the walls of the structure that rose from the water's edge.

According to George S. Bryan in *The Great American Myth*, an earthwork was constructed at this location during the 1700s. In 1803, a small military post was established. By 1817, it had become the Washington Arsenal. Eventually, a federal penitentiary consisting of some 160 cells was located here, the prison operating side by side with the manufacture and storage of arms and ammunition.

It was at this former penitentiary that the boat carrying the corpse arrived. Here, a wide door opened, and Lafayette Baker tossed the stern rope to a man who appeared in the opening holding a lantern. As the boat was pulled close to the door, Baker told the man to help him lift the body out. The corpse was removed from the boat and placed just inside the open doorway. Baker and Sampson then climbed out of the craft and entered the building through the same opening.

According to Baker, the three men lifted the corpse and, following the man with the lantern, carried it down a concrete hallway to a cell, purportedly to a vault where ammunition was once stored. Major Eckert, who was present in the building at the time but not at the actual interment, testified before a House Judiciary Committee hearing on May 30, 1867, that the burial occurred in the largest room in the arsenal building. It was thirty square feet.

In the middle of the room (some writers claim a corner), a portion of a concrete slab had been removed and a shallow grave excavated. The body, enclosed in canvas, was dropped in. Some claim that the body was placed in a musket case and the name "Booth" printed on the underside of the lid. It has also been written that the body was placed in an ammunition case. Dirt was shoveled and scraped in and the concrete slab replaced.

Assistant Surgeon General G. L. Porter was present at the burial and later wrote that two men "picked up the body . . . still in its wrapping of gunny sacking, and enshrouded in an army blanket, and deposited it in the shallow hole." Oddly, he made no mention off a wooden case. No one present at the burial ever saw the body.

Moments later, Lafayette and Luther Baker, along with Sampson, left the penitentiary the way they came in and climbed into the boat. As the massive door closed behind them, Sampson rowed away.

The overt secrecy and extreme measures surrounding the disposal of the body remain curious. Did officials fear that the corpse would be disinterred and recognized as belonging to someone other than Booth? Stanton claimed that the secret burial was undertaken simply for the purpose of preventing the assassin from being made the subject of Rebel rejoicing. On the other hand, a common practice during this time was to publicly display the bodies of slain leaders and notorious criminals as well as photograph them. The disposal of the body that the government claimed was Booth represented a noted and curious departure from that practice.

Accusations of a hoax soon reverberated across Washington and the rest of the country. Rumors abounded that the man taken from the burning barn in Virginia was *not* John Wilkes Booth. The *Constitutional Union* printed that the so-called capture, death, and burial of Booth was a fraud and maintained that the assassin had escaped. The Richmond *Examiner* wrote that Booth had indeed escaped.

Several days later, Lafayette Baker formally closed the case on John Wilkes Booth. Following that, he called for a meeting with the twenty-six detectives who had worked on the investigation and pursuit. Each of the detectives was given a $5,000 bonus for their contribution, but only if they signed a form stating that they had no further interest in the case. Each man signed. This begs the question: If the pursuit and death of the man who the government insisted was John Wilkes Booth had been conducted honestly and competently, why would this have been necessary?

During the month of September 1867, according to Bryan, the War Department decided to tear down a portion of the Old Arsenal Penitentiary building and improve the grounds. These plans made necessary the removal of the body touted by the government as that of John Wilkes Booth as well as the bodies of Atzerodt, Herold, Payne, and Mary Surratt. The latter four were buried in the yard following their executions on the gallows for their participation in the plot to assassinate President Lincoln.

On October 1, all five bodies were disinterred and carried to an arsenal warehouse, a little-used building with thick walls, a stone floor, and a heavy iron door. The warehouse was located on the eastern side of the parade ground. Inside, the five bodies were reburied in a trench eight feet wide and six feet deep. According to official documents, the body identified as John Wilkes Booth was placed at the extreme right.

On February 15, 1869, President Andrew Johnson signed an order to have Booth's body dug up and delivered to John Weaver, the sexton of Baltimore's Christ Church. The executive order came in response to a request submitted five days earlier by Edwin Booth.

On that same afternoon, men of the Ordnance Corps dug up the body. The bodies of Mary Surratt and David Herold had been removed weeks earlier and handed over to claimants. The name "John Wilkes Booth," printed in capital letters, was barely legible on the top of the slightly decayed box. Documents relating to the earlier burial stated that different lettering was on the underside of the lid.

Four troopers carried the box to an awaiting wagon provided by the War Department. Around 6:00 p.m., the vehicle pulled up to the back door of the undertaking firm of Harvey and Marr, 335 F Street. Ironically, the alley in which the wagon was halted was the same one from which Booth fled on the night of April 14, 1865.

The old ammunition box in which the body had been placed was badly decayed, as was the body within. The skin was dark brown and shriveled, and the skull was detached from the neck. The undertaker's son noticed at the time that only one shoe accompanied the body. According to historian Oldroyd, the body was formally identified by a dentist who claimed to have filled Booth's teeth. As the body lay in the Harvey and Marr funeral home, a number of people came and "positively" identified what they stated was a remarkably well-preserved corpse of John Wilkes Booth—this in spite of the fact that the body had never been adequately prepared for burial and was little more than a skeleton at the time.

A Miss Blanche Chapman viewed the body and described it as a skeleton with little of the remains left, all the flesh having disappeared. She also noted that now associated with the body were an old army shoe and a boot cut open at the top. Strangely, additional footwear had appeared with the body between the time that it arrived at the funeral parlor and when Chapman observed it.

The body was placed in a plain coffin, carried to the train station, and delivered to Baltimore, arriving at 9:00 p.m. From the station, it was delivered to Sexton Weaver's quarters on Fayette Street. It arrived wrapped in two army blankets on February 15.

News of the removal and delivery of the body circulated throughout the area. On the afternoon of February 16, a large crowd of people gathered outside Weaver's. Hundreds were allowed to view the body, which now reposed in a mahogany casket covered with a hinged glass plate in a back room of Weaver's. An article in the February 16 edition of the *Baltimore American* stated that a skeleton devoid of flesh was transferred from the box to a metal coffin. On one foot, continued the article, was an old army shoe. On the other foot was a boot cut open at the top.

During the days of February 16 and 17, dozens of people came by to gaze at the body. In spite of the fact that only a skeleton lay in the coffin, many offered "verification" that it was, indeed, that of John Wilkes Booth.

One of those who viewed the body was Basil Moxley, a longtime doorkeeper at Ford's Theater and a man who knew Booth well. Years later, Moxley stated that the corpse he viewed at Sexton Weaver's had red hair and was not Booth but rather another man.

Moxley also claimed that he had once been present during a meeting between Edwin Booth and a private detective where they discussed the notion that the corpse was not that of the famous actor and that the president's assassin was still alive. During the early 1900s, Moxley maintained that the burial of the government-identified corpse, whoever it had been in life, was arranged to pacify Booth's mother. He said that the entire Booth family, as well as a number of friends, were aware of this innocent deception. Moxley was adamant that the body delivered to Sexton Weaver by the government was not that of Booth. Moxley also declared that Sexton Weaver was involved in the deception and was well aware that the body was not Booth's.

While the body was at Weaver's, it was also viewed by Colonel William P. Pegram, a childhood friend of Booth. In a written statement, Pegram related that the body was clothed in a dark suit and that a long cavalry boot was still on the right leg while on the left was the other boot, which had been cut to make a kind of a shoe. At the time, Booth's left boot, which had been left at Dr. Mudd's house, was in the possession of the U.S. government. Apparently, the Confederate uniform in which the dead man was buried was exchanged for a dark suit.

Joseph Booth stated that if the body was indeed that of his brother John, it should have only one filled tooth in the head. A dentist was not present, but Sexton Weaver produced a dental chart. Charles Bishop, an actor who requested permission to view the body, looked in the mouth of the corpse, identified only one filled tooth, and pointed it out to all in attendance. This differs markedly from the report of the government-appointed dentist Merrill, who allegedly examined Booth's teeth during the inquest four years earlier and found two fillings. Colonel Pegram also stated that he saw only one filling. A third examiner, Henry C. Wagner, found only one filling in the mouth.

Rumors surfaced once again that the body laid out on display at Weavers was a substitute for Booth's. Several former Confederate officers came forward and, after examining the corpse, stated that the body was not that of the assassin.

The body that lay in repose at Weaver's was eventually buried in Baltimore's Green Mount Cemetery. From all descriptions and available evidence, it was not the body of John Wilkes Booth and may not even have been the same body that was examined aboard the *Montauk*.

To confuse matters even more, according to the Green Mount Cemetery records there appears to have been two burials of the body. One occurred around midnight following the arrival of the body at Baltimore in February 1869. The second took place on June 26 of the same year. Those present during the February interment stated that there were no services. For the June burial, there were services conducted in the Episcopal church.

The controversy, confusion, and contradictions surrounding the body identified by the U.S. government as John Wilkes Booth have never been resolved. Washington officials, including Stanton and Baker, remained steadfast in their positions that the body was that of the assassin. Given the circumstances relative to their involvement in the conspiracy, they could hardly have stated otherwise. Further, given the deception devised and promoted by these two men, it would be difficult to find much truth in anything they had to say about the matter.

During the years that have passed since the event at the Garrett farm, a growing number of researchers maintain quite the opposite—that the evidence for the body being that of Booth is weak and contradictory and lacks substance and verification. Many government files relating to the pursuit and capture of John Wilkes Booth, as well as information regarding the inquest, were hidden away and labeled top secret during the days following the original burial. Years later, after the authorities were forced to open the secret files, many key documents were missing. Booth's diary, which had been in the possession of Secretary of War Edwin Stanton, was found. Eighteen pages were missing, having been torn out.

On June 9, 1893, as funeral services for Edwin Booth were ending in New York City, most of the interior of Ford's Theater collapsed into a pile of rubble. It was subsequently explained that the tons of filing cabinets and boxes provided too much of a strain on the floors. Destroyed in the collapse were records of the Army Medical Corps that were stored there, including the surgeon general's reports on the inquest of the body that the government maintained was that of John Wilkes Booth.

NINETEEN

♦♦♦

Tracking John Wilkes Booth

While James William Boyd was dying on the front porch of Richard Garrett's house, John Wilkes Booth, accompanied by Ed Henson and Henry Johnson, was escaping westward across the state of Virginia. Following the farcical inquest aboard the *Montauk*, Colonel Lafayette Baker was growing concerned over the numerous reports filtering in that Booth was still alive. If true, he thought, the damage the actor could do to highly placed government officials was inestimable.

In order to pursue the leads relative to Booth, Baker called in Luther, Andrew, and Earl Potter and ordered them to follow up on reports that a man answering to Booth's description, accompanied by a white man and a black man, was seen passing through the settlement of Orange Court House by way of Fredericksburg.

Desperate for some concrete information about Booth, Provost Marshal O'Bierne was also sent to Fredericksburg on a tip that the assassin and two companions were seen in the area. When he arrived, however, O'Bierne found no real evidence that the men had passed that way.

After reaching the Orange Court House, forty miles west of Fredericksburg, the Potter brothers interviewed a black man who, on being shown a photograph of Booth, said that it was the same man who spent the night at his cabin. The man paid him five dollars. Acting on leads, the Potters continued westward toward Stanardsville, twenty miles away.

At Stanardsville, a merchant told the detectives that three men similar to the ones described had passed through the town on Friday, April 28. The merchant showed the Potters a barn in which the three men slept. Before leaving, he said, the strangers purchased some goods from his store, including a ham, several canned goods, and some oats.

The Potters traveled from Stanardsville a few miles down the road to Lydia, where they encountered a widow who told them that the same men spent the night in her house on Saturday, April 29. They paid for their room with the ham they purchased in Stanardsville. By this time, the Potters were convinced that the man they were following was John Wilkes Booth and that he was riding with Ed Henson and Booth's longtime valet, Henry Johnson. To their dismay, the Potters lost the trail at Lydia. In spite of riding several miles out from the town in different directions, they found no evidence of Booth's passage.

On May 2, as the detectives passed back through Lydia on their way to Washington, they were approached by a black youth about eight years of age. The lad asked them if they were still looking for the three men they inquired about during their earlier visit. When they admitted they were, the boy told the detectives that he knew where the men had been hiding and that his father had brought them food and coffee. He would take them to the place, he said, for twenty dollars. The detectives paid the boy, who then led them out of town.

The Potters followed the youth along a trail that wound back and forth across the bottom of a dry gully. Near the head of the gully, the boy pointed to a small cave a quarter of a mile away and said that that was where the men spent several nights. Luther and Andrew Potter went to the location and found enough evidence to convince them that their quarry had lain up there for several days. After questioning the young boy further, they learned that the men had spent one week in the cave.

Back in the town of Lydia, the brothers paused to examine a map. Beginning at Stanardsville, they drew a nearly straight line that ran through the towns of Lydia and Elton, across the Shenandoah River, and on to Harrisonburg, all locations they had already investigated. Looking closely at the map of Harrisonburg and the surrounding area, Andrew Potter offered the opinion that they did not go far enough in their search. After studying the map, he suggested that they travel on to the small community of Linville.

Once in Linville, they located a man named Louis Pence, a farmer who neighbors said rode a horse that was given to him by one of the three strangers who had come to town a few days earlier. During interrogation, Pence acknowledged that he accepted the horse, along with some money, from a man who asked to spend the night at his farm. The stranger was accompanied by two men; one was white and the other black. When shown a photograph of Booth, Pence tapped it and said that it was the likeness of the man who paid him the horse, except that the man had no mustache.

After assuring the concerned Pence that he was not in any kind of trouble, Andrew Potter asked him what became of the three men. Pence said that he took them to meet friends at Harpers Ferry.

If Pence was correct, Booth was circling back toward the east. Then it suddenly occurred to the detectives that Booth owned a farm near Harpers Ferry on the Potomac River where Maryland, Virginia, and West Virginia come together. The farm had been purchased from Michael O'Laughlin, who had won it in a card game. They made haste to that location. On arriving, they found no sign of Booth, nor did they find any indication that anyone had been there recently.

During the time that the Potters were searching Booth's farm, the assassin may have actually returned to Washington. According to Eisenschiml, a man named Hill (a printer and a friend of Booth) was walking down the capital's E Street when he spotted what appeared to be a woman hobbling on a crutch a short distance ahead of him. Hill believed that the person was Kate Robinson, and he strode forward to inquire about her injury. When she turned to face Hill on his arrival, the printer was startled to find himself looking into the face of John Wilkes Booth in disguise. Booth subsequently fled.

Dressing as a woman was not foreign to Booth. His sister Asia once recalled that as a young man, John "dressed himself in a petticoat and draped a shawl around [himself]. . . . He put on my long trained dress and walked before the long glass, declaring that he would succeed as Lady Macbeth." On another occasion, Asia wrote that her brother "dressed in my skirts [and] . . . a tiny bonnet then in fashion and went out across the fields. The men took off their hats as they passed in their work." Clearly, John Wilkes Booth demonstrated an early competency with female dress.

The trial of those deemed as conspirators in the assassination of President Abraham Lincoln—George Atzerodt, David Herold, Lewis Payne, and Mary Surratt—proceeded swiftly. It commenced on May 9. The suspects were arraigned on May 10, convicted and sentenced to die on June 30, and hanged on July 7. The uncommon speed of the trial was unheard of in American jurisprudence. Convicted as accessories in the assassination were Sam Arnold, Dr. Samuel Mudd, Michael O'Laughlin, and Ned Spangler. They were sentenced to prison on Dry Tortugas, a remote island several miles west of the Florida Keys.

The selection of this location has long confused historians. Normally, prisoners such as these would have been confined in one of the federal prisons in Washington or New York. It has been suggested that Stanton wanted these four isolated from potential interrogators and secretly hoped that they would die of fever. Records show that Michael O'Laughlin perished from yellow fever while incarcerated on Dry Tortugas on September 23, 1867. As will soon be pointed out, that was not true.

As the weeks passed, the public reaction to the assassination, the trial, and the executions died down. Lafayette Baker, along with Luther and Andrew Potter, remained concerned that the assassin was still alive and dangerous to those involved in the plot to remove the president.

On September 23, Andrew Potter, along with National Detective Police detective William Bernard, arrived by train at Harrisburg, Pennsylvania, for a hunting vacation. As the two men stepped off the train, the Harrisburg constable approached and stated that he had news that might interest them.

Pulling the detectives aside and speaking in a low voice, the constable told them that three men had been in town for several days and left only two days earlier. He told Potter and Bernard that he recognized one of the men, a black man, as Henry Johnson. The other two men, he said, wore full beards. The constable also said that on the morning of September 21, the three men had boarded a train for New York City.

Realizing that he was once again on the trail of Booth, Andrew Potter sought and found the train conductor, who in turn verified the constable's assessment. As it turned out, the conductor had known Henry Johnson for years. One of the other men, he said, walked with a bad limp and used a cane. When the conductor described the third man, Potter recognized him immediately as Ed Henson.

The conductor told Potter that the three men got off the train in Philadelphia, so the two detectives immediately headed for that city. On arriving, they questioned the crew of the train and learned that the three men had left that same afternoon, continuing on to New York City. There, however, the trail grew cold once again.

According to his papers located in the Neff-Guttridge Collection at Indiana State University, Andrew Potter accumulated enough information to suggest that Booth, Henson, and Johnson, along with Booth's wife Izola, lived off and on at the actor's Harpers Ferry farm from October through part of November 1865.

In November, Booth, Henson, and Johnson, all wearing disguises, departed for Pennsylvania, where Booth allegedly met with Kate Scott, a former lover. Scott, according to an affidavit she signed, stated that Booth was alive months after the killing at Garrett's barn and that he visited her in Pennsylvania. She also claimed that she was pregnant with Booth's child. After leaving Scott's home, the three men traveled to New York City.

Nothing more was heard of the three escapees until the third week of December 1865. A few days before Christmas, Henry Johnson, carrying three valises, was spotted by a detective in the New York City train station. When he noticed the man approaching, Johnson ran and disappeared into the crowd.

The same afternoon that Johnson was spotted in New York, Booth's wife Izola was recognized in a Baltimore train station. She, like Johnson, vanished into the crowd when a policeman approached her. Before the year was out, Lafayette Baker and the Potters received several more reports of Booth, Henson, Johnson, and Izola being identified in several different locations along the eastern seaboard.

Baker finally arrived at a decision. He told the Potters that the search for Booth was officially closed. The Potters, however, insisted that the assassin was still at large and encouraged Baker to keep searching. According to Andrew Potter, Baker told them that all of the rewards had been paid on Boyd, who was dead and buried as Booth, and that the chase was permanently called off.

As time passed, additional evidence accumulated that suggested that Booth traveled to Canada and from there to England. Izola remained in Maryland. In England, Booth allegedly married Elizabeth Burnley, a woman he had known prior to the assassination. There is evidence that he changed his name to John Byron Wilkes, a name he once used during his early days as an actor. He remained in England for several years and then traveled to India, where, some are convinced, he died. There exists other evidence, however, that the assassin, John Wilkes Booth, returned to the United States.

TWENTY

✦✦✦

The Return of the Assassin

Almost from the moment the mortally wounded man dressed in Confederate garb was dragged out of Richard Garrett's burning barn on the morning of April 26, 1865, whispers and rumors began circulating that the victim was not John Wilkes Booth. By the time the body reached the Washington Navy Yard, many were saying that the assassin had escaped and that the government was passing off the body of a Confederate spy as that of the actor. A few days later, similar rumors were even spreading throughout Europe and had been picked up and printed by the foreign press.

Subsequent events, all culminating in the burial of a body in Baltimore's Green Mount Cemetery, provided for considerable doubt that the man who assassinated President Abraham Lincoln had actually been captured and killed. A Democratic congressman named Eldridge, a member of an 1867 congressional investigation committee, noted all of the confusion surrounding the body and openly expressed uncertainty about its true identity.

If the corpse that was buried in the Old Arsenal cell was not that of Booth, then who was it? The most compelling evidence to date supports the notion that it was not Booth but rather James William Boyd. If that is true, then what became of the assassin, John Wilkes Booth?

By the 1930s, at least twenty different people had been identified as or made claims to be Booth. Some could easily be dismissed as frauds, imposters, or cases of mistaken identity. Others, however, have puzzled investigators and generated considerable reevaluation of the events surrounding the capture and death of the president's assassin. Some of the more noteworthy cases and sightings are presented here.

For many years following the assassination, Booth was allegedly seen in various parts of the world, sometimes acting in plays, sometimes attending the theater, and sometimes just walking down the streets of San Francisco, Rome, Paris, or Vienna. Many of these reports were undoubtedly false, springing from creative minds. Once in a while, however, a story would come to light that carried some level of credibility.

In June 1865, a scant two months following the assassination of Lincoln, two men came aboard the *Mary Porter*, a schooner that was docked in Havana, Cuba. The skipper for the 800-ton ship was Thomas Haggett. During the war, Haggett, using the *Mary Porter*, smuggled contraband through the Union blockades. When his home in New Orleans was burned to the ground by Union troops, Haggett and his wife moved aboard the ship.

Mrs. Haggett, writing in 1898, stated that one of the men who arrived on board the *Mary Porter* was very haggard and emaciated and was suffering from a broken leg as well as mental strain. Haggett told his wife that the man was John Wilkes Booth and that he wanted him to have her cabin for a few days.

Several days later, the *Mary Porter* arrived at Nassau in the Bahamas to deliver a load of sugar. Here the man identified as Booth left the ship, telling Mrs. Haggett that he was on his way to England. Before leaving, he presented her with a ring bearing a large diamond in a gold setting. Mrs. Haggett claimed that Booth died a natural death in England several years later.

During August 1866, Lieutenant William M. Tolbert, an officer aboard the Confederate privateer *Shenandoah*, got into a heated discussion with a southerner in a Calcutta, India, bar. The southerner claimed that he possessed information that Booth was alive and well and hiding in Ceylon. Booth was allegedly spotted in Ceylon on a number of other occasions over the years.

One interesting experience came from Andrew Jackson Donelson, once a close companion of Booth. Donelson claimed to have encountered the assassin on a Pacific island in the late 1860s. Donelson, who had served in the Army of the Confederacy, was working as first mate on a ship sailing from San Francisco to Shanghai. On arriving at the Palau Islands, some 600 miles east of the Philippines, Donelson, along with several crew members, went ashore for water and supplies.

During the process of obtaining needed supplies, Donelson encountered five men and a woman, all Americans. The leader of the group advanced toward Donelson and extended his hand in greeting. According to Donelson, it was John Wilkes Booth. In an article that appeared in a St. Louis newspaper and quoted by George S. Bryan, Donelson stated that "there was no mistaking [Booth's] identity."

The man who Donelson claimed was Booth asked the seaman not to tell anyone of his whereabouts for at least a year. Booth introduced the woman as his wife and said that the other four men were not aware of his identity. According to Donelson, Booth told him that his escape had taken him to Mexico, South America, Africa, Turkey, Arabia, Italy, and China. In China, he claimed, he played the title role in *Richard III* before American residents and naval officers.

On the island, Booth handed Donelson a gold medal and asked him to deliver it to his brother Edwin. The same medal, according to Donelson, had once been awarded to Edwin Booth by "the citizens of New York."

In 1870, a stranger arrived in the tiny town of Forestville in northern California's Sonoma County, fifty miles northwest of San Francisco. In this part of California, a number of southern secessionists found refuge. The stranger gave his name as Thomas Jerome, but in a short time the residents came to believe that it was John Wilkes Booth. Jerome, incidentally, was a Booth family name. According to one story, a Secret Service officer arrived in Forestville seeking to interrogate Jerome. On learning this information, Jerome fled from the region, returning only when the operative was called back to Washington.

Jerome bore a remarkable resemblance to Booth. When Forestville residents were later shown photographs of Booth, they identified the images as Jerome. Jerome himself never claimed to be Booth, and a subsequent handwriting analysis failed to link him to the actor. Another investigation reported that Jerome's real name was Thomas McGittigan and that he had originally come from Philadelphia.

During the early 1880s, an Episcopal minister going by the name of James G. Armstrong lived in Richmond, Virginia. Armstrong looked remarkably like Booth, loved the theater and attended it often, and manifested certain dramatic skills during his sermons. Armstrong also walked with a cane as a result of a pronounced limp. His left leg, he once stated, had been broken in a fall. Armstrong also had a scar on the back of his neck, a scar that corresponded to the one mentioned by

Dr. Frederick May and that was the result of the removal of a tumor from a man he believed was Booth.

Armstrong was once called into court to testify in a lawsuit against the church. During the questioning, an attorney for the plaintiff asked him point blank if he was John Wilkes Booth. Armstrong did not deny the association, replying merely that he was on trial as James Armstrong, not John Wilkes Booth.

In 1884, Armstrong left Richmond for Atlanta. In 1888, he resigned his post with the church and became a paid lecturer. His favorite topics were *Hamlet* and *Richard III*. During this time, it was reported, he confessed to his wife that he was, in fact, John Wilkes Booth.

In the late 1880s, Edwin Booth was performing in an Atlanta theater, and Armstrong was in the audience. During the play, the elder Booth chanced to look on the features of Armstrong and, startled, paused in his monologue. At 1:00 the following morning, Edwin Booth was transported by carriage to Armstrong's home, where the two visited for several hours. What the two men discussed was never revealed.

On another occasion, an Atlanta hotel guest was gazing out the window of the dining room when Armstrong passed by on the sidewalk outside. The guest, visibly disturbed, pointed at Armstrong and told diners at a nearby table that the man who just walked by was John Wilkes Booth. When they informed him that it was the Reverend James G. Armstrong, the guest replied that though that might be the name he went by in Atlanta, his real name was John Wilkes Booth.

Armstrong died in 1891. Because of persistent rumors that he might have been Booth, the New York *Herald* undertook an investigation in 1903 into the mysterious minister's past. The *Herald* concluded that Armstrong could not have been Booth, claiming that it discovered evidence that the minister was living in western Ohio during the time the actor was known to be residing in New York and Baltimore.

A provocative case of a man believed by some to be Booth involved a resident of Morgan County, Tennessee, from 1866 to 1885. One day, a stranger who gave his name as Sinclair arrived in Wartburg, forty miles west of Knoxville. He checked into the hotel, where he remained for many weeks. Sinclair stayed to himself, preferring to remain in his locked room for days at a time.

During one of his few strolls through town, Sinclair accidentally lost a small portfolio. It was found later. It contained a handwritten account providing intimate details of the assassination of President

Abraham Lincoln, details that would have been known only to one who had participated.

During his stay at the hotel, Sinclair fell ill and had to be attended by a physician. While suffering from a period of high fever, Sinclair, according to the doctor, screamed out the names Atzerodt, Herold, Payne, Mudd, and Spangler. Before his fever broke, he also told the doctor that his real name was not Sinclair but Booth.

Sinclair resided in Wartburg for almost twenty years. In 1885, a visitor came to town. After descending from a carriage, he spotted Sinclair walking along the sidewalk. The stranger walked up to him, extended his hand, and greeted him as Booth. Sinclair turned and hurried away. He was never seen again after that day.

During the time that ex-soldier, statesman, and lawyer General Albert Pike resided in Washington, D.C., he became a fan of the theater and attended numerous performances. One of his favorite actors was John Wilkes Booth. One evening in 1885 in Fort Worth, Texas, Pike was drinking with old friend and newspaperman Colonel M. W. Connolly in the barroom of the Pickwick Hotel. As the two men conversed, Pike's gaze wandered to the mirror behind the bar. There, he saw the image of a man he recognized immediately. Turning, he stared directly at the customer seated a few tables away and exclaimed, "My God! It's John Wilkes Booth!" With that, the man at the table jumped up and ran out of the bar.

Several years following the events at the Garrett farm, Edwin Booth, accompanied by his mother, was in England for a series of performances. Following a play one evening, Edwin and Mrs. Booth were driving away from the theater when the mother, looking out of the carriage window, spotted a man across the street and screamed, "Johnnie! There goes Johnnie!" Edwin had to hold on to her to keep her from leaping out of the vehicle. While struggling to calm down his mother, Edwin looked out the window, saw the man, and was heard to exclaim, "My God! It *is* Johnnie!"

Edwin left the carriage and pursued the man, overtaking him some distance away from the carriage. He spent several minutes conversing with him but never revealed the substance of the conversation.

Another Booth showed up in Sewanee, Tennessee. He lived and worked there as a cabinetmaker and went by the name of John W.

Booth. When questioned about his name, the cabinetmaker replied only that he was a distant cousin to the famous assassin. The Sewanee Booth had wavy black hair, a black mustache, and dark eyes; weighed 145 pounds; and was described by Sewanee residents as a man who knew quite a bit about the theater.

On February 25, 1872, the Sewanee Booth married Louisa Payne, the daughter of a Presbyterian minister. During the evening following the ceremony, the Sewanee Booth pointed to a scar on one of his legs and told his new wife that it was the result of a break he had suffered during a fall on the stage when he killed President Abraham Lincoln. He went on to tell her that he would soon receive $100,000 from the group that was responsible for the assassination of Lincoln.

On July 21, 1872, the Sewanee Booth, his wife, and her son from a previous marriage moved to Memphis, where Booth took a job in a cottonseed mill. On two occasions, a group of men were spotted stalking him. When he became aware of this, he moved his family to new quarters.

One evening, Booth did not return home from his job. When his wife went to the mill, she was told that two men arrived and exchanged what appeared to be secret signs with her husband, and then the three left together. The Sewanee Booth was never seen again. A few months later, Louisa Booth gave birth to a daughter, Laura Ida Booth.

The Louisa Payne and Laura Ida Booth claims are not particularly convincing. On the other hand, the discovery of another woman, who many contend is the real daughter of John Wilkes Booth, deserves some considered attention.

TWENTY-ONE

***

Booth's Secret Families

During the 1890s, Ogarita Booth Henderson had been identified and referred to as the daughter of the assassin. Although she was often seen wearing a brooch containing a small portrait of John Wilkes Booth, she denied the association. Henderson was also active in the theater. Several who knew Booth stated that Ogarita possessed the same features, hair, eyes, and high brow of the assassin.

In 1937, a book titled *This One Mad Act* was published and purported to tell the true story of John Wilkes Booth and his secret wife and family. The author was listed as Izola Laura Forrester, allegedly the daughter of Ogarita Henderson and granddaughter of John Wilkes Booth. Author George S. Bryan was highly critical of the book and claimed that Izola Forrester was actually a woman named Mann Page, who once worked as a staff writer for a newspaper. It was no secret that Page was, in fact, a nom de plume often used by Forrester, and while her inexperience as a researcher of history is apparent from time to time in the book, her contentions are rather compelling.

In the book, Forrester writes that her grandmother, Izola Mills D'Arcy, met Booth in Richmond, where the actor was appearing with a stock company. Others have contended that they met while both were involved in smuggling quinine to Confederate hospitals. Not long afterward, Forrester says, Booth and D'Arcy were married in Cos Cob, Connecticut, on January 9, 1859. Booth would have been twenty years of age.

The newlyweds decided to keep the marriage secret, a decision that has created some confusion among researchers. The fact is that actors and actresses of the day often posed as single before the public simply because it was good for business. Booth's own father, Junius Brutus Sr., married his first wife at twenty years of age and kept her, along with the birth of two children, a secret from the theatergoing public for many years. They were, in fact, left behind in England when Junius came to the United States.

After the marriage to Izola, John continued acting, mostly in Richmond, and his wife continued to live in the Shenandoah Valley. In time, she moved onto Booth's farm near Harpers Ferry. On October 23, 1859, Ogarita, the mother of author Forrester, was born to John Wilkes and Izola.

Ogarita grew up to be a noted stage performer who initially went by the name Ogarita Wilkes and later Rita Booth. Ogarita died in Binghamton, New York, on April 12, 1892. An obituary that appeared in the *New York World* noted that she was the daughter of John Wilkes Booth and stated that several people "who knew Booth . . . noted in her the clear-cut features . . . the curly hair and high brow" of the actor. It was also pointed out in *This One Mad Act* that the mother of Henry Johnson, Booth's valet who played an important role in his escape, worked for Izola D'Arcy at one time.

Following the assassination, Izola changed her name, moved to Baltimore, and lived with John Henry Stevenson, a longtime friend of Booth and Izola. Stevenson was an alias of Michael O'Laughlin, who the government claimed had died from yellow fever in prison on Dry Tortugas. According to Stevenson's diary, an agent named W. G. Pollock paid him a visit while he was in prison. Pollock interrogated Stevenson about where Booth had hidden the gold, silver, and treasury bonds he was paid by the higher-echelon members of the plots to kidnap and kill Abraham Lincoln. Although Stevenson had no knowledge of Booth's cache of wealth, he agreed to help, believing that it was a way to escape for all time the horrors of the prison. Pollock arranged for Stevenson to be officially declared dead and shipped him to Washington, D.C., where they expected him to reconnect with Izola and learn the location of the gold.

Izola told Stevenson that Booth had arrived at the farm shortly after the assassination and spent time there recuperating from his broken leg. In December 1867, Stevenson and Izola dug up Booth's cache of gold and silver and fled to California, where she met with Booth aboard a ship. The next day, the ship set sail for the Palau Islands.

Researchers are convinced that the woman introduced as Booth's wife to the sailor Andrew Jackson Donelson on the Palau Islands in the late 1860s was Izola. Stevenson remained for a time in California, where he purchased and operated a smelter.

Stevenson and Izola eventually married in 1870. For most of her life, she lived in fear that her children, going under the name Booth, would be scorned. Izola, however, remained in contact with the Booth family, particularly John's sister, Rosalie, who apparently provided Izola with money. Izola and her two children were also acquainted with John Matthews, another friend of the family and a fellow actor.

During the autumn of 1868, according to Forrester, Izola D'Arcy Booth, in the company of Stevenson, returned to California to meet once again with her husband in San Diego. She remained for several months. After spending time with Booth, she returned to Baltimore, where she eventually gave birth to a son, Harry Jerome, on February 27, 1870. Harry was reared with the Stevenson surname.

As a youth, Harry bore what Forrester referred to as "a striking resemblance" to Booth. When Harry was a young man, he was told by Stevenson just a few days before his death that he was not his son, that his real father was John Wilkes Booth.

In 1894, Harry was the featured entertainment at a banquet. Seated in the audience was an elderly guest of a family member. Following Harry's performance, the stranger walked up to him and, with tears in his eyes, embraced the young man.

"Don't you remember me, Mr. Booth?"

The stunned Harry grew upset with the stranger and asked why he was addressed in such a manner. The old man, according to Izola Forrester, said, "Because that is your name, sir." He went on to introduce himself as George Whyte Smith and explained that he had been in the employ of the Booth family years ago, eventually moving on to work with John Wilkes's sister, Rosalie. Whyte went on to say that he recalled a young Harry visiting Rosalie's house with the mother, Ogarita, and that Whyte used to hold him on his lap and feed him cake. Harry died in 1918.

Author Forrester also wrote of a man named Colonel John Young, who claimed that he received a number of letters during the 1890s from a man who signed them "John Wilkes." Wilkes lived in Bombay, India, and the letters arrived from that city as well as from Calcutta, Shanghai, and the island of Ceylon. Young claimed that he became friends with John Wilkes during an Asian journey in 1871 and that the two maintained a correspondence. While spending time with his new friend, Young met "a Negro named Henry," who accompanied Wilkes on his travels. This must have been Henry Johnson.

Young also recalled the account of a man names James Kelly, a former actor who stayed in touch with many theatrical performers. Kelly met Booth in 1858 and for a time acted with him in the same stock company. Kelly also knew Booth's valet, Henry Johnson.

During the 1870s, Kelly traveled to New York City on business from his home in Grand Rapids, Michigan. While strolling down Broadway Avenue, Kelly encountered Henry Johnson and spoke to him. Johnson appeared nervous and tried to get away. During the conversation, Kelly asked Johnson what he was doing, and the black man replied that he had been working for Edwin Booth "ever since Master John got away." Under rigorous questioning, Kelly got from Johnson the story that Booth, accompanied by Henry, eventually sailed to Liverpool, England, where they remained for a short time. From there, he said, they traveled to Bombay.

Persisting, Kelly said that he obtained Booth's Bombay address from the valet and wrote his old friend a letter. To his utter surprise, he received a response from "John Wilkes." According to Kelly, the handwriting on the letter was identical to Booth's signatures on some old theater posters he possessed. Booth, as a young man, often acted under the name "John B. Wilkes." Colonel Young stated that he was convinced Edwin Booth was entirely aware that his brother was alive and living in Bombay.

In 1926, Izola Forrester discovered another piece of compelling evidence that Booth survived. During his frantic ride through the streets of Washington following the assassination, Booth encountered his friend Billy Andrews, who presented Booth with his silk cravat and scarf pin. Like many others who knew Booth, Andrews had been jailed for a time as a conspirator but was eventually released. Years later, he moved to New York, where he dabbled in politics and became a special counsel for the president of the Erie Railway.

One evening, Andrews told a number of assembled friends about his encounter with Booth on the streets of Washington on that night of April 14, 1865. What stunned the assembled guests, however, was when Andrews admitted that, four years later, the pin had been returned to him by Izola D'Arcy Booth.

In 1932, author Forrester located and visited with Harry Jerome Stevenson's ex-wife. During the interviews, the former Mrs. Harry Stevenson, now Mrs. Godfrey, told Izola that she had known all along that Harry was the son of John Wilkes Booth and that he was born five years following the assassin's escape.

In 1882, Izola Booth Stevenson moved to Connecticut and the town of Canterbury, where she somehow managed to live well. Although no one knew for certain from where her fortune came, it was often suggested that she received support from the Booth family. Throughout her life, she never spoke of John Wilkes Booth or of the death of Abraham Lincoln. She did, however, wear a medallion around her neck that contained a photograph of the actor. In addition, several photographs of Booth hung on the walls of her home.

As a child, Izola Forrester played with her grandmother's collection of seashells. Years later, when the shells were examined, it was discovered that they came from a species known to exist only in the Palau Islands in the Pacific Ocean.

Forrester died on March 6, 1944. Her search for the truth about her grandfather has added to the growing evidence that John Wilkes Booth, the assassin of President Abraham Lincoln, escaped and returned.

There exists compelling evidence that John Wilkes Booth also fathered a child with Kate Scott. Booth and Scott met during the onset of the Civil War and maintained a relationship throughout. During their affair, she learned that Booth was married and had a child. On December 8, 1865, Scott gave birth to a daughter. She never identified the father as Booth until shortly before her death in 1911.

Three months following the assassination of President Lincoln, Scott received a letter from Booth. In September, the two met and spent several days together. Booth told Scott that he had plans to travel to India, where he intended to live for a time. For the next ten years, Scott received letters from Booth postmarked from India and England. Then the letters stopped, and Scott was convinced that Booth died in India around 1880.

TWENTY-TWO

The Strange Case of David E. George

One of the most highly publicized and perplexing accounts relative to the return of John Wilkes Booth involves a man known at different times as John St. Helen and David E. George. In his book *The Escape and Suicide of John Wilkes Booth*, author Finis L. Bates writes of meeting St. Helen in Granbury, Texas, a quiet little town forty miles southwest of Fort Worth. Bates was a young lawyer who had recently opened an office in Granbury. St. Helen dropped by one day and asked Bates to defend him against a charge of running a saloon without a license in the nearby town of Glen Rose. St. Helen admitted to Bates that he was, indeed, guilty of the charge but stated that he would resist appearing at a federal court hearing in Tyler. The barkeeper told Bates that his real name was not John St. Helen and that he was concerned that his true identity might be discovered. The risk, he said, was too great.

Several weeks later, St. Helen moved to Granbury. In his book, Bates described St. Helen as having "more money than was warranted for his stock in trade." According to Bates's notes, St. Helen had "penetrating black eyes" that manifested "desperation and a capacity for crime." He also said that St. Helen showed an "intimacy with every detail of theatrical work" and often kept theater-related periodicals in his room. St. Helen could recite most of Shakespeare's plays and was particularly fond of *Richard III*. Townspeople remembered St. Helen as "vain."

Late one night in 1877, Bates was summoned to St. Helen's bedside. He was seriously ill, said the author, and he confided in Bates that he did not think he would live. St. Helen told Bates to search under his pillow, where he would find a tintype. Bates searched for and retrieved it, a tintype that bore the image of John St. Helen.

St. Helen told the lawyer, should he die, to please send the tintype to Edwin Booth in Baltimore with a note stating that the man in the picture had passed away. St. Helen then placed a hand on Bates's forearm and told him that he was John Wilkes Booth, the assassin of President Abraham Lincoln. The stunned Bates promised that he would, if necessary, send the picture to Edwin. He sat up with the sick St. Helen through the night.

St. Helen remained seriously ill for several weeks but finally began improving. When he was able, he invited Bates to walk with him some distance out of town. During the walk, St. Helen once again told the lawyer that he was Booth, and he pleaded with Bates to keep the knowledge secret.

According to St. Helen, Andrew Johnson was the principal instigator of the assassination of Lincoln. St. Helen related that he, Booth, did in fact visit with Johnson on the afternoon of April 14 only four hours before the assassination and that the vice president informed him that it had been arranged for General Grant to be out of town and that the way had been cleared to allow the assassin to escape into Maryland.

For his part, Bates respected the confidentiality of St. Helen's admission, though he was initially disbelieving. Throughout their conversation, St. Helen related a number of other details relative to the murder of Lincoln, the subsequent escape from Ford's Theater, and the flight through the Maryland and Virginia countryside.

Some of St. Helen's descriptions and information, as told to Bates, have been questioned by researchers. Others, however, maintain that they could have come only from someone with intimate experience regarding the events surrounding the assassination, particularly those associated with the flight of the assassin. How, then, could St. Helen have been aware of Booth's movements and other aspects of the escape that were virtually unknown to historians? If St. Helen were merely an imposter, one must wonder why he did not relate commonly accepted and widely publicized aspects of the assassination and escape. Instead, he provided versions somewhat different from the accepted ones, versions that, on investigation, bear some level of credibility—more, in fact, than many of the government's conclusions.

One particularly telling piece of information concerns the diary. The official version relates that it was taken from the pockets of the dying man at Garrett's farm. According to journals and papers analyzed by researchers Balsiger and Sellier, Booth's diary was lost in a grove of trees where he camped with Henson near Gambo Creek after escaping into Virginia. St. Helen related that, on April 22, he had "discovered that he lost his diary, some letters, and a picture of my sister" by the time he reached Port Royal on the Rappahannock River. St. Helen's story is consistent with the Gambo Creek version. Since this information did not come to light until 100 years later, there is no way that he could have learned it from another source.

St. Helen also told Bates that on April 24, he fled westward through West Virginia and Kentucky, eventually making his way to Mississippi and thence to Indian Territory. After spending some time in the American West, he went into Mexico, where he disguised himself as a priest. From Mexico, he traveled in 1866 or 1867 to California, where he said he met with his mother and older brother in San Francisco.

St. Helen arrived in Texas after spending a year in New Orleans, where he went by the name of Ney and taught school there. He eventually settled in Glen Rose, Texas, where he assumed the name John St. Helen and operated a saloon. In October 1872, he moved to Granbury.

A few months following St. Helen's revelations, lawyer Bates moved to Memphis, Tennessee, where he established what eventually became a successful law practice. In his spare time, he began reading everything he could find pertaining to the assassination of President Abraham Lincoln and related events. The more he studied, the more he grew convinced that John St. Helen was telling the truth, that he was, in fact, John Wilkes Booth.

In January 1898, Bates wrote to Secretary of War Russell A. Alger, explained that he possessed evidence that Booth was still alive, and inquired if such information was important to the War Department. Alger replied that it was not.

On January 13, 1903, the body of a man named David E. George was transported from his room at the Grand Avenue Hotel in Enid, Oklahoma, to the undertaking establishment of W. B. Penniman. George, known around town as a handyman and house painter, had committed suicide earlier that morning. George was also known by Enid residents to be an alcoholic and perhaps even a drug addict since he regularly took morphine. He died from a strong dose of strychnine.

While Penniman's assistant, W. H. Ryan, was embalming the body, Reverend E. C. Harper walked in. Harper was a Methodist preacher who had just completed a funeral service in the outer room. Harper glanced down at the body of George and cried out, "Do you know who that is?"

When assistant Ryan said that he did not, Harper explained that the body belonged to none other than John Wilkes Booth, the assassin of President Abraham Lincoln. He told Ryan that "George" had confessed his identity to Mrs. Harper three years earlier. Mrs. Harper subsequently made a statement wherein she confirmed that she had gone to the funeral parlor on January 15 and identified the corpse of David E. George as the man who admitted to her in El Reno, Oklahoma, in 1900 that he was John Wilkes Booth.

During the next few days, newspapers around the country carried the story that the man believed by some to be Booth had died in Enid. In a short time, Enid officials began receiving letters from Laura Ida Booth, who claimed that George was her father. Subsequent investigation, however, arrived at the conclusion that the Sewanee Booth could not have been George.

In Memphis, Finis Bates read the article and wondered if the dead man named David E. George might be the man he once knew as John St. Helen. Bates departed Memphis and arrived in Enid on January 23. The following morning, he went to view the body. From a folder, he withdrew the tintype of John St. Helen and held it up next to the face of the corpse. It was, according to Bates, the same man.

For several days, the body remained on display at Penniman's establishment. Because it went unclaimed, it was eventually placed in a back room where it was stored for years. Finally, Finis Bates came forward and took possession of the body.

It was subsequently learned by Bates that George had worked as a house painter in El Reno, Oklahoma. When he was not working (which was most of the time), he just hung around retail establishments and occasionally the police station. Bates also discovered that George regularly received large amounts of money from mysterious sources. George, like St. Helen, was getting money from the Booth family. Bates learned that, at his death, George was worth $30,000 and carried a $5,000 life insurance policy. When George left El Reno for Enid, he owed money to several people.

In April 1900, George, in a fit of depression, swallowed a large amount of prescription drugs and sincerely believed that he was going to die. While still barely conscious, he told a Miss Young, who was to become the wife of Reverend Harper the following year, that he had a confession to make. He told her that he had killed "one of the best men who had ever lived, Abraham Lincoln." He asked the woman to

bring him a pen and paper, and when she did, he scribbled, "I am going to die before the sun goes down." He signed it, "J. Wilkes Booth."

George recovered from the suicide attempt and several weeks later
moved from El Reno to Enid, sixty-five miles to the north. Blanche de
Bar Booth, daughter of Junius Brutus Booth and niece of John Wilkes,
told a story of what may have been a near encounter with her famous
uncle. During a 1902 visit to Enid, Blanche Booth responded to a
knock on her hotel door. Without opening it, she asked who was there.
The voice on the other side said that it was "Johnnie." Members of the
Booth family always called John Wilkes "Johnnie." Believing that a
joke was being played on her by an actor friend, Blanche replied that
she did not wish to be disturbed. The voice on the other side said that
he would call later, and then a card was slipped under the door. The
name on the card was "John Wilkes Booth." On the morning of January 13, 1903, while staying at Enid's Grand Central Hotel, George
swallowed a large amount of strychnine and died a short time later.

Were John St. Helen and David E. George the same men? More
importantly, were they John Wilkes Booth?

Some critical researchers, Bryan foremost among them, contend that
Bates worked hard to make the two men appear to be the same and,
in so doing, purposely altered some of the facts. In spite of Bryan's
contentions, St. Helen and George shared many of the same characteristics: they looked alike, they drank heavily, they were inclined to be
loud and boisterous on occasion, they were known to launch into extended soliloquies and poetry, and both carried a gun. Both men were
apparently well educated, and both were intimate with the theater and
with Shakespeare. While living in El Reno, George was remembered as
having participated in a number of amateur productions and providing excellent performances.

Both St. Helen and George dressed in the manner of Booth. Bates
noted that both men wore "a black semi-dress style suit, of the best
fabrics, always with the turndown Byron collar and dark tie . . . tailor
made, new and well-pressed, his pants well creased, his shoes new
patent leather and his hat a black Stetson derby."

George possessed certain physical characteristics that were similar
to those of Booth. The only officially recognized comparison study of
the day, the Bertillon Examination, evaluated the features of David
E. George and John Wilkes Booth and found some compelling similarities. Developed by Alphonse Bertillon, the test involved sitting and

standing height, length of the outstretched arms, length and breadth
of the head, the length of the right ear, as well as features such as
scars, eye color, and other markings. Although imperfect, the test
concluded that the shape of George's head, specifically the structure of
the forehead, as well as the contour of the face around the eyes and the
jawline, bore a striking resemblance to Booth. The Bertillon analysis
also revealed that the structure of the nose, particularly the bridge,
the indenture of George's left nostril, and the distance from nose to
mouth, bore some resemblance to Booth's. Other features described by
the analysis included a cocked right eyebrow manifested by both men,
the ears, and the striking similarity of their hands.

Many skeptics state that the eyes of David E. George were enough
to dismiss the claim that he was Booth. George's eyes, as described by
the mortician, were blue gray. According to a number of government
documents, Booth's eyes were black. Asia Booth, the actor's sister,
wrote that they were hazel.

George, according to Bates, bore the marks of a broken right leg,
not the left that Booth broke when his horse fell on him. Others who
claimed to have examined the body stated that they found no evidence
of a break at all. George's signature as "J. Wilkes Booth," according to
some analysts, bore little resemblance to Booth's handwriting. Others,
however, insist that there were certain critical similarities.

A Doctor Clarence True Wilson told a writer in 1932 that he had
conducted a thorough study of the George–Booth similarities and was
convinced that they were one and the same man. Wilson was also
quoted at stating that he learned that the man who died at Garrett's
farm was named Boyd and that Booth lived long afterward, only to
finally die in Enid. Wilson claimed that he was in possession of the
George mummy for three years, during which time he studied it extensively.

Bates showed photographs of St. Helen and George to a number of
people who had known Booth. The city editor of the El Reno newspaper was a man named Brown, who had lived in Washington, Baltimore, and New York during the 1860s; regularly attended the theater;
and saw Booth numerous times. On being shown the photographs of
George, Brown stated that he had never met the man, but the pictures
were those of John Wilkes Booth.

Brown, who was serving in the army at the time of the assassination,
was in Washington when the body of the man killed in Virginia arrived
on the *Montauk*. He told Bates that "there was a belief, quite general

among members of the federal army with whom I came in contact, that the body . . . was not that of John Wilkes Booth."

Bates showed photographs of Booth to L. Threadkell, who once employed John St. Helen as a teamster in 1867. Threadkell unhesitatingly identified the images as those of St. Helen.

Bates also showed the tintype of St. Helen and photographs of George to Joseph Jefferson in April 1903. Jefferson had known Booth since childhood, was a fellow actor, and performed in many of the same plays with him. After examining the images closely, Jefferson looked up at Bates and said, "This is John Wilkes Booth."

One particularly compelling piece of evidence is related to Booth's signet ring, a piece of jewelry that he was seldom without. It will be remembered that the ring was not found on any finger of the man killed at Garrett's farm. David E. George wore a similar ring. Some time before expiring from the dose of strychnine, George told a neighbor that, on spotting the approach of two law enforcement officers, he feared that he would be identified. He pulled the ring from his finger and swallowed it.

The mummy of David E. George was examined by a group of seven physicians at Chicago's Northwestern University in December 1931. The group was headed by Dr. Otto L. Schmidt. At one time, Schmidt was the president of the prestigious Chicago Historical Society. Another member of the team was Dr. Lewis L. McArthur, one of the county's leading X-ray specialists at the time.

The George mummy was subjected to X-rays and dissection. During the examination, according to their report, the team found evidence of a broken leg, although it was never stated whether it was the right or the left.

The most astounding discovery, however, was that of a ring embedded slightly in the flesh of the body cavity. Although the surface of the ring had been modified somewhat as a result of the action of digestive juices, it was believed that the initials "JWB" could be discerned on its face. Dr. Schmidt subsequently wrote that the team could safely say that the body they worked on was that of John Wilkes Booth.

Still, there were people who maintained that there was nothing in the personalities of John St. Helen or David E. George to suggest that they could have been Booth. Booth was regarded by most as being handsome, vital, magnetic, and brilliant and possessing a restless and irresistible energy. He was dynamic, and people were attracted to him.

According to Izola Forrester, there was "no such compelling quality about either [St. Helen or George]." The two, she states, were "ordinary, commonplace . . . without distinction or education, and without a trace of Booth's mannerisms or artistic ability." Since she had never met either man, it remains unclear how she came to these conclusions.

The truth is that the evidence for St. Helen being George and either or both being Booth remains intriguing and provocative yet inconclusive. Given the available facts, a number of researchers are convinced that David E. George was the assassin John Wilkes Booth. According to Roscoe, most of those discrediting the George mummy as being that of Booth have been journalists, not professional detectives or medical personnel.

The fate of the David E. George mummy presents yet another mystery. At one point, Bates offered to sell the mummy to the *Dearborn Independent* for $1,000. Another time, he offered it to Henry Ford for $100,000. Both declined to purchase it. During the 1920s and 1930s, Bates leased or sold the mummified corpse to a carnival promoter who charged patrons twenty-five cents to view "The Assassin of President Abraham Lincoln." The body was still being displayed during the 1940s. After that, the promoter went bankrupt and moved to Declo, Idaho, where he placed the mummy in a chair on his front porch and charged neighbors ten cents to see it. The mummy eventually disappeared, and to this day no one is certain of its whereabouts. It is reputed to exist in a private collection somewhere.

In 1990, three research pathologists at the Regional Forensic Center in Memphis, Tennessee, undertook a search for the so-called Booth mummy. They were convinced that George was Booth and believed that they could prove it. To date, however, the mummy has not been found.

TWENTY-THREE

◆◆◆

Analysis

For those who have studied the Lincoln assassination and the flight, pursuit, and alleged capture and killing of John Wilkes Booth in depth, an array of somewhat disturbing elements are apparent. Following the assassination of President Abraham Lincoln, a number of aspects of Booth's escape are well documented. Others, however, are sketchy, contradictory, inferred, and even falsified and are subject to a wide variety of interpretations.

Far too much of the official record as it relates to the events at Garrett's farm, the body, and the burial are suspect, confusing, and, more often than not, contradictory. The more one studies extant materials related to these cases, the more one comes away convinced of ineptitude on the part of the government, cover-up, and conspiracy. Reading between the lines, one can detect no small amount of fear in the minds and hearts of many of the government officials involved.

Another problem with the official documents related to the assassination is the fact that access to such information—and thus research and scholarship oriented toward the plight of John Wilkes Booth—was stifled for seventy years. The War Department kept the files of the so-called assassination conspiracy, along with those associated with the pursuit and killing of Booth, under lock and key for seven decades. During the time the materials were hidden away from the public, it is suspected (and for ample reason) that many important documents were removed. Some have suggested that hiding the documents from the public eye was done in order to protect government officials from implication in Lincoln's assassination and Booth's escape. Researcher Theodore Roscoe hints that the military censorship was intended to "conceal the survival of John Wilkes Booth." Still others have maintained that the secrecy was intended to keep the public from finding out about the massive incompetence associated with the investigation and pursuit.

To add to the confusion, most traditional writers of Booth history and the Lincoln era have essentially perpetuated the government's version of events by resorting to available official documents and government-approved transcriptions as gospel. Far too much of the existing "history" is little more than a repetition of materials quoted from the works of earlier writers who in turn obtained it from federal files.

Author William Hanchett states that "professional historians allowed the assassination to fall through the gaps separating the two traditional fields of historical scholarship—the Civil War and Reconstruction. [Booth and Lincoln] did not seem to belong to one or the other." As a result, most of what Americans think they know about John Wilkes Booth is simply not true.

As new documents, journals, diaries, and papers are discovered and become available, they do little to support the traditional (i.e., government) position on the events related to the assassination. The truth is that they accomplish quite the opposite—the more that is learned about this period in American history, the more it becomes apparent that Booth was never captured and killed by the authorities but rather escaped to live for several more decades.

Ultimately, what the researcher is faced with is an incredible amount of contradiction, obfuscation, doubt, and questions regarding the veracity of the traditional and "accepted" version of the escape, capture, and killing of the assassin. In researching government documents related to these very important events, one comes away with the feeling that elected and appointed officials could not be trusted to tell the truth. What, then, is the truth?

For purposes of analysis and summary, critical and conflicting aspects of Booth's case are herein summarized and considered. They include the following:

1. The diary
2. The David Herold–Ed Henson conundrum
3. The Lewis Payne–Lewis Powell conundrum
4. The body of the man killed at Garrett's farm
5. The disposal of the body
6. The question of suicide

7. The role of Edwin Booth
8. The return of the assassin, John Wilkes Booth

THE DIARY

One of the greatest mysteries surrounding John Wilkes Booth is related
to the diary that the government claimed was found on the body of the
man killed at Richard Garrett's farm. Some writers call it a personal
diary, while others refer to it as a memorandum book. Some have
identified it as a notebook. It has been described on several occasions
as being bound by red Moroccan leather. Elsewhere, it is identified
as black. Author Chamlee wrote that it was "an outdated 1864 diary
[used] mostly as scratch paper . . . [and serving] as a combination
wallet and notebook." In the end, there appears to be little agreement
as to what the object was.

According to most historical accounts, a "diary" was found among
the possessions of the dead man. It was handed around to some of the
soldiers present, for some accounts mention that a number of them
made copies of the contents. Ultimately, the diary was confiscated by
Lieutenant Colonel Everton Conger, along with the rest of the victim's
belongings, and taken to Washington.

On arriving at the capital, Conger turned over all of the items, including the diary, to Lafayette Baker, who in turn delivered them to
Secretary of War Stanton. Stanton examined each item and retuned
them to Lafayette Baker, all except the diary. Stanton kept the diary
overnight and on the following day gave it to Major Thomas Eckert,
who allegedly locked it in a War Department safe. When the diary was
removed from the safe two years later, eighteen pages were missing.

Another curious mystery associated with the so-called diary is that
it was not introduced as evidence during the conspiracy trial. All of
the other items taken from the victim—knife, revolver, compass, and
more—were placed before jurors as evidence. Of all of those items, the
diary would have been regarded, without question, as the single most
vital and important piece of evidence associated with the conspiracy.

John Francis Wilson wrote that many were aware of the existence
of the diary at the time of the conspiracy trial. Critics of the government claim that Stanton (and perhaps others) suppressed the diary
as evidence because it contained information critical of government
leaders. The missing pages, it is believed, were excised by someone in
order to remove evidence of such.

On one of the pages that remained in the diary, Booth wrote that he intended to return to Washington to "clear my name." What could he possibly have meant by this, and how did he intend to do it? In the diary, Booth used words like "we" and "our," indicating that he was not alone in his efforts. Did clearing his name have anything to do with the missing pages? Did the diary contain incriminating evidence? It would be easy to conclude such a thing. Otherwise, why was it kept secret for two years, and why were pages removed?

Congressman Benjamin Butler speculated that Booth's diary could have proved who it was who changed Booth's purpose from capture to assassination. Butler also suggested that the person who would benefit most from Lincoln's death was Vice President Andrew Johnson.

Yet another mystery revolves around the copies of the diary made by the soldiers at Garrett's farm on the morning of April 26, copies that were verified by Lafayette Baker. What was it about the diary that caused the troopers, who were exhausted from riding and pursuit and no sleep for twenty-four straight hours, to take the time and trouble to make copies of the book? Did it contain some relevant, perhaps provocative information? If so, would not Baker, Conger, or Doherty have taken charge of the document and not allowed the soldiers access to it? Once Stanton learned that copies of the diary had been made, he immediately ordered all of them turned over to him at once. This remains curious since an examination of the extant pages reveals little of major import.

Lieutenant Colonel Conger also admitted making a copy of the diary while it was in his possession before he turned it over to Baker. It will be recalled that the lieutenant colonel's name was mentioned in the diary. It will also be recalled that Conger and Booth were acquaintances. What became of Conger's copy is not known.

A third mystery concerns the eighteen missing pages. During questioning in 1867, Lafayette Baker stated with confidence that the diary he examined in 1867 was not in the same condition as the one he delivered to Stanton in 1865. Since that time, he said, it had been "mutilated."

When the diary was initially found, according to Baker, there were no pages missing. Baker recalled that there was a great deal more to the diary when he first saw it, and he remembered reading portions of it that contained passages not present in the one retrieved in 1867. Baker also related that he remembered seeing a drawing of a house in the diary he first examined, a drawing not found in the 1867 version.

He further stated that cards and pieces of paper with names were also missing from the back cover's pocket. Conger, after examining the diary in 1867, stated that he thought it read a little differently from the one he examined two years earlier.

Stanton, on the other hand, claimed that the eighteen pages were missing from the diary when it was given to him, conflicting with statements made by Baker, Conger, and Eckert. If the diary did possess evidence incriminating to him, that is what he would be expected to say.

Experts who have examined the diary closely, according to Bryan, declare that it is evident that a heavy knife lopped away the missing pages in one batch. Is it likely that Booth could have done such a thing? Or is it more likely, as many have suggested, that Stanton removed all of the pages? The remaining edges of the cut pieces show that they had been written on.

The findings of Balsiger and Seller provide for more mystery. They contend that Booth's diary was found at a temporary campsite near Gambo Creek on April 22, examined by Andrew and James Potter, and then delivered to Stanton soon afterward by National Detective Police detectives Bernard and Dooley. Stanton, according to the papers of George Julian, showed the diary to him, John Conness, Thomas Eckert, and Zachariah Chandler. According to Julian, all agreed that the diary contained incriminating evidence.

If the above is true, how does one account for the diary found on the body of the man at Garrett's farm? One possibility is that James William Boyd carried a similar diary. Another possibility—and one that has been suggested over the years—is that the "official" Booth diary was a forgery masterminded by government officials and planted on Boyd. This notion has been bandied about by researchers for over a century, but logic dictates that it does not make sense. If this is true and if the soldiers made copies of it that were subsequently confiscated, what would have been the purpose?

The diary found on the body, according to the government, contained several photographs of women known to consort with Booth. While many apparently examined the diary at Garrett's farm, there was never any mention of photographs until the diary was in the hands of Stanton in Washington, D.C. The missing pages of Booth's diary, according to Balsiger and Sellier, were found among the papers of Stanton's descendants in 1977. Whatever the truth, the fact remains that the diary, one of the most valuable pieces of information and evidence in the entire Lincoln assassination episode, was kept hidden for two years by Stanton and was clearly tampered with before it was finally brought forth.

THE DAVID HEROLD–ED HENSON CONUNDRUM

History generally records that Booth, in the company of David Herold, fled across portions of Maryland and Virginia, eventually arriving together at the farm of Richard Garrett on the morning of April 26. Given a thorough evaluation of the traditional accounts, along with a close and critical examination of documents in private collections that have come to light during the past few decades, historians would be well served to reexamine the so-called facts regarding these two men and their respective roles.

The introduction of the mysterious Ed Henson into the activities of the last few days of John Wilkes Booth is, in part, the result of the research of evidence encountered in the Andrew Potter papers. These materials and their subsequent interpretations have forced serious and unbiased researchers to reconsider some aspects of the man who is said to have accompanied Booth. At least five pertinent factors must be considered in a comparison analysis of these two important figures: appearance, logistics, identification by others, personality and behavior, and the isolation of David Herold by the government authorities following his capture.

According to the information available, the two men, Herold and Henson, were similar in appearance. Henson was somewhat older, but if the photograph of this enigmatic character in the Neff-Guttridge Collection at Indiana State University is authentic, it is easy to see how the two men could be confused with one another.

Henson was allegedly involved in smuggling supplies and medicine to the southern army along with Booth. He eventually settled in Washington, D.C., and continued to have occasional contact with him. Herold likewise was often found in the company of the actor—running errands, fetching, and essentially serving at Booth's beck and call. The possibility exists, therefore, that one could have been mistaken for the other.

Evidence shows that David Herold crossed from the capital to Maryland on the afternoon of April 14 in the company of another and was miles away at the time of the assassination and Booth's escape. Henson, on the other hand, allegedly crossed the Navy Yard Bridge only minutes after Booth and joined up with him at Good Hope Hill. Unfortunately, neither of these events can be proven. Despite the lack of proof, however, there exists some compelling evidence that suggests that Herold was arrested by the National Detective Police on April 16 and was already in custody at the time of the initial organized pursuit of Booth. Considered by itself, this information does not carry much weight. Considered in the light of other evidence, particularly the problems associated with the identification of Herold along with Herold's own testimony, it takes on more significance.

The only basis on which a determination was made that David Herold was the man who crossed the Navy Yard Bridge minutes after Booth is the testimony of Nailor's Stable employee John Fletcher, who, in fact, never saw him up close. During the trial, when the bridge guard Silas T. Cobb was called on to identify Herold as that man, he was clearly uncertain, stating that Herold was somewhat taller and had a darker complexion. Dr. Mudd's stable hand, who had spoken with Henson, was called forth to examine the prisoners, among them Herold. Asked if he had ever seen any of them before, the hand replied in the negative. When Herold was pointed out, he was asked if he had ever seen the man before. The stable hand replied that he had not. There exists, therefore, no irrefutable evidence on which to base the contention that Herold crossed the bridge behind Booth.

The identification provided by Dr. Samuel Mudd likewise does nothing to convince anyone that it was Herold who accompanied Booth to the physician's house near Bryantown on the morning of April 15. During his interrogation by authorities, Mudd was shown a photograph of Herold and asked if it was the man who accompanied Booth. Mudd replied, "I do not recognize it as that of this young man . . . I asked his name. He gave it as Henston [sic]." In other words, within only a few days following the visit to Mudd's house, the doctor did not recognize David Herold as the man who traveled with Booth and stayed with him there.

Perhaps the most telling differences between Herold and Henson are associated with their respective personality and behavior. Since Henson was an accomplished smuggler, it is not unreasonable to assume that he possessed a respectable level of self-confidence, maturity, and composure. He likely had a keenly developed sense of adventure since he so readily agreed to accompany Booth on his flight.

According to testimony, the man with Booth dealt expeditiously with Surrattsville tavern proprietor John Lloyd. At Mudd's house, he quickly and confidently assumed a number of responsibilities, including taking the initiative to approach the house, make introductions, ask directions, converse with Mudd, and aid the ailing Booth.

On arriving at the farm of Samuel Cox, Booth's companion consulted with the guide Oscar (also identified as Oswald) Spann, paid him twelve dollars, and warned him that if he mentioned the incident, he would be killed. While hiding in the pine thicket near Cox's farm, he took charge, acted maturely and responsibly, constructed a lean-to, and removed the horses a significant distance away so that they would not attract passing cavalrymen. The tricky crossing of the Potomac River was clearly handled by a man experienced with such things, a man not inclined to panic during an emergency.

Such behavior and competence was not evident in David Herold. Herold was characterized by several different witnesses as "doltish," "trifling," "a mere boy," and "slightly retarded." During the conspiracy trial, soldier Willie Jett described Herold as "not . . . very self-possessed, his voice trembled very much, and he was a good deal agitated." The Herold family physician said that Herold was "very lightly trivial . . . with . . . the mind of an eleven-year-old child." These characteristics do not in any way represent the personality and behavior of the man who accompanied Booth through the trials and agonies during the flight through Maryland and Virginia. Furthermore, the competence and poise manifested by the man who was with Booth at Surratt's Tavern, Dr. Mudd's residence, the Cox farm, and crossing the Potomac River was not at all evident in the reactions of the terror-stricken young man who was captured at Garrett's barn.

There are so many clear and obvious differences between David Herold and the man who rode with Booth that it is rather surprising that this was not noted and commented on by historians. A thorough and logical analysis of these events encourages one to conclude that Herold and Booth's companion were two different men.

Two additional factors should concern the serious Booth researcher as it relates to David Herold. First, why was there such a rush to try, convict, and hang the young man as well as the other conspirators? Second, why was Herold never permitted to testify during the trial or speak to anyone for the entire time he was in custody?

Given the available evidence, the only logical conclusion is that the man who accompanied John Wilkes Booth during his escape into Maryland and Virginia was not David Herold. The only other possibility is Ed Henson.

And what became of Ed Henson? The Potter papers suggest that Henson traveled with Booth and Henry Johnson to Europe; later returned to Fort Wayne, Indiana, where he changed his name to Edwin Henderson; married; and lived out the remainder of his life as a farmer.

THE LEWIS PAYNE–LEWIS POWELL CONUNDRUM

Descriptions of the man called Lewis Payne (or Paine) offered in dozens if not hundreds of publications about the conspiracy and assassination of Lincoln add more disorder and bewilderment to an already confusing and contradicting series of events. Writers have referred to Payne as "lacking mental capacity," having a "weak and sluggish intellect," "crazy," "demented," "mentally unbalanced," "insane," and "illiterate." Men such as this do not make good conspirators or spies. Conversely, a man sometimes identified as Lewis Powell is described as "almost sophisticated," "immaculately clad," "literate," and a man who played chess and euchre in the company of refined ladies. It is clear that the above are the descriptions of two different men.

Regarding the role of Payne–Powell in the conspiracy to assassinate Secretary of State William Seward, consider for a moment the strange events surrounding his capture. It will be recalled that Payne was taken into custody at Mary Surratt's boardinghouse, where he arrived late one evening while the occupants were being questioned by detectives. If Payne had actually attacked Seward, would he have been so stupid as to blunder into the Surratt house while Washington detectives were present and while there was a police vehicle parked outside? Such a thing is highly unlikely.

Payne told the detectives that he had been hired to dig a trench and came to find out what time he could begin work in the morning. Would a man who had been described as immaculately clad and almost sophisticated work at trench digging? Again, not likely. Not only did Payne not resist the arresting officers, but he appeared not to have the slightest idea of what was happening. Such is not consistent with the behavior of a guilty man.

Furthermore, Detective C. H. Rosch, who was among the officers at the Surratt house, observed that Payne did not behave as a man who had attacked the secretary of state, left him for dead, and surely knew that he was being searched for by law enforcement authorities. According to Rosch, who was guarding the front of the Surratt boarding-house while the occupants were being questioned inside, he watched Payne approach the building. Rosch stated that the newcomer peered at the porch number of each house as he passed. At 11:20 p.m., according to Rosch, he saw Payne with a pickax over his shoulder go up the steps of the Surratt house, check the address, knock, and also ring the bell.

Searching for addresses would seem odd for a man who, according to the government, was already well acquainted with the Surratt boardinghouse, had stayed there from time to time, and was used to entering and leaving it at will. On the other hand, the behavior of the man described by Rosch is consistent with one who had never been there before.

On seeing Payne, Mary Surratt proclaimed to the officers that she did not know the man and had never seen him before. Anna Surratt, Mary's daughter, who had spent time with Lewis Powell, denied ever seeing Payne before.

Seward's butler, William Bell, identified Payne as the secretary's assailant from a lineup at General Augur's headquarters. William E. Doster, defense attorney for Payne and Atzerodt, maintained in court that the lineup was rigged.

If Payne and Powell were two different men who were look-alikes, that may, in part, explain many of the discrepancies in the historical record. Payne's movements were hard to follow during the unfolding of the conspiracy. If Payne was constantly confused with Powell, then it is easy to see how such a thing could happen.

Lewis Powell and John Wilkes Booth had been acquaintances for years. Because of Powell's apparent intelligence and his passion for the theater as well as his involvement in smuggling medicines into the South, it appears as though he could have been a suitable companion to the actor. Lewis Payne, on the other hand, possessed not a single one of the characteristics prized by Booth.

In another mysterious development, Lewis Payne, following his arrest, was placed in the personal custody of Major Thomas T. Eckert. This was normally the job assigned to an ordinary detective. Eckert kept Payne in complete isolation, allowing no one near him but himself. Why an assistant secretary of war was assigned such a menial task remains unexplained. Deductively speaking, it is possible that Lewis Payne had been set up. If so, it was in the best interests of those involved to keep him isolated and incommunicado. Following Payne's execution, his body went unclaimed. Had it been the body of Lewis Thornton Powell, it would have been claimed by at least one of several family members known to live nearby.

It is apparent that most historians and other researchers, working with information and documents made available by the government, were unaware that Payne and Powell were two different men. Given the varying descriptions of the two men, it is difficult to understand how they could have been confused in their interpretations, mixing the two different identities and activities. Such mistakes are not unknown in historical research.

THE BODY OF THE MAN KILLED AT GARRETT'S FARM

The man who was shot and killed at Garrett's farm and placed on board the *Montauk* had little in common with John Wilkes Booth. Although Booth and James William Boyd shared several similarities, the obvious differences between the two men are numerous, clear, and convincing.

With regard to similarities, both had comparable facial features, both had the same initials, both had their initials tattooed on some part of their body, both were approximately the same height and weight, both were southern sympathizers, and both had an injured leg. While these half dozen similarities might seem remarkable, the differences between the two men were so striking that it begs enormous indulgence on the part of any researcher to remotely consider that the man killed at Garrett's farm and delivered to authorities on the *Montauk* and John Wilkes Booth were the same. Following is a summary of the most striking differences:

1. The man killed at Garrett's had a "long, scraggly" mustache. Booth did not possess one, having shaved it off while at Dr. Mudd's house on April 15. When ferryman Rollins transported Booth across the Rappahannock River on April 25, he noted that his passenger had no mustache. Numerous witnesses who saw the body mentioned the mustache. The laws of endocrinology do not provide for a man going from a cleanly shaven face to possessing a long, scraggly mustache in such a short time. It is impossible.

2. The man at Garrett's had red hair. Booth's hair was jet black.

3. Booth was twenty-six years old. The body at Garrett's was much older. James William Boyd was forty-three years old.

4. The body that lay on the deck of the *Montauk* was described as thin, gaunt, and starved. Marshal John L. Smith, who had seen Booth only a few days prior to the assassination, said that he looked well and fleshy. According to Thomas Jones, Booth had been fed well during his stay at the pine thicket near Cox's farm. Jones carried abundant food to Booth and his companion. It is inconceivable that Booth's condition would have gone from fleshy to gaunt and starved in so short a time.

5. It has been established with reasonable certainty that Booth broke his left leg. It was the left leg that was treated by Dr. Mudd. According to Dr. John Franklin May, the corpse on the *Montauk* had a broken right leg. Boyd's ailment was on his right leg.

6. It was stated that the man killed at Garrett's wore brogans similar to those worn by Confederate soldiers. The left boot removed from the foot of Booth, which was in the possession of the War Department, was never compared to the footwear on the corpse.

7. It was never established with certainty whether the initials "JWB" had been tattooed on the left or right hand, wrist, or arm.

8. Booth was known to carry large amounts of money. It has also been established that when he escaped, he had $6,500 in his possession. The man killed at Garrett's had no cash among his possessions. It is inconceivable that Booth could have spent $6,500 during his escape.

9. Booth's personal keys were not found on the body. A set of keys found in the pockets of the coat belonging to the dead man did not fit anything that belonged to Booth.

10. Booth's personal watch, which he carried at all times, was not found on the dead man.

11. Booth's signet ring, which he was never without, was not found on the corpse.

12. The clothing worn by Booth during his escape, as described by Thomas Jones and others, was a suit of black broadcloth, the very same suit he wore when he shot the president. During his escape, he did not carry a change of clothes. The man killed at Garrett's farm wore the uniform of a Confederate army officer. James William Boyd was a captain in the Confederate army.

13. It is clear from an analysis of testimony that no one among the party that captured and killed the man at Garrett's farm was absolutely certain of his identity.

14. Conflicting, evasive, and confusing testimony by Dr. May and others regarding the body that the government claimed was Booth does nothing to establish a specific identity. On close examination, May's testimony has the earmarks of one that was at most coerced and at least tempered. In addition, it is apparent that the written statement pertaining to his examination of the body was modified by someone after it had been transcribed and submitted.

15. Not a single person who could have authoritatively identified John Wilkes Booth was invited by the government to the inquest.

If the man killed at Garrett's farm had truly been Booth, researchers today would not be faced with the disturbing number of exceedingly contradictory elements. It causes the serious investigator or scholar to wonder what actually took place on the morning of April 26, 1865. The events of that time and place have generated opposing testimony and reporting to the degree that one can safely conclude that no one is reasonably certain of what took place or who was killed.

The circumstances under which the man was shot and killed are likewise perplexing. No one knows for certain who fired the fatal shot, and no one was certain of the identity of the body. It seems strange that twenty-six troopers and three officers could not take a single crippled man alive if, indeed, that was their intention.

One must ask, Why the contradicting and conflicting testimony regarding the body of the man the government identified as John Wilkes Booth? Why the veil of secrecy thrown over the matter by the federal government? Either the authorities were aware of their mistakes and sought to hide them, or they were incredibly inept (or both). The disaffirming testimony regarding the man killed at Garrett's and placed aboard a government vessel is matched only by the confusion and contradiction relative to the disposal of the body.

THE DISPOSAL OF THE BODY

The traditionally accepted version of how the military disposed of the alleged body of John Wilkes Booth has it interred in the floor of a cell in the Old Arsenal Penitentiary. Such was the testimony of Colonel Lafayette Baker, one that has been entered into the official record.

Baker's testimony and those of others intended to support it, however, offer immediate contradictions. In some versions, the body is placed in a musket box; in others, an ammunition box; and, in still others, a canvas shroud. To compound the confusion, other versions of the disposal have surfaced over the years.

In direct conflict with Baker's testimony, General Charles A. Dana stated that, to his certain knowledge, "the body was . . . buried under a slab in the Navy Yard and a battery of artillery hauled over it to obliterate any trace." Detective William B. Wood maintained that the body was removed from the *John S. Ide* by Lafayette and Luther Baker after docking in Washington, placed in a rowboat, and transported to a small island twenty-seven miles downstream where it was buried. An unidentified man who claimed to have witnessed this burial corroborated Wood's version and added that the body was buried in quicklime.

Yet another version was provided by Captain E. W. Hilliard, who stated that he was one of four men who removed the body from the Old Arsenal Penitentiary cell and transported it ten miles down the Potomac River where it was sunk. Hilliard also claimed that the government manufactured the tale of Booth being buried just to placate the public.

An article in the June 21, 1930, *Denver Republican* stated that there were two bodies taken from the *Montauk*. One was delivered to the Navy Yard, and the other was carried out to sea and dumped overboard.

In a startling revelation, retired Colonel James Hamilton Davidson, former commander of the 122nd Infantry, offers another version. At the time of the assassination, Davidson was in command of a post located at Portsmouth, Virginia. He claimed that the head of the Secret Service, Colonel Lafayette Baker, approached him on the evening of April 27 and requested a private meeting. Baker told Davidson that he brought into Portsmouth the body of Booth. Under orders from Baker, Davidson, along with six soldiers, carried the body to a warehouse basement, dug a grave, interred the body, and covered it with sand, limestone, and dirt.

Not only have several different versions of the disposal of the body been offered, but it must be pointed out that in each case no one ever got a look at the corpse, nor was it subjected to photographs save for the one ordered by the government, which was subsequently hidden away. Furthermore, in direct contrast with the practice of the day, the body was not placed on public display. In an additional departure from the custom of the day, the body was not turned over to relatives, as occurred with Charles J. Guiteau, the assassin of President James Garfield, and with Leon Czolgolsz, the assassin of President William McKinley.

Regarding the official version describing the disposal of the body, along with all of the other versions presented above, pertinent questions need to be asked: Why was the government keeping the body from being seen or scrutinized? Why were members of the Booth family not permitted to view the body? Why was the government, in effect, hiding the body of the man who it claimed was John Wilkes Booth? A number of answers can be offered, but only one carries with it any logic: the body was not that of the assassin.

In response to a request from Edwin Booth, President Andrew Johnson ordered the body of "John Wilkes Booth" disinterred from the Old Arsenal Penitentiary and delivered to the Harvey and Marr Funeral Home in Washington, D.C. If the body had been buried on an island or dumped into the Potomac River or the Atlantic Ocean as some have claimed, then it could not have been dug up from the grounds of the penitentiary. In other words, the removal of the body had to correlate with Baker's—and therefore the government's—version relating to the disposal of the body.

Rather than just put an end to the web of contradiction and confusion associated with the body, the disinterment and reburial only added to the doubts. The only truth that can be determined regarding the reburial is that a body was delivered by the government to the undertaker's shop in Washington. Following that, there occurred another series of conflicting testimonies and observations.

First, when the body arrived at the funeral home, it was wearing a black suit. Sometime between the killing in the barn and the delivery of the body, someone apparently removed the Confederate officer's uniform that it was wearing when it was dragged out of the barn and replaced it with a black suit.

Second, according to the son of one of the undertakers, the body showed up wearing only one boot. Within a day, a second boot miraculously appeared. And why boots? The body at Garrett's was wearing Confederate army–issued brogans.

Although the body on display at Sexton Weaver's house in Baltimore was described as being only a skeleton, it was "positively" identified as John Wilkes Booth by a number of observers. Booth family friend Basil

Moxley, however, confirmed what many were already thinking—the body was not that of Booth, and family members knew it.

The prevailing evidence suggests that the body delivered to Baltimore was not the body of Booth and perhaps not even the same body that was identified on the *Montauk*. Were the bodies switched? If so, by whom? It may be that the government, on the request of Edwin Booth, was forced to provide a body. There exists the distinct possibility that there may have been several bodies that were substituted at one time or another for that of John Wilkes Booth.

THE QUESTION OF SUICIDE

In spite of the government's conclusion that Sergeant Boston Corbett fired the shot that killed John Wilkes Booth, there is ample evidence that the man in Garrett's barn shot himself. The absolute truth will likely never be known, but serious doubt and suspicion surrounded the contention that the trooper committed the deed, and the only reasonable and logical explanation is that the fugitive died by his own hand.

The man in the barn, on being advised that he was under arrest, stated that he would never be taken alive. All of his actions, according to writer John Francis Wilson, were consistent with those of a desperate man who meant to kill himself if capture were imminent.

W. F. Ferguson was told by one of the troopers present at the Garrett barn that the man shot himself. Lieutenant Colonel Everton J. Conger stated that the victim had the appearance of a man who put a pistol to his head and shot himself. Throughout his life, Conger never wavered from his contention. An experienced officer, Conger had seen many men die in battle and knew the nature of wounds.

As stated in chapter 16, the bullet entered the fugitive's neck on the right side and, following a downward course at an angle of twenty degrees, penetrated three vertebrae and passed out the left side. If he were shot from any significant distance, according to Eisenschiml, he would had to have been standing with his head and a portion of his torso bent sharply to the right and with his profile to the right wall and parallel to the door. According to witnesses, the man in the barn did no such thing; he remained upright from the time he rose from the piled hay where he had been sleeping.

On the other hand, continues Eisenschiml, the wound incurred by the fugitive could have been self-inflicted "if he had held a pistol to the right side of his head and shot low." Since the fugitive had thrown away his crutch and rifle, had drawn his handgun, and was reacting under duress, Eisenschiml's argument is a strong one. Lieutenant Ruggles also believed that the man killed himself. "No one saw Corbett fire," he stated, "and one chamber of Booth's revolver . . . was empty."

A simple trigonometric ratio can demonstrate the impossibility that the man in the barn was shot by Corbett or anyone else. Assuming that the man was standing in the center of the forty-eight-foot-wide barn, that would place the alleged shooter approximately twenty-four feet away and having to shoot through a four-inch-wide space between the barn planks. If this happened—and assuming that the shooter was the same height as the victim—the trajectory of the bullet would have been flat. Given the twenty-degree angle at which the ball penetrated the neck, however, the shot could have come only from a point fourteen feet five inches above the ground. That did not happen. For the sake of argument, let's position the victim only five feet from the shooter. Given the same twenty-degree angle and employing the trigonometric ratio, the shot would had to have come from a height of seven feet nine inches above the ground. In fact, Boston Corbett was only five feet five inches tall, slightly less than three inches shorter than Booth. The mathematics proves that the man in the barn was not shot by anyone outside the structure.

Despite the logical and compelling argument for suicide, some maintain that the man in the barn was shot not by Corbett but by Conger, who carried a pistol. At the time, Baker was convinced that Conger did the killing and held that belief throughout the rest of his life. No one at the site sought to examine Conger's handgun.

As commanding officers, Baker, Conger, and/or Doherty could have ordered an examination of the firearms to determine which was used in the shooting. The truth is that not a single weapon was examined other than the victim's. According to David Miller Dewitt, had a legitimate autopsy been conducted on the body, it would have "disclosed the caliber of the pistol and the size of the ball with which the wound was inflicted." The War Department was in possession of the weapons carried by the dead man, and it would have been a simple task to examine them.

It must also be realized that the examination of the body that was placed aboard the *Montauk* revealed what appeared to be a burn on the back of the neck. Such a burn, it has been suggested, could have resulted from the firing of a pistol at close range, as happens in a suicide.

THE ROLE OF EDWIN BOOTH

Some researchers suspect that Edwin Booth knew of his brother's escape all along and played an important role in keeping it secret. During his later years, Basil Moxley stated that Edwin knew all along that his brother had gotten away and that the body delivered to the funeral home was merely a substitute.

On those rare occasions after April 1865 when Edwin Booth spoke of his brother, it was always in the present tense, never the past. In addition, a man named Colonel John Young, who claimed that he corresponded with Booth while the latter was living in India, said that he was convinced that Edwin knew John as alive and residing in Bombay at the time.

When the alleged body of Booth lay in state at Sexton Weaver's quarters in Baltimore, Edwin never once looked at it to determine if it was his own brother, even though he was the one who requested that it be moved to that location for burial in the family plot to pacify his mother. Longtime Booth family friend Basil Moxley claimed that Edwin knew all along that it was not John.

According to papers in the Neff Collection, Henry Johnson, Booth's valet, returned to Maryland after serving his longtime employer in England and India. Within days of his return, he went to work for Edwin and remained with various members of the Booth family in Maryland and Massachusetts until he died.

THE RETURN OF THE ASSASSIN, JOHN WILKES BOOTH

Did John Wilkes Booth escape from federal authorities following the assassination of President Abraham Lincoln? The evidence is compelling and strong and suggests that he did. Did he travel to foreign countries, only to return to the United States and die here? Again, evidence is plentiful and mounting and invites more research and investigation, but at this point there exists no incontrovertible proof one way or another. However, the writings of Izola Forrester and Finis Bates, along with the eyewitness accounts of others, leave us with little doubt that he did.

Of the twenty or so men who have been identified as John Wilkes Booth over the years, most can be dismissed for lack of appropriate evidence. Researchers, however, keep returning to examine the possibility that John St. Helen/David E. George might have been the assassin. Unfortunately, the mummy remains missing. Should it ever be located, a DNA test would determine a Booth family connection. The mummy, like Booth himself, remains elusive. Hope is held out that it will someday be located. Maybe, as sometimes happens, a tenacious researcher will also stumble onto an old trunk containing important documents that can prove or disprove the contentions regarding the assassin of President Abraham Lincoln. Until then, patient, rational, and logical analysis of the evidence continues to put the lie to the official version of the capture and death of John Wilkes Booth and points toward the likelihood that he escaped.

Bibliography

Books

Abbott, Abbott A. *The Assassination and Death of Abraham Lincoln, President of the United States of America.* New York: American News Company, 1865.

Arnold, Samuel Bland. *Defense and Prison Experiences of a Lincoln Conspirator, Statements and Autographed Notes.* Hattiesburg, MS: Book Farm, 1943.

Baker, Lafayette C. *History of the United States Secret Service.* Philadelphia: King and Baird, 1868.

Balsiger, David, and Charles E. Sellier. *The Lincoln Conspiracy.* Los Angeles: Schick-Sunn Classic Books, 1977.

Basler, Roy P. *The Lincoln Legend.* Boston: Houghton Mifflin, 1935.

Bates, David Homer. *Some Recollections of Abraham Lincoln.* New York: Grafton Press, 1906.

———. *Lincoln in the Telegraph Office.* New York: D. Appleton-Century, 1907.

Bates, Finis L. *Escape and Suicide of John Wilkes Booth, Assassin of President Lincoln.* Memphis: Pilcher Printing, 1907.

Beyer, William Gilmore. *On Hazardous Service.* New York: Harper and Brothers, 1912.

Bishop, James A. *The Day Lincoln Was Shot.* New York: Harper and Brothers, 1955.

Borrenson, Ralph. *When Lincoln Died.* New York: Appleton-Century, 1965.

Bryan, George S. *The Great American Myth.* New York: Carrick and Evans, 1940.

Buckingham, J. E. *Reminiscences and Souvenirs of the Assassination of Abraham Lincoln.* Washington, DC: Press of Rufus H. Darby, 1894.

Burnett, Henry L. *Some Incidents in the Trial of President Lincoln's Assassins.* New York: D. Appleton, 1891.

———. *Assassination of President Lincoln and the Trial of the Assassins.* New York: Ohio Society of New York, 1906.

Campbell, Helen Jones. *The Case for Mrs. Surratt.* New York: G. P. Putnam's Sons, 1943.

Campbell, W. P. *The Escape and Wanderings of John Wilkes Booth until Final Ending of the Trail by Suicide in Enid, Oklahoma, January 12, 1903.* Oklahoma City: Self-published, 1922.

Carter, Samuel. *The Riddle of Dr. Mudd.* New York: G. P. Putnam's Sons, 1974.

Chamlee, Roy Z. *Lincoln's Assassins: A Complete Account of Their Capture, Trial, and Punishment*. Jefferson, NC: McFarland, 1924.

Clark, Asia Booth. *The Elder and Younger Booth*. Boston: James R. Osgood, 1882.

———. *A Memoir of John Wilkes Booth by His Sister, The Unlocked Book*. Edited by Eleanor Farjeon. London: Faber and Faber, 1882.

Cottrell, John. *Anatomy of an Assassination*. New York: Funk and Wagnalls, 1966.

Crozier, R. H. *The Bloody Junto; or, The Escape of John Wilkes Booth*. Little Rock, AR: Woodruff and Blocker, Huntington Library, 1949.

Cuthbert, Norma B., ed. *Lincoln and the Baltimore Plot*. San Marino, CA: Huntington Library, 1869.

Dewitt, David Miller. *The Assassination of Abraham Lincoln and Its Expiation*. New York: Macmillan, 1909.

Dye, John Smith. *A History of the Plots and Crimes of the Great Conspiracy*. New York: Self-published, 1866.

Eisenschiml, Otto. *Why Was Lincoln Murdered?* Boston: Little, Brown, 1937.

———. *In the Shadow of Lincoln's Death*. New York: Wilfred Funk, 1950.

Ferguson, William F. *I Saw Booth Shoot Lincoln*. Cambridge, MA: Houghton Mifflin, Riverside Press, 1930.

Flower, Frank A. *Edwin McMasters Stanton*. Akron, OH: Sadfield Publishing, 1905.

Forrester, Izola. *This One Mad Act*. Boston: Hale, Cushman, and Flynt, 1937.

Fowler, Robert H. *Album of the Lincoln Murder*. Harrisburg, PA: Stackpole Books, 1965.

Garrett, Pat F. *The Authentic Life of Billy the Kid*. Santa Fe: New Mexico Printing and Publishing, 1882.

Good, Timothy S. *We Saw Lincoln Shot: One Hundred Eyewitness Accounts*. Jackson: University Press of Mississippi, 1995.

Gorham, George C. *Life and Public Services of Edwin M. Stanton*. 2 vols. Boston: Houghton Mifflin, 1899.

Grant, Ulysses S. *Personal Memoirs of U.S. Grant*. Vols. 1–3. New York: Charles L. Webster, 1886.

Gutman, Richard J. S., and Kellie O. Gutman. *John Wilkes Booth Himself*. Dover, MA: Hired Hand Press, 1979.

Hall, James O. *Notes on the John Wilkes Booth Escape Route*. Clinton, MD: Surratt Society, 1979.

Hanchett, William. *The Lincoln Murder Mysteries*. Chicago: University of Illinois Press, 1983.

Harris, Thomas Mealey. *The Assassination of Lincoln, a History of the Great Conspiracy: Trial of the Conspirators by a Military Commission and a Review of the Trial of John H. Surratt*. Boston: American Citizens Company, 1897.

Higdon, Hal. *The Union vs. Dr. Mudd*. Chicago: Follett, 1964.

Jameson, W. C. *Billy the Kid: Beyond the Grave*. Boulder, CO: Taylor Trade Publishing, 2005.

Johnson, Bryan Berkeley. *Abraham Lincoln and Boston Corbett*. Waltham, MA: Lincoln and Smith Press, 1914.

Johnson, Robert Underwood, and Clarence Clough Buel. *Battles and Leaders of the Civil War*. Vol. 4. New York: The Century Company, 1888.

Jones, Evan R. *Lincoln and Stanton, Historical Sketches.* London: Frederick Warne, 1875.

Jones, Thomas A. *J. Wilkes Booth. An Account of His Sojourn in Southern Maryland after the Assassination of Abraham Lincoln, His Passage across the Potomac, and His Death in Virginia.* Chicago: Laird and Lee, 1893.

Kauffman, Mike. *American Brutus: John Wilkes Booth and the Lincoln Conspiracies.* New York: Random House, 2004.

Kimmel, Stanley. *The Mad Booths of Maryland.* 2nd ed. New York: Dover, 1969.

Kunhardt, Dorothy Meserve, and Philip B. Kunhardt Jr. *Twenty Days.* New York: Castle Books, 1965.

Lamon, Ward H. *Recollections of Abraham Lincoln.* Chicago: A. C. McClurg, 1895.

Laughlin, Clara E. *The Death of Lincoln: The Story of Booth's Plot, His Deed and the Penalty.* New York: Doubleday, 1909.

Lewis, Lloyd. *Myths after Lincoln.* New York: R. Hart, 1886. Reprint, New York: Harcourt, Brace, 1929.

Logan, John A. *The Great Conspiracy.* New York: A. R. Hart, 1886.

McCarty, Burke. *The Suppressed Truth about the Assassination of Abraham Lincoln.* Philadelphia: Burke McCarty, 1924.

McLaughlin, Emmett. *An Inquiry into the Assassination of Abraham Lincoln.* New York: Lyle Stuart, 1963.

Mearns, David C. *The Lincoln Papers.* Garden City, NY: Doubleday, 1948.

Morse, John T., Jr. *Abraham Lincoln.* Boston: Houghton Mifflin, 1921.

Mudd, Samuel A. *The Life of Dr. Samuel A. Mudd.* Edited by Nettie Mudd. New York: Neale Publishing, 1906.

Oldroyd, Osborn H. *The Assassination of Abraham Lincoln, Flight, Pursuit, Capture, and Punishment of the Conspirators.* Washington, DC: Self-published, 1914.

O'Reilly, Bill, and Martin Dugard. *Killing Lincoln: The Shocking Assassination That Changed America Forever.* New York: Henry Holt, 2011.

Pinkerton, Allan. *Spy of the Rebellion.* New York: G. W. Carleton, 1883.

Pittman, Ben, comp. *The Assassination of President Lincoln and the Trial of the Conspirators.* New York: Funk and Wagnalls, 1954.

Poore, Benjamin Perley. *The Conspiracy Trial for the Murder of the President. And the Attempt to Overthrow the Government by the Assassination of Its Principal Officers.* Boston: J. E. Tilton, 1865.

Pratt, Fletcher. *Stanton, Lincoln's Secretary of War.* Westport, CT: Rumford Press, 1949.

Robertson, David M. *Booth: A Novel.* New York: Doubleday, 1997.

Roscoe, Theodore. *The Web of Conspiracy: The Complete Story of the Men Who Murdered Abraham Lincoln.* Englewood Cliffs, NJ: Prentice Hall, 1959.

Samples, Gordon. *Lust for Fame: The Stage Career of John Wilkes Booth.* Jefferson, NC: McFarland, 1982.

Shelton, Vaughan. *Mask for Treason: The Lincoln Murder Trial.* Harrisburg, PA: Stackpole Books, 1965.

Skinner, Otis. *The Mad Folk of the Theater.* New York: Bobbs-Merrill, 1928.

Smoot, R. M. *The Unwritten History of the Assassination of Abraham Lincoln.* Baltimore: John Murphy Company, 1904.

Starkey, Larry. *Wilkes Booth Came to Washington.* New York: Random House, 1976.

Starr, John W., Jr. *Lincoln's Last Day.* New York: Stokes, 1922.

Steers, Edwin. *Blood on the Moon: The Assassination of Abraham Lincoln.* Lexington: University Press of Kentucky, 2001.

Stern, Philip Van Doren. *The Man Who Killed Lincoln.* New York: Random House, 1939.

Tanner, James. *While Lincoln Lay Dying.* Philadelphia: Union League of Philadelphia, 1868.

Tarbell, Ida M. *The Life of Abraham Lincoln.* New York: Macmillan, 1928.

Townsend, George Alfred. *The Life, Crime, and Capture of John Wilkes Booth.* New York: Dick and Fitzgerald, 1865.

Walker, Dale L. *Legends and Lies: Great Mysteries of the American West.* New York: A Tom Doherty Associates Book, 1997.

Weichmann, Louis J. *A True History of the Assassination of Abraham Lincoln and the Conspiracy of 1865.* Edited by F. E. Risvold. New York: Knopf, 1975.

Wilson, John Francis. *John Wilkes Booth: Fact and Fiction of Lincoln's Assassination.* Boston: Houghton Mifflin, 1929.

ARTICLES

Arnold, Samuel Bland. "Lincoln Conspiracy and Conspirators." *Ohio State Journal,* December 10–20, 1902.

Baker, L. B. "An Eyewitness Account of the Death and Burial of J. Wilkes Booth." *Journal of the Illinois State Historical Society,* no. 39 (December 1946).

Crook, William H. "Lincoln's Last Day." *Harper's Monthly,* September 1907.

Davis, William C. "The Lincoln Conspiracy—Hoax?" *Civil War Times Illustrated,* November 1977.

DeMotte, William H. " The Assassination of Abraham Lincoln." *Journal of the Illinois State Historical Society,* no. 20 (October 1927).

Doherty, Edward P. "Pursuit and Death of John Wilkes Booth: Captain Doherty's Narrative." *Century Magazine,* January 1890.

Ford, John T. "Behind the Curtain of a Conspiracy." *North American Review,* September 1888.

Fowler, Robert H. "Was Stanton behind Lincoln's Murder?" *Civil War Times,* August 1961.

———. "New Evidence in the Lincoln Murder Conspiracy." *Civil War Times Illustrated,* February 1965.

Fulton, Justin D. "Behind the Purple Curtain: Lincoln's Assassins." *Christian Heritage,* April/May 1979.

Garrett, Richard Baynham. "A Chapter of Unwritten History . . . Account of the Flight and Death of John Wilkes Booth." *Virginia Magazine of History and Biography,* no. 71 (October 1963).

Garrett, William H. "True Story of the Capture of John Wilkes Booth." *Confederate Veteran Magazine,* April 1921.

Giddens, Paul H. "Ben Pitman on the Trial of Lincoln's Assassins." *Tyler's Quarterly Historical and Genealogical Magazine,* July 1940.

Gleason, D. H. L. "Conspiracy against Lincoln." *The Magazine of History,* February 1911.

Hall, James O. "The Mystery of Lincoln's Guard." *Surratt Society News,* May 1982.

Hanchett, William. "Booth's Diary." *Journal of the Illinois State Historical Society,* no. 72 (February 1979).

Head, Constance. "Insights on John Wilkes Booth from His Sister Asia's Correspondence." *Lincoln Herald,* no. 82 (Winter 1980).

———. "John Wilkes Booth as a Hero Figure." *Journal of American Culture,* no. 5 (Fall 1982).

King, Horatio. "The Assassination of President Lincoln." *New England Magazine,* December 1893.

Laughlin, Clara. "The Last Twenty-Four Hours of Lincoln's Life." *Ladies' Home Journal,* February 1909.

May, John F. "The Mark of the Scalpel." *Records of the Columbia Historical Society* 8 (1910).

McBride, Robert W. "Lincoln's Body Guard." *Indiana Historical Society Publications* 5 (1911).

Morris, Clara. "Some Reflections of John Wilkes Booth." *McClure's Magazine,* February 1901.

Moss, M. Helen Palms. "Lincoln and Wilkes Booth as Seen on the Day of the Assassination." *Century Magazine,* April 1909.

Munroe, Seaton. "Recollections of Lincoln's Assassination." *North American Review,* April 1886.

Peck, Harry Thurston. "Dewitt's Assassination of Abraham Lincoln." *Bookman,* April 1909.

Porter, George Loring. "How Booth's Body Was Hidden." *Magazine of History,* no. 38 (1929).

Rankin, Mrs. McKee. "The News of Lincoln's Death." *American Magazine,* January 1909.

Reid, Albert T. "Boston Corbett: The Man of Mystery of the Lincoln Drama." *Scribner's Magazine,* July 1929.

Ruggles, M. B. "Pursuit and Death of John Wilkes Booth: Major Ruggles' Narrative." *Century Magazine,* no. 39 (January 1890).

Shepherd, William G. "Shattering the Myth of John Wilkes Booth's Escape." *Harper's Magazine,* November 1924.

Skinner, Otil. "The Last of John Wilkes Booth." *American Magazine,* November 1908.

Speed, James, "The Assassins of Lincoln." *North American Review,* September 1888.

Stimmel, Smith. "Experiences as a Member of President Lincoln's Body Guard." *North Dakota Historical Quarterly,* January 1927.

Surratt, John H. "Lecture on the Lincoln Conspiracy." *Lincoln Herald,* no. 51 (December 1949).

Taylor, W. H. "A New Story of the Assassination of Lincoln." *Leslie's Weekly,* March 26, 1908.

Tilton, Clint C. "First Plot against Lincoln." *National Republic,* February 1936.

Tindal, William. "Booth's Escape from Washington." *Records of the Columbia Historical Society* 18 (1915).

Townsend, George Alfred. "How Wilkes Booth Crossed the Potomac." *Century Magazine*, April 1884.

Weik, Jesse W. "A New Story of Lincoln's Assassination." *Century Magazine*, February 1913.

NEWSPAPERS

Arnold, Samuel B. "The Lincoln Plot." *Baltimore American.* December 20, 1902, and June 6, 1903.

Baltimore American, February 16, 1869.

Black, F. L. "David E. George as John Wilkes Booth." *Dearborn Independent*, April 25, 1925.

———. "Identification of J. Wilkes Booth." *Dearborn Independent*, May 2, 1925.

Boston *Sunday Globe*, December 12, 1897.

Hathaway, Carson C. "What the Mark of the Scalpel Tells." *Dearborn Independent*, February 7, 1925.

McNutt, Michael. "Sleuths Seek Mummified Mystery Body." *Saturday Oklahoman and Times*, June 22, 1991.

New York *Tribune*, April 15, 1865.

New York *World*, April 5, 1892.

Sciolino, Elaine. "Assassins Usually Miss the Larger Target." *New York Times*, November 12, 1995.

Washington *Daily Morning Chronicle*, April 15, 1865.

DOCUMENTS

Baker-Yull-Cooley Collection, Archives of Michigan, Michigan Library and Historical Center, Lansing, MI.

Neff-Guttridge Collection, Cunningham Memorial Library, Indiana State University, Terre Haute.

Office of the Provost Marshal, National Archives, Washington, DC.

Records of the District of Columbia, Police Blotter, Detective Corps, April 14–19, 1865. National Archives, Washington, DC.

Records of the Judge Advocate General, Investigation and Trial Papers—Assassination of President Lincoln. Microfilm 599. National Archives, Washington, DC.

Index

Note: *Italic* page numbers indicate illustrations.

Abbott, Ezra W., 95
acting career, of Edwin Booth, 9
acting career, of John Wilkes Booth,
    8–10; debut, 8; earnings in, 10;
    Edwin Booth on brother's potential,
    8; interest and performances after
    "death," 165, 166, 174; jealousy
    of father and brother (Edwin), 9;
    Lincoln's attendance at performance,
    10; popularity and celebrity in, 9–10
acting career, of Junius Brutus Booth,
    7–8
Adamson, Bernard, 101–2
age, of Booth vs. Boyd, 149, 193
alcohol, Booth's consumption of: on day
    of assassination, 47–48, 50, 51, 59;
    after kidnapping attempts, 39; after
    South's defeat, 43
Alger, Russell A., 176
Allen, Aquilla, 101–2
Allen's Creek, 78, 99
Allen's Fresh (Maryland), 99, 112, 113
American Brutus (Kauffman), 90
American Party, 8
Anacostia River: bridge across, 73;
    Herold's crossing of, 143, 187–88;
    planned crossing in kidnapping plot,
    32, 34, 35, 44
Anacostia River, Booth's flight across,
    69, 69–71; alternate version of, 86–
    88, 90–91, 93, 187–88; traditional
    version of, 72–73
Anderson, Mary J., 46, 68, 89–90

Andrews, Billy, 172
Andrews, Sally, 10
Appomattox (Virginia), surrender at, 41
Armstrong, James G., Booth living as,
    165–66
Arnold, Samuel Bland, *30*; arrest of,
    103, 105; as Booth classmate, 8;
    decision to leave plot, 39; evidence
    implicating, 75; imprisonment
    of, 160–61; kidnapping plot
    involvement, 29, 34, 35, 38;
    treatment during imprisonment, 106
assassin: body of, treatment vs. other
    assassins, 196; Booth's notoriety as,
    vii, 6
assassination of Lincoln, 51–61; Booth's
    diary entries on, 42–43; Booth's
    plot for, 42–50; Booth's threat of,
    43; Lincoln's dream about, 53;
    opportunity at inauguration, 37;
    premature reports of, 53; president
    pronounced dead, 76, 95; rumors,
    plots and threats of, 15–16; shooting
    at Ford's Theater, 1, 59–60;
    Stanton's dismissal of information,
    42
Atlanta (Georgia), Booth living as
    Armstrong in, 166
Atzerodt, Andreas, *31*, 31–32; arrest of,
    79; on day of assassination, 50, 52;
    disinterment and reburial of body,
    154; evidence implicating, 75; flight
    of, 75, 76; imprisonment of, 145;

kidnapping plot involvement, 30–38;
misidentified as Seward assailant,
66; name screamed by Sinclair
(Booth), 167; name signed to Booth's
accusatory letter, 47; on Powell's
identity, 62; refusal to participate in
assassination plot, 52, 59; trial and
execution of, 160
Augur, Christopher C.: flight information
reported to, 73; help sought in
Seward attack, 64–65; Payne
investigated at office of, 104–5, 191

Badden, Joseph, 117, 118
Bahamas: Booth sighting after "death,"
164; kidnapping plot plans for, 44
Bainbridge, A. B., 125–26, 148
Baker, Lafayette, 27, 40–41;
assassination plot reported by, 42;
Booth's capture announced by, 144;
Booth's diary and, 119, 122–23,
184–87; closing of case on Booth,
153, 162; disposal of body, 151–53,
194–96; on Garrett Farm shooter,
198; identification of body as
Booth's, 144–46, 150–51, 156, 162;
knowledge of kidnapping plots, 27,
40–41; Powell as agent reporting to,
63; pursuit of Booth, 76, 81, 96–97,
102, 107, 124; pursuit of Booth after
"death," 158–62
Baker, Luther, Jr.: on Identification
Committee, 146; identity of body
investigated by, 143–45; pursuit
and capture by, alternate version of
(Boyd), 124–39; pursuit and capture
by, traditional version of (Booth),
81–84; responsibility for body,
140–45, 151–53, 195
Baltimore (Maryland): Booth's wife in,
162, 170; viewing and reburial of
body in, 154–56, 196–97, 199
Baltimore American (newspaper), 155
Baptist's Alley, 46, 68, 89–90
barn, on Garrett farm: Booth and Herold
in (traditional version), 82–84; Boyd
and Herold in (alternate version),
130–39
Barnes, James V., 36
Barnes, J. K., 145–51

Bates, Edwin, 89
Bates, Finis L.: belief in George, St.
Helens and Booth as same man,
177–81, 199; interest in
assassination, 176; letter on Booth's
survival, 176; mummy in possession
of, 181; relationship with St. Helens
(Booth), 174–76; tintype given to,
174–75
Beale, Frank, 107
Beckwith, Captain, 125
Bell, William, 64–66, 78, 104–5, 191
Belle Isle Prison, raid to free Union
prisoners from, 14–15
Benjamin, Judah, 26
Bernard, William, 24, 109, 161, 186
Bertillon, Alphonse, 178–79
Bertillon Examination, 178–79
Billy the Kid, 2–4
Bingham, John A., 142–43, 146
Bishop, Charles, 156
boardinghouse, Surratt's. *See* Surratt,
Mary, boardinghouse of
body identified as Booth's, 1, 84,
140–57, 192–94; age of, 149, 193;
belongings found on, 138, 193;
as Boyd's body, 131–39, 192–94;
broken leg of, 146, 150; burial of,
152–53, 194–96; clothing of, 193;
dental evidence of, 146, 151, 156;
deterioration of, 145; diary found on,
184–86; disinterment and reburial
of, 154–56, 163, 196–97; disposal
of, 151–53, 194–97; documents on
destroyed or missing, 157; exposure
and starvation of, 149, 193; footwear
of, 139, 155, 193, 196; freckles on,
149; hair analysis of, 151; hair color
of, 139, 155, 192; Herold's referral
to as Boyd, 141; Herold's silence on,
142–45; Identification Committee on,
145–51; investigators' challenge of,
143–45; mismatch of Corbett's gun
to wounds, 135; money missing from,
193; mustache of, 143, 149, 150,
192; not Booth's or Boyd's, possibility
of, 149; photography of, 146,
150–51, 195; physician's questions
about, 148–50, 165–66, 193, 194;
rumors about, 153, 156; scars of,

147, 148–50; suicide as cause of
death, 135, 148–50, 197–99; tattoo
on, 147–48; transport of, 140–41;
wounds on, 135–37, 146, 197, 198
boot, Booth's, 80, 81, 139, 156
Booth, Asia (sister), 8; description of
Booth, 11–12; description of Booth
dressing as woman, 160; description
of tattoo, 147
Booth, Blanche de Bar (niece), 6–7, 178
Booth, Edwin (brother), 8; body
requested by, 154, 196; Booth's
jealousy of, 9; Booth's valet working
for, 172, 199; contact with Booth
after "death," 165, 166, 167; funeral
of, 157; knowledge of Booth's escape,
155, 172, 199; photograph of,
used to identify assassin, 116, 151;
political discussions forbade by, 10;
regard for Booth's acting, 8; tintype
intended for, 174
Booth, Elizabeth (sister), 8
Booth, Frederick (brother), 8
Booth, Henry Byron (brother), 8
Booth, Izola D'Arcy. *See* D'Arcy, Izola
Mills
Booth, James (blacksmith), 97
Booth, Johnny (blacksmith's son), 97
Booth, John Wilkes: author's family
relationship to, vii–viii; birth of, 7;
children of, 162, 168, 169, 170, 171,
173, 177; early life of, 7–8; notoriety
of, vii, 6. *See also* acting career;
body; death; diary; escape; family;
flight; pursuit
Booth, Joseph (brother), 8, 156
Booth, Junius Brutus (father), 7–8;
acting career of, 7; acting lessons
from, 8; Booth's jealousy of, 9; death
of, 8; secret marriage of, 169–70;
slave ownership by, 7
Booth, Junius Brutus, Jr. (brother), 8
Booth, Laura Ida (daughter), 168, 177
Booth, Mary Ann (sister), 8
Booth, Ogarita. *See* Henderson, Ogarita
Booth
Booth, Rita. *See* Henderson, Ogarita
Booth
Booth, Rosalie (sister), 8, 171
Bowman, William T., 34

Boyd, "David," Herold introduced as,
126, 130
Boyd, James William: age of, 149; death
of, mistaken for Booth's, 131–39,
192–94; diary carried by or planted
on, 186; escape from custody, 108–9;
flight of, 92–93, 108–39; forced
cooperation in pursuit of Booth,
107–8; Garrett farm events, 126–39;
hair color of, 139, 192; implicated
in assassination, 96; kidnapping plot
involvement, 23, 36, 37; leg injury
of, 22, 81, 116–17, 150, 192–93;
murder committed by, 43, 92, 96,
107; as Union informant, 22–23, 24
Boyd, John W.: Booth introduced as, 81;
Boyd (James W.) introduced as, 126
Boyle, Frank, fatal resemblance to
Booth, 120
Boyle, John H., Boyd's crime attributed
to, 43
briefcase, Booth's, 52
broken leg. *See* leg fracture, Booth's
Bronson, Spencer, 89
Brown, Fanny, 10
Brown (newspaper editor), George
identified as Booth by, 179–80
Browning, William A., 18–20, 47
Bryan, George S.: on Booth's appearance
and personality, 6, 8, 12; on Booth
sightings after "death," 165; on
identity of Booth's granddaughter,
169; on kidnapping plot, 24; on Old
Arsenal Penitentiary, 152
Bryantown (Maryland): investigators
in, 105, 109, 125; meetings of
kidnapping conspirators in, 17,
24–25; Mudd imprisoned in, 116;
Mudd's location near, 74–77, 91,
97–98; on route in kidnapping plot,
44
Buckingham, John, 52, 59
burial, of body identified as Booth's,
152–53, 194–96
burn, vs. scar on body identified as
Booth's, 148–50, 198
Burnley, Elizabeth (wife), 162
Burns, Francis, 56, 58, 59
Burnside, body identified as Booth's
aboard, 145

Burroughs, John: Booth's assault of, 69;
  Booth's horse held by, 50, 58,
  68–69
Butler, Benjamin, on contents of Booth's
  diary, 185
Butler, Major General, 89

California, Booth's life after "death" in,
  170, 171
Canada: acting tours in, 10; activities
  of Surratt (John) in, 25; Booth's
  escape to, 122, 162; Booth sightings
  in, 122; Booth's visits to, 23, 27–28;
  Confederate activities in, 17–18,
  23–28, 37; Confederate raids
  conducted from, 18; Confederate
  soldiers fleeing to, 17; Confederate
  underground to, 74
Canterbury Music Hall, 28
Carvoe, John, 93
censorship: of Booth's diary (missing
  pages), 157, 185–86; of records,
  182–83
Ceylon, Booth sightings in, 164, 171
Chamlee, Roy Z.: on Booth's diary, 184;
  on identification of Powell, 62
Chandler, Zachariah, 123, 186
Chapman, Blanche, disinterred body
  viewed by, 155
Chase, Salmon P., 15, 37
childhood, Booth's, 7–8
children, Booth's: daughter with D'Arcy,
  169, 170; daughter with Payne, 168,
  177; daughter with Scott, 162, 173;
  son with D'Arcy, 171
Clarke, John Sleeper (brother-in-law),
  11
Clay, Clement C., 17–18, 23
"clear my name" passage, in Booth's
  diary, 115, 185
Clifford, James, 46
Cobb, Clarence E., 151
Cobb, Silas: Booth's injury not observed
  by, 90; crossings permitted by,
  alternate version, 86–88, 188;
  crossings permitted by, traditional
  version, 72–73; identification of
  Booth, 151
Colfax, Schuyler, 54
Collins, Charles M., 146, 147

Confederate Secret Service, Booth as
  member of, 23
Confederate States of America: Booth's
  espionage activities for, 11; Booth's
  smuggling for, 11, 23; Booth's
  support of, 6–7, 10; military losses
  of, 36, 40; surrender of, 41
Conger, Everton J.: Booth pursued and
  captured by, 81–84, 103; Booth's
  diary and, 119, 184–87; Boyd and
  Herold pursued and captured by,
  124–39; knowledge of kidnapping
  plot, 40; responsibility for body,
  140–41; as shooter on Garrett Farm,
  135, 198; on suicide at Garrett
  Farm, 197
Connecticut, Booth's wife living in,
  172–73
Conness, John: Booth's diary and,
  119, 123, 186; kidnapping plot
  involvement, 28, 29, 39–40
Connolly, M. W., 167
conspiracy: to assassinate Lincoln,
  42–50; to declare Booth dead, 1–5,
  139, 156–57; to kidnap Lincoln,
  15–41. *See also specific conspiracies*
Constitutional Union (newspaper), 153
Cooke, Henry, 26–27, 119
Cooke, Jay, 26–27, 119
Corbett, Thomas P. "Boston," 127–29,
  128; as Garrett farm shooter, 84,
  135–36, 197–99; life after shooting,
  136; mental stability of, 84, 127–29,
  136; reward received by, 136
corpse. *See* body identified as Booth's
cotton, speculation in, 26–28, 36
Cox, Samuel: aid to Booth during flight,
  77, 99–101, 189; kidnapping plot
  involvement, 34
Crawford, A. M. S., 89–90
Crowningshield, William W., 146, 147
Cuba, Booth sighting in, 164
Czolgolsz, Leon, 196

Dahlgren, Ulric, 14–15
Dana, Charles A., 195
Dana, David D., 96
D'Arcy, Izola Mills (wife): arrest for
  smuggling, 19; in Baltimore, 162,
  170; Booth's escape acknowledged

by, 170; daughter with Booth, 169,
170; financial support of, 172–73;
granddaughter of, 169–73; life after
Booth's "death," 170–73; living
on farm near Harpers Ferry, 170;
marriage to Stevenson (O'Laughlin),
170–71; Palau Island shells in home
of, 173; pin given to Booth returned
by, 172; secret marriage to, 11, 19,
169–70; son with Booth, 171
Davidson, James Hamilton, 195
Davis, Jefferson: Booth's letter to,
23; Booth's meeting with, 26;
representatives in Canada, 17–18;
Union plans to kill, 15, 19–20
Davis, Thomas, 80
Dawson, Charles, 146, 147, 151
death, Booth's: author's doubts about,
vii–viii; Boyd's mistaken for, 131–39,
192–94; conspiracy to declare,
1–5, 139, 156–57; funeral services
after, 156; as George, in Oklahoma,
176–81; as goal of high-ranking
conspirators, 102, 123, 144;
identification of body, 1, 84, 140–57,
192–94; in India, reported, 162;
mummy of George (Booth), 180,
181; traditional version of, 82–85.
See also body identified as Booth's;
sightings of Booth, after "death"
death, Lincoln's, 76, 95
Deery's Saloon, 43, 47, 50
dental evidence, 146, 151, 156
Derringer pistol, Booth's, 52, 60
Dewitt, David Miller: on Atzerodt, 32;
on Booth's appearance and skills,
11–12; on Herold, 30; on pursuit
of Booth, 96; on Stanton, 21; on
wounds of body identified as Booth's,
198
diary, Booth's, 184–87; assassination
plot in, 42–43; Baker and, 119,
122–23, 187–90; "clear my name"
passage in, 115, 185; copies made
of, 184–85; description of, 184;
flight accounts in, 78, 108, 115,
118–19; forgery of, 186; found on
body identified as Booth's, 184–86;
loss and discovery at Gambo Creek,
118, 119, 122, 175–76, 186;

missing pages of, 157, 185–86;
official cover-up of, 123, 184–87;
photographs of women tucked
in, 119, 186; rediscovery of, 157;
Stanton and, 42, 122–23, 157; St.
Helen's knowledge about, 175–76
disinterred body, 154–56, 163, 196–97
disposal of body, 151–53, 194–97
DNA testing, 200
documents: censorship of, 182;
contradictions in, 182; discovery of
new, 4, 183; missing or destroyed,
157; in possession of Stanton
descendants, 42, 47, 186; secrecy of,
182–83; study of, 2–4
Doherty, Edward P.: escort of prisoner
Herold, 140–42; pursuit and capture
by, alternate version (Boyd), 124–39;
pursuit and capture by, traditional
version (Booth), 81–84
Donelson, Andrew Jackson, 164–65, 170
Dooley, Ernest, 109, 186
Doster, William E., 191
Dr. Booth (nickname), 11
drinking. *See* alcohol
Dry Tortugas: conspirators imprisoned
on, 160–61; O'Laughlin's reported
death on, 161, 170
Dugard, Martin, 12
Dunn, Alphonso, 28

Early, Jubal, 36
Eckert, Thomas, 55; assassination plot
knowledge of, 42; Booth's diary and,
123, 184, 186; on Identification
Committee, 145; interrogation of
Payne (Powell), 105; kidnapping
plot knowledge of, 28, 41; Payne
in custody of, 191–92; refusal of
Lincoln's invitation to play, 54;
sabotage by suspected, 86–87;
Seward attack role alleged, 63;
testimony on burial of body, 152
Edeline, Walter, 97
education, Booth's, 7–8
Eisenschiml, Otto: on Booth's return to
Washington, 160; on death at Garrett
farm, 136, 139, 197–98; on Herold's
interrogation, 143
Eldridge, Congressman, 163

Emerson, E. A., 43
engagement, 10–11, 19
England: Booth's father in, 7; Booth's
    intended escape to, 94; Booth's life
    after "death" in, 162, 164, 167, 172,
    173, 199; kidnapping plot plans for,
    44
Enid (Oklahoma), Booth living as
    George in, 176–81
erysipelas, 20
escape, by Booth: acting and theater
    interests after, 165, 166, 174;
    analysis of, 199–200; author's belief
    in, viii; Booth family knowledge of,
    155, 165, 166, 167, 170, 172, 178,
    199; closing of official case, 153,
    162; letters from Booth, 171–72,
    173; life after, 160–81; money and
    wealth in, 170, 174, 177; officials
    tracking Booth after "death,"
    158–62; return to United States after,
    162, 199–200; return to Washington
    after, 160, 167; rumors about,
    153, 156, 158, 163. See also flight;
    sightings
espionage: Booth's, for South, 11;
    Boyd's, for Union, 22–23, 24;
    Confederate activities in Canada,
    17–18, 23, 27–28
Ewing, General, 120
Examiner (newspaper), 153
execution, of conspirators, 160

facial hair, of body identified as Booth,
    143, 149, 150, 192
family, Booth's, 7–8; author as member
    of, vii–viii; knowledge of escape, 155,
    165, 166, 167, 170, 172; secret,
    162, 168, 169–73. See also children;
    marriage; specific members
Ficklin, Benjamin, 105
fire, in Garrett barn, 83–84, 133–35
Fitzpatrick, Honora, 103
Fletcher, John: in alternate account of
    bridge crossing, 87–88, 93, 188;
    in traditional account of bridge
    crossing, 72–73
flight, Booth's: alternate version of,
    86–139; Booth's diary accounts of,
    78, 108, 115, 118–19; crossing of

Potomac, 80–81, 113–15; from
    Ford's Theater, 67–71, 89–90;
    Garrett farm events in, 1, 70–71,
    81–84; Henson identified as
    companion during, 87–88, 119, 187–
    90; Herold identified as companion
    during, 72–74, 87–88, 187–90; map
    of route, 114; roadblocks avoided
    during, 92; route out of Washington,
    69, 69–71; sightings reported,
    120; St. Helen's description of,
    176; Surrattsville stop during, 74,
    89–93; traditional version of, 72–85;
    treatment of broken leg during,
    74–77, 90, 94–98. See also escape
Florida Keys, conspirators imprisoned
    in, 160–61
footwear: on body identified as Booth's,
    138, 193, 196; Booth's boot, 80, 81,
    139, 156; on disinterred body, 155
Forbes, Charles, 57, 58, 59
Ford, James, 46, 53, 68
Ford, John T., 44–45
Ford's Theater, 44–46, 95; Booth's
    familiarity with, 35; Booth's flight
    from, 67–71, 89–90; Booth's
    movements between boxes, 59–61,
    61; Booth's plans to kidnap Lincoln
    at, 29, 32, 35, 37–38; Booth's
    preparations in, 46–50; collapse
    of interior, 157; history of, 44–45;
    layout and design of, 45, 46, 48–49,
    49; Lincoln left unprotected at, 50,
    53–61; Lincoln's frequent attendance
    at, 45–46; Lincoln's insistence on
    attending play, 53; popularity of, 28,
    45–46; presidential box of, 48–49,
    49; shooting of Lincoln at, 1, 51–61
Forestville (California), Booth sighting
    in, 165
Forrester, Izola Laura (granddaughter),
    169–73; book attributed to, 169,
    170, 199; death of, 173; identity
    challenged, 169; on St. Helen or
    George as Booth, 181
Fort Wayne (Indiana), Henson living
    in, 190
Fredericksburg (Virginia): Booth's flight
    to, 122, 126; tracking Booth to, 158
"Freedom," Booth's cry of, 60

Freeman, Ned, transport of body by, 140–42
funeral: of Booth (Edwin), 157; of Booth (John Wilkes), 156; of Lincoln, 79–80

Gambo Creek campsite, 118–19, 175–76, 186
Gardner, Alexander, 146, 150–51
Garfield, James, assassin of, 196
Garrett, Cora, 126, 127
Garrett, John "Jack": actions at farm, 82–83, 126–34; arrest and imprisonment of, 145
Garrett, Kate, 126
Garrett, Lily, 126, 127
Garrett, Pat, 2
Garrett, Richard: reputation for aiding southerners, 81, 126; statement on identity of body, 144; testimony on shooting, 135. *See also* Garrett farm
Garrett, Richard, Jr., 126
Garrett, William: actions at farm, 83, 126; arrest and imprisonment of, 145
Garrett farm: alternate version of killing on (Boyd's death), 127–39, 192–94; Conger as shooter on, 135, 198; Corbett as shooter on, 84, 135–36, 197–99; last words of man killed on, 137–38; map of, *137*; return of investigators to, 143–44; suicide as possibility in death on, 197–99; traditional version of killing (Booth's death), 1, 70–71, 81–84
Gautier's Restaurant, 38
George, David E.: body claimed by Bates, 177; body identified as Booth, 176–77; Booth living as, 174, 176–81, 199–200; leg injury of, 179; mummy of, 180, 181, 199–200; personality of, vs. Booth's, 180–81; resemblance to Booth, 178–79; resemblance to St. Helen, 178; ring swallowed by, 180; suicide attempt of, 177–78; suicide of, 176, 180
Georgia, Booth living as Armstrong in, 166
German, Effie, 10
Gerry, Margarite Spalding, 16–17
Gleason, D. H. L., 26, 34

Godfrey, Mrs., 172
gold, speculation in, 26–28
Gourlay, Jennie, 59
Granbury (Texas), Booth living as St. Helen in, 174–76
Grant, Julia, 53–54
Grant, Ulysses: Booth's encounter with carriage, 50; military advance on Richmond, 41; refusal of president's invitation to play, 53–54; on Stanton, 22
The Great American Myth (Bryan), 6, 152
Green, Dan, 115–17, 120–21
Green, Mrs., 117, 120
Greene, Thomas, 24
Green Mount Cemetery (Baltimore), reburial of body in, 156, 163
Grey, Alice, 10
Grover's Theater, 28, 37
guards, for Lincoln: assignment during kidnapping threats, 28; lack of protection at Ford's Theater, 50, 53–61
Guiteau, Charles J., 196
Gurley, Phineas, 95

Haggett, Mrs., Booth sighting by, 164
Haggett, Thomas, 164
"Hail to the Chief," playing at Ford's Theater, 56–57
hair color, of body identified as Booth, 139, 155, 192
Hale, John P., 10, 36
Hale, Lucy Lambert, 10–11, 19
Hamlet (Shakespeare), 9, 166
Hanchett, William: on failure of historians, 2, 183; on hatred of Lincoln, 15; on shooting at Garrett farm, 136
handwriting, 165, 172, 179
Hansell, Emerick "Bud," 65
Harbin, Thomas H., 117, 118
Harper, E. C., 176–77
Harper, Mrs., 177
Harpers Ferry (West Virginia), Booth farm near: Booth's acquisition of, 160; Booth's stay after "death," 160, 161; Booth's wife living on, 161, 170

Harris, Clara: attendance of play
    with Lincolns, 54, 56–61; seat in
    presidential box, 57, 60
Harris, Ira, 54
Harrisburg (Pennsylvania), tracking
    Booth in, 161
Harrison, Fannie. See Turner, Ella
Harvey and Marr Funeral Home, 154,
    196
Havana (Cuba), Booth sighting in, 164
Hawk, Harry, 60, 67–68, 89
Hay, John, 11
Henderson, Edwin, Henson's name
    change to, 190
Henderson, Ogarita Booth (daughter),
    169, 170
Henson, Ed: appearance, vs. Herold,
    187; as Booth's companion in
    flight, 87–126, 187–90; on day of
    assassination, 47–48, 59; fate of,
    190; name change of, 190; officials
    tracking after Booth's "death,"
    158–62; personality and behavior,
    vs. Herold, 188–89; smuggling
    experience of, 187, 188–89
Herald (newspaper), 166
hero, Booth envisioning self as, 34–35,
    44
Herold, David Edgar, 30, 31;
    appearance, vs. Henson, 187; arrest
    of, 102; after assassination, alternate
    version of activities, 97, 102–3,
    107–39; as Booth's companion in
    flight, 72–85; as Booth's companion
    in flight, misidentification of, 87–88,
    187–90; as Boyd's companion in
    flight, 108–39; description and
    picture on wanted poster, 110–12,
    111; disinterment and reburial of
    body, 154; escape from custody, 108–
    9; forced cooperation in pursuit of
    Booth, 103, 107–8; interrogation of,
    102–3; kidnapping plot involvement,
    30–38; Mudd's failure to identify,
    116; name of conspirator withheld,
    70–71; name screamed by Sinclair
    (Booth), 167; name signed to Booth's
    accusatory letter, 47; politics of, 43;
    as prisoner, 140–41; reward offered
    for, 79, 110, 120; Seward attack

involvement, 59, 62–66; silence of,
    142–45, 189; suppressed statement
    of, 142–43; surrender of, 83, 133;
    trial and execution of, 160
Hilliard, E. W., 195
Holloway, Lucinda, 126, 131, 132
Holmes, Mary Ann (mother), 7, 167,
    176
Holmes, Oliver Wendell, 11
Holt, Joseph, 142–43, 146, 147
horse(s): abandoned by Powell, 66;
    acquired by Booth, 46–47, 49–50,
    66; fall on Booth, as cause of broken
    leg, 89–90; given to Pence after
    Booth's "death," 159–60; killed, in
    Booth's hiding place, 77, 101; police
    need for, 93; stolen, in flight from
    Washington, 72–73, 87–88, 93
Horton, Ann, 10

Identification Committee, 145–51; lack
    of personal knowledge of Booth,
    146; membership of, 145–46;
    witnesses handpicked by government,
    146–47
identification of body. See body
    identified as Booth's
identities, alternate. See Armstrong,
    James G.; George, David E.; Sinclair;
    St. Helen, John
inauguration, Lincoln's second, 36–37
India: Booth's life in after "death," 162,
    164, 171, 199; Booth's reported
    death in, 162, 173
Indiana, Henson living in, 190
Indiana State University, 161, 187
initials, shared by Booth and Boyd, 23,
    100, 125, 127, 147–48, 180, 192–93
inquest, 145–51

Jenny B. (patrol boat), 102, 109, 117,
    119, 120
Jerome, Thomas, Booth living as, 165
Jett, W. S. "Willie": aid to Booth during
    flight, 82; aid to Boyd and Herold,
    125–26; dying man's question to,
    138; escape of, 142; escort for body
    identified as Booth's, 140–41; forced
    participation in pursuit, 131
Johnnie (nickname), 7, 167, 178

John S. Ide (steamer), transport of body on, 140–45, 195

Johnson, Andrew: assassination involvement alleged, 174, 185; Booth meeting with, 19; Booth's plot to kidnap, 44, 52; Booth's plot to kill, 52; Booth's visit to office on day of assassination, 47, 174; order to disinter body, 154, 196

Johnson, Henry: as Booth's companion in flight, 121–22, 126; on day of assassination, 43; employment by Booth (Edwin), 172, 199; "ever since Master John got away," 172; mother's employment by Booth's wife, 170; officials tracking after Booth's "death," 158–62; sightings after Booth's "death," 171–72

Jones, Thomas: aid to Booth during flight, 77, 80, 100–101, 110–14, 149, 193; Booth's payment to, 113–14; on Booth's tattoo, 147; encounters with searchers, 110, 112; kidnapping plot involvement, 34

Kauffman, Mike, 90
Keene, Laura, 53, 68
Keim, W. R., 75
Kelly, James, 171–72
Kenzie, Wilson D., 138–39
kidnapping plots against Lincoln, 15–41; Booth proposed as leader of, 17; Booth's first attempt, 35; Booth's second attempt, 37–38; Booth's third attempt, 38–39; Booth's fourth attempt, 39; Booth's fifth attempt, 39; Booth's sixth attempt, 39; Booth's seventh attempt, 40; Booth's dismissal as leader of, 35–36, 37; Booth's plan on day of assassination, 43–44, 52; Booth's pursuit of original mission, 37–41; Booth's recruitment for, 20; Booth's recruits for, 29–34; Boyd as leader of, 23, 36, 37; Confederate, 23–28; financing of, 20, 23; Mudd's involvement in, 17, 24–25; Radical Republican, 22–23, 24, 29, 40–41; as ransom for Confederate prisoners, 29, 34–35; weapons purchased for,

24; Weichmann's exposure of Booth's, 26, 34

Kilpatrick, Judson, 14–15
Kirby, Wallace, 101–2
Knights of the Golden Circle, 6
Know-Nothings, 8

Lamon, Marshall Ward: financial speculation by, 26–27; named in Booth's accusatory letter, 47; warnings to Lincoln about plots, 16–17, 28

Landes, Henry Washington, 145
last words, of man slain on Garrett farm, 137–38

Leale, Charles, 70
leg fracture, Booth's: injuries in men suspected of being Booth vs., 165–66, 168, 179; injury in body identified as Booth's vs., 146, 150, 192–93; Mudd's treatment of, alternate version of, 90, 94–98; Mudd's treatment of, traditional version of, 74–77; pain from, 74, 77, 94, 97, 100; timing and cause challenged, 89–90

leg injury, Boyd's, 22, 81, 116–17, 150, 192–93

letters sent by Booth, after "death," 171–72, 173

Lincoln, Abraham, *16*; armed escort for, 28; attendance at Booth performance, 10; Booth's hatred of, 10, 11, 36, 43, 50; Booth's notoriety as assassin of, vii, 6; death of, 76, 95; dismissal of warnings by, 16–17, 28; dream about assassination, 53; enjoyment of theater, 28, 45–46; funeral for, 79–80; reelection and second inauguration of, 36–37; Stanton's dislike of, 22; unpopularity of, 15–16. *See also* assassination; kidnapping plots

Lincoln, Mary Todd: eagerness to attend play, 53; reaction to shooting, 69, 70; seat in presidential box, 57, 60; sponsorship of Parker (guard), 54, 55–56

Lincoln, Robert Todd, involvement with Booth's fiancée, 11

Linville (Virginia), tracking Booth in, 159–60

Liverpool (England), Booth's escape to, 172

Lloyd, John: aid to Booth during flight, alternate account of, 91, 95, 105, 189; aid to Booth during flight, traditional version of, 74; alcoholism of, 105; arrest of, 105; interrogation and cooperation of, 105; kidnapping plot involvement, 38

Lomax, L. L., 24

Lovett, Alexander, 79, 80, 101–2, 116

Lucas, Charlie, confusion over Booth vs. Boyd, 121, 125

Lucas, William: aid to Booth, 81, 118; aid to Boyd and Herold, 120–21

Lydia (Virginia), tracking Booth in, 158–59

Maddox, James, 50

"the major," Booth's references to, 51–52

Manchester (New Hampshire), premature report of Lincoln's assassination in, 53

marriage: to Burnley, 162; to D'Arcy, 11, 19, 169–70; to Payne, 168. *See also specific women*

Martin, Patrick C., 17, 20, 23, 24

Maryland: birth and upbringing in, 7–8; flight and pursuit in, alternate version of, 86–121; flight and pursuit in, traditional version of, 72–81. *See also specific sites and events*

Mary Porter (schooner), 164

Matthews, John, 49–50, 171

May, John Franklin: identity of body questioned by, 148–50, 165–66, 193, 194; summoned as witness, 146, 148

McArthur, Lewis L., 180

McClellan, George B., 20

McGittigan, Thomas, 165

McKinley, William, assassin of, 196

McPhail, J. L., 147–48

Memphis (Tennessee), Booth living as Booth (John W.) in, 168

Merrill, William, 146, 151, 156

Metz, Lucinda, 76

Middletown (New York), premature report of Lincoln's assassination in, 53

money: bonus awarded detectives, 153; Booth's payment to Jones, 113–14; Booth's wealth after "death," 170, 174, 177; earnings from acting, 10; financing of kidnapping plots, 20, 23; missing, on body identified on Booth's, 193; rewards offered, 79, 102, 105, 110, 120, 136; speculation and kidnapping plot, 26–28, 36

Montauk (vessel): conspiracy suspects imprisoned aboard, 145; inquest conducted aboard, 145–51; removal of body from, 151–53; transfer of body to, 145, 192; two bodies removed from, possibility of, 195

Montgomery, J. B., 145, 152

Moore, William G., 146

Moxley, Basil, 155, 196–97, 199

Mudd, George (brother of doctor), 101

Mudd, George (cousin of doctor), 79

Mudd, Mary, 80, 97–98

Mudd, Samuel, 25; arrest of, 80, 116; Booth's identity concealed from, 75, 94–95, 101; discussion about fugitives, 79, 101; Henson vs. Herold as visitor to, 188–89; imprisonment of, 160–61; interrogation of, 79, 101, 116, 188; investigation of, 79, 80; kidnapping plot involvement, 17, 24–25; name screamed by Sinclair (Booth), 167; Powell's horse acquired from, 66; surveillance on home, 101–2; treatment of Booth's leg, alternate version, 90, 94–98; treatment of Booth's leg, traditional version, 74–77

Muehlenberger, Dr., hair analysis by, 151

mummy, of George (Booth), 180, 181, 199–200

Munroe, Seaton, 146, 147, 150

mustache, of body identified as Booth, 143, 149, 150, 192

Nailor's Livery, 72–73, 87–88

name of assassin withheld, 70–71, 91–92

Nassau (Bahamas), Booth sighting in, 164

National Detective Police: Baker as chief of, 40–41; capture and recruitment of Boyd, 22–23. *See also* Baker, Lafayette

National Hotel: body identified as Booth's by clerk of, 146, 147; Booth's activities on assassination day, 43–44, 47, 50; search of Booth's room, 75; storage of items for kidnapping at, 35

National Intelligencer (newspaper), Booth's letter to, 47, 50

Navy Yard Bridge, 73; Herold's crossing of, 143, 187–88; planned crossing in kidnapping plot, 32, 34, 35, 44

Navy Yard Bridge, Booth's flight across, 69–70; alternate version of, 86–88, 90–91, 93, 187–90; route left open, questions about, 90–91; traditional version of, 72–73

Neff–Guttridge Collection, 161, 187, 199

newspapers: Booth's letter to *National Intelligencer*, 47, 50; premature reports of Lincoln assassination in, 53; rumors about Booth's escape, 153

New York City, tracking Booth in, 161–62

nicknames, 7, 11, 167, 178

Nilgai, Whippet, 102–3, 117, 119

Nixon, Richard, 3

O'Bierne, Major, 121, 125, 158

Oklahoma, Booth living as George in, 176–81

O'Laughlin, Michael: arrest of, 103, 105; Booth's acquisition of farm from, 160; on day of assassination, 43–44, 51–52; death reported, 161, 170; decision to leave kidnapping plot, 39; flight of, 74; imprisonment of, 145, 160–61; kidnapping plot involvement, 29, 35–38; life after "death," 170–71; marriage to Booth's wife, 170–71; on Powell's identity, 62; Stevenson as alias for, 170

Old Arsenal Penitentiary: disposal and burial of body at, 152–53, 194–97; reburial of bodies on grounds, 154

Old Capital Prison: Boyd's work as Union informer at, 22–23, 24; history of, 24

Oldroyd, Osborne H.: on disinterred body, 154; on transport of body identified as Booth's, 141

O'Reilly, Bill, 12

O'Sullivan, Timothy, 146

Our American Cousin (play), 51, 53

Oxford Hall, 28

Page, Mann, identity of Booth's granddaughter vs., 169

Palau Islands: Booth life after "death" in, 164–65, 170; shells, in home of Booth's wife, 173

Parker, John, 28, 54–59; ineptitude vs. role in plot, 57–58; Lincoln left unprotected by, 57–61; mysteries surrounding, 55; sponsorship by first lady, 54, 55–56

Payne, Lewis: appearance and demeanor, vs. Powell, 190; arrest and punishment in Powell's stead, 62–63, 66, 78, 103–4, 190–92; body unclaimed, 193; confusion over name/identity, 32, 62–63; description on wanted poster, 108; disinterment and reburial of body, 154; Eckert's custody of, 192–93; imprisonment of, 106, 145; inconsistencies in case of, 190–92; lawyer's argument for, 191; name screamed by Sinclair (Booth), 167; trial and execution of, 160

Payne, Louisa: daughter born to, 168, 177; marriage to Booth, 168

peace negotiations: Booth's help in reestablishing, 19; Booth's knowledge about, 18–19; Dahlgren raid and end to, 15

"Peanut John." *See* Burroughs, John

Peddicord, J. M., 151

Pegram, William P., 155–56

Pence, Louis, 159–60

Pendel, Thomas, 28, 54

Penniman, W. B., funeral home of, 176–77

Pennsylvania, tracking Booth in, 161–62

Petersburg (Virginia), Union capture of, 40

Peterson, William, Lincoln carried to
    home of, 70
photographs: of body identified as
    Booth's, 146, 150–51, 195; of Booth,
    used to confirmed sightings after
    "death," 159, 179–80; in Booth's
    diary, 119, 186; of Edwin Booth,
    used to identify assassin, 116, 151;
    on wanted poster, 110–12, *111*
physical appearance, Booth's, *9*, 11–12;
    attractiveness to women, 9, 10, 12;
    body identified as Booth's vs., 139,
    143, 146–51, 192; comparison to
    George, 178–79; concealed, from
    Mudd, 75, 94–95, 97–98, 101;
    description and picture on wanted
    poster, 108, 110–12, *111*; description
    by sister, 11–12; fashion sense, 10;
    good looks, 10, 11–12; men slain
    for resemblance, 120; on night of
    assassination, 52–53; scars, 12;
    tattoo, 12
Pike, Albert, 167
Pittman, Benn, 37, 86
politics: Lincoln's reelection and second
    inauguration, 36–37; passion for, 10;
    support for Southern cause, 6–7, 10;
    support of McClellan, 20
Pollock, W. G., 170
Porter, G. L., 148, 153
Port Tobacco (Maryland): Atzerodt's
    activities in, 30–32; Booth's flight
    toward, 74, 76, 81, 92, 94, 96;
    investigators in, 102, 108, 109, 110;
    planned crossing in kidnapping plot
    at, 35, 44
posters, wanted, 79, 102, 105, 108,
    110–12, *111*
postmortem examination, 145–51
Potomac River: Atzerodt's activities on,
    30–31; Booth's crossing of, 80–81,
    96, 109, 113–15, 117; Boyd and
    Herold's crossing of, 109, 115–16;
    Jenny B. (patrol boat) on, 102, 109,
    117, 119, 120; planned crossing in
    kidnapping plot, 35, 44; transport
    of body identified as Booth's on,
    140–45. *See also* Anacostia River
Potter, Andrew: diary discovered by,
    186; fugitives pursued by, 102–3,

107–9, 117, 118–26; identity of body
    challenged by, 143–45; papers of,
    161, 187, 190, 199; pursuit of Booth
    after "death," 158–62
Potter, Earl, 42, 158–62
Potter, James, 119, 186
Potter, Luther: fugitives pursued by,
    102–3, 107–9, 119, 122; identity of
    body challenged by, 143–45; pursuit
    of Booth after "death," 158–62
Powell, Lewis Thornton, 32–34, *33*;
    appearance and demeanor, vs. Payne,
    190; assassination plot involvement,
    48, 52; attack on Seward, 59, 62–66,
    78; as Booth companion, 191;
    confusion over name/identity, 32,
    62–63; kidnapping plot involvement,
    32–38, 40; name signed to Booth's
    accusatory letter, 47; Payne arrested
    and punished in his stead, 62–63,
    66, 78, 103–4, 190–92; service as
    Confederate soldier, 32; as Stanton's
    agent, 63
presidential box, Ford's Theater, 48–49,
    49; Booth's movements toward, 59–
    61, *61*; Lincoln's arrival in, 56–57;
    scene after shooting, 68, 70; seating
    arrangement in, 57, 60; tampering
    by Booth, 48–49
prisoner(s): Confederate, Boyd
    as informant on, 22–23, 24;
    Confederate, kidnapping Lincoln
    to ransom, 29, 34–35; conspirators
    as, 104–6, 145, 160–61; Herold as,
    140–41; Union, Kilpatrick raid to
    free, 14–15
Pumphrey, James W., 46–47, 49
pursuit, of Booth: alternate version of,
    86–139; bonus paid to participants
    in, 153; Booth's diary accounts of,
    78; closing of official case, 153,
    162; command post for, 96; death
    of Booth as goal of high-ranking
    conspirators, 102; from Ford's
    Theater, 68–71; Garrett farm
    events in, 1, 70–71, 81–84; name
    of assassin withheld, 70–71, 91–92;
    pledge extracted from participants
    in, 153; police falling behind in, 93;
    rejoicing over capture, 144; reward

money in, 79, 102, 105, 110, 120, 136; sightings of Booth reported during, 120; Stanton's role in, 75, 79, 90–92, 96, 102; tracking after "death," 158–62; traditional version of, 72–85; wanted posters in, 103, 105, 108, 110–12, *111*

Queen, William, 17, 24
Queensbury, Mrs., 81, 113, 117

Radical Republicans: opposition to Lincoln, 15–16; plot to kidnap Lincoln, 22–23, 24, 29, 40–41. *See also* Stanton, Edwin McMasters
Rappahannock River: Booth's crossing of, 81, 96, 109, 121–22; Boyd and Herold's crossing of, 109, 120, 122, 125; transport of body identified as Booth's across, 140
Rathbone, Henry Reed: attendance of play with Lincolns, 54, 56–61; knife wound of, 67; reaction to shooting, 67, 69; seat in presidential box, 57, 60
Raybold, Tom, 46
razor, used by Booth, 80, 97, 116
reburial, 154–56, 163, 196–97
"Revenge for the South!," Booth's cry of, 60
reward money, 79, 102, 105, 110, 120, 136
reward posters, 103, 105, 108, 110–12, *111*
Richard III (Shakespeare), 8, 10, 165, 166, 174
Richards, A. C., 73, 93, 95
Rich Hill (Cox farm), 77, 99–101
Richmond (Virginia): Booth living as Armstrong in, 165–66; Booth's meetings in, 26; Kilpatrick's raid to free Union prisoners, 14–15; Union plans to destroy, 15, 19–20; Union threat to, 36, 40
ring, Booth's. *See* signet ring, Booth's
Ritterspaugh, Jacob, 68
Robey, Franklin, 100
Robinson, George, 65
Robinson, Kate, Booth mistaken for, 160

Rollins, William: forced participation in pursuit, 129, 131; identification of Booth, 151, 192; transport of Booth, 82, 121, 129; transport of Boyd and Herold, 125
romances, 10–11; engagement to Hale, 10–11, 19; involvement with Surratt (Anna), 34; involvement with Surratt (Mary), 10; marriage to Burnley, 162; marriage to D'Arcy, 11, 19, 170–71; marriage to Payne, 168. *See also specific women*
Rosch, C. H., 190–91
Roscoe, Theodore: on Atzerodt, 32; on body identified as Booth's, 147; on Booth's attractiveness, 10; on Booth's preparations at theater, 60; on censorship of documents, 182–83; on first lady, 56; on hoods covering prisoners' heads, 105; on kidnapping plot, 38; on mummy, 181; on Powell, 32; on pursuit of Booth, 93, 96; on Spangler, 32; on Stanton, 20–21; on wanted poster, 110
Rowland (Woodland), Henry, 80, 101, 113
Ruggles, Mortimer B., 125–26, 198
Ryan, W. H., 176–77

Sampson (Stebbins), Edwin H., 151–52
Sanders, George N., 18, 27–28
San Diego (California), Booth's life after "death" in, 171
Sawyer, Frederick A., 89
scars, Booth's, 12; scars of body identified as Booth's vs., 147, 148–50; scars of men suspected of being Booth vs., 165–66, 168
Schmidt, Otto L., 180
Scott, Kate: child with Booth, 162, 173; letter from Booth received after "death," 173; relationship with Booth after "death," 161–62, 173
Seaton Hall, 28
secrecy, of documents, 182–83
secret family, 169–73; daughter with D'Arcy, 169, 170; daughter with Payne, 168, 177; daughter with Scott, 162, 173; granddaughter, 169–73; son with D'Arcy, 171

secret wife. *See* D'Arcy, Izola Mills
Seventh Street Hospital, plans to kidnap
    Lincoln at, 38–39
Sewanee (Tennessee), Booth living in,
    167–68
Seward, Augustus, 65
Seward, Fanny, 65
Seward, Frederick, 64
Seward, William H.: assailant of
    identified/misidentified, 62–63,
    66, 78, 104–5, 190–92; attack on,
    59, 62–66; Booth's plot to kidnap,
    44, 52; Booth's plot to kill, 52, 59;
    carriage accident and injuries of,
    63
Shakespeare, William, 174, 178;
    Hamlet, 9, 166; *Richard III*, 8, 10,
    165, 166, 174
Shelton, Vaughan, 62–63
Shepherd, Julie Adeline, 89
Sheridan, Phillip, 36
Sherman, William Tecumseh, 36
siblings, 8. *See also specific siblings*
"Sic semper tyranis!," Booth's shout of,
    67, 89
sightings of Booth, after "death":
    analysis of, 199–200; as Armstrong
    in Richmond and Atlanta, 165–66;
    as Booth (John W.) in Tennessee,
    167–68; Booth photographs used to
    confirm, 159, 179–80; in California,
    170, 171; dressed as woman, 160;
    early, reported to officials, 158–62; in
    England, 162, 164, 167, 172, 173,
    199; on farm near Harpers Ferry,
    160, 161; as George in Oklahoma,
    176–81; in India, 162, 164, 171,
    173, 199; noteworthy cases, 163–81;
    in Palau Islands, 164–65, 170,
    173; return to Washington, 160; as
    Sinclair in Tennessee, 166–67; as St.
    Helen in Texas, 174–76
sightings of Booth, during pursuit,
    120
signature, Booth's, 172, 179
signet ring, Booth's: missing on body
    identified as Booth's, 138, 193;
    presence in noteworthy Booth
    sightings, 164, 180
Sinclair, Booth living as, 166–67

slaves: Booth family ownership of, 7;
    Booth's contempt for, 8, 43; freed,
    citizenship for, 43
Smith, Alexander, 28
Smith, George Whyte, 171
Smith, H. B., 63
Smith, John L., 193
smuggling: by Atzerodt, 32; by Booth,
    11, 23; by Booth's wife, 19; by
    Henson, 187, 188–89; by Powell,
    191
South. *See* Confederate States of
    America
Spangler, Edman "Ned," 32, *33*; arrest
    of, 103, 105; on day of assassination,
    50, 58, 68; imprisonment of, 160–
    61; kidnapping plot involvement, 32;
    name screamed by Sinclair (Booth),
    167
Spann, Oscar (Oswald), 189
speculation, financial, 26–28, 36
Spellman, William, farm of, 115–16
spying. *See* espionage
Stanardsville (Virginia), tracking Booth
    in, 158
Stanton, Edwin McMasters, 20–23, *21*;
    Booth's death as goal of, 102, 123,
    144; Booth's diary and, 42, 122–23,
    156, 184–87; Corbett complaint
    dismissed by, 136; dislike of Lincoln,
    22; dismissal of assassination
    plot information, 42; documents
    possessed by descendants of, 42, 47,
    186; early life of, 21; identification
    of body as Booth's, 156; kidnapping
    plot involvement alleged, 22–23,
    40–41; Lincoln protection possibly
    compromised by, 53–54; mental
    health of, 20–21, 42; personality of,
    21; photography of body as property
    of, 150–51; pursuit of Booth led by,
    76, 79; pursuit of Booth possibly
    undermined by, 90–92, 96; reaction
    to capture of Booth, 144; refusal of
    president's invitation to play, 53;
    telegraph lines of tapped, 41, 76;
    treatment of prisoners ordered by,
    105–6
Star, Ella. *See* Turner, Ella
Starr, Nellie. *See* Turner, Ella

Stebbins (Sampson), Edwin H., 151–52
Stephens, Alexander, 26
Stevenson, Harry Jerome (son), 171–72
Stevenson, John Henry: as alias for O'Laughlin, 170; marriage to Booth's wife, 170–71. *See also* O'Laughlin, Michael
Stewart, Joseph B., 68–69
Stewart, Richard, 81, 118–19
St. Helen, John: accusation against Johnson (Andrew), 175; Booth living as, 174–76, 199–200; diary knowledge of, 175–76; flight described by, 176; George as same man, 176–81; personality, vs. Booth's, 180–81; photograph matched, 179–80; theater interests of, 174; tintype possessed by, 174–75
St. Joseph (Minnesota), premature report of Lincoln's assassination in, 53
St. Timothy's Hall (school), 7–8
suicide: attempted by George (Booth), 177–78; committed by George (Booth), 176, 180; Garrett farm death as, 135, 148–50, 197–99
Surratt, Anna: arrest of, 78, 103; attraction to Booth, 34; Payne not recognized by, 191
Surratt, Isaac, 110
Surratt, John H., Jr., *26*; on day of assassination, 43–44; description and picture on wanted poster, 110–12, *111*; evidence implicating, 52, 75; kidnapping plot involvement, 23, 25, 34–40; pursuit of, 79, 105, 110–12; reward offered for, 79, 110, 120
Surratt, Mary: arrest of, 78, 103, 105; Booth's visits on day of assassination, 44, 49; disinterment and reburial of body, 154; evidence implicating, 52; imprisonment of, 106, 145; investigation of, 75, 78; Payne not recognized by, 191; romantic involvement with Booth, 10; tips against, 75, 78; trial and execution of, 160. *See also* Surratt's Tavern
Surratt, Mary, boardinghouse of, *104*; arrest of Payne (Powell) at, 74, 78, 103–4, 190–91; Booth's visits on day of assassination, 44, 49; investigators at, 75 78; storage of weapons at, 24; Weichmann as boarder at, 25, 34, 44, 78
Surratt's Tavern: Booth's flight to, 74, 91; equipment and weapons stashed at, 38, 74, 91; Henson vs. Herold as Booth's companion at, 189; meeting of kidnapping conspirators at, 38. *See also* Lloyd, John
Surrattsville (Maryland): Booth's flight to, alternate version of, 89–93; Booth's flight to, traditional version of, 74; investigators in, 95, 105; kidnapping plot in, 37–38, 44; underground route through, 74
surrender, Confederate, 41
survival, Booth. *See* escape; sightings
swamps, Booth hiding in, 77, 78–79, 97, 99–102
Swann, Oswald, 99–100

Taft, Charles Sabin, 89
Taltavul, Peter, 59
Taltavul's Tavern, 39, 50, 58–59
tattoo, 12, 100, 125, 127, 147–48, 192–93
telegraph lines: severing, after Lincoln shooting, 86–87; Stanton's, tapping of, 41, 76
Tennessee: Booth living as Booth (John W.) in, 167–68; Booth living as Sinclair in, 166–67
Texas, Booth living as St. Helen in, 174–76
theater: Lincoln's enjoyment of, 28, 45–46; popular sites in Washington, 28. *See also* acting career; *specific theaters*
This One Mad Act (Forrester), 169, 170
Thompson, Jacob, 17–18, *18*, 23, 27–28
Thompson, John C., 34
Threadkell, L., 180
Todd, G. B., 89
Tolbert, William M., 164
Townsend, George Alfred, 11–12
Tucker, Beverly, 18, *19*, 27–28
Tudor Hall (Booth family home), 7
tumor, removed from Booth, 148, 165–66

Turner, Ella, 10
"Tyler," Booth identified as, 75, 94–95, 97–98

underground route, Confederate, 74, 91
upbringing, 7–8
Urquhart, Dr., 84, 138

valet, Booth's. *See* Johnson, Henry
Virginia: Booth living as Armstrong as, 165–66; Garrett farm killing in, 1, 70–71, 81–84, 126–39; pursuit of Booth in, 80–84, 115–39; tracking Booth after "death" in, 158–60. *See also specific sites and events*

Wade, Benjamin, 28, 29
Wagner, Henry C., 156
wanted posters, 103, 105, 108, 110–12, *111*
Wardell, James A., 150
Washington, D.C.: Booth's flight from, alternate version of, 86–88; Booth's flight from, traditional version of, 72–74; Booth's return to, after "death," 160, 167; Booth's route out of, *69*, 69–71; kidnapping plot's planned escape from, 32, 34, 35, 44; transport of body identified as Booth's to, 140–41
Washington Penitentiary, conspiracy suspects held in, 105–6
Watkins, Thomas H., 43, 92, 96, 107
Watson, William, 120
wealth, Booth's, in life after "death," 170, 174, 177
weapons: Booth's, during flight, 101; Booth's, in assassination, 52, 60; Booth's marksmanship with, 26; mismatch of Corbett's gun to fatal wounds, 135; purchases for kidnapping plot, 24; in Seward attack, 64; storage at Surratt boardinghouse, 24; storage at Surratt's Tavern, 38, 74

Weaver, John H., 155–56, 196–97, 199
Webb, William B., 28
Weed, Thurlow, 119
Weichmann, Louis: assassination day conversation overheard by, 44; Booth's flight route described by, 92; Booth's kidnapping plot exposed by, 26, 34; as companion of Surratt (John), 25; Surratt (Mary) implicated by, 78
Welling, James C., 47
Western, Helen, 10
Wilkes, John (namesake), 7
Wilkes, John B. (Byron), Booth's usage of name, 162, 172
Wilkes, Ogarita. *See* Henderson, Ogarita Booth
Williams, Captain, pursuit of Booth, 110
Williams, William, 105
Wilmington (North Carolina), Union capture of, 36
Wilson, Clarence Truth, 179
Wilson, John Francis: on Booth's diary, 184; on Booth's personality, 7; on suicide at Garrett Farm, 197; on tattoo, 148
Withers, William, Jr., 56–57, 68
wives. *See specific women*
women: Booth dressing as, 160; Booth's attractiveness to, 9, 10, 12; photos in Booth's diary, 119, 186. *See also* romances
Wood, James, 38
Wood, William B., 195
Woodland (Rowland), Henry, 80, 101, 113
Woodward, Joseph Janvier, 146

Young, John, 171
Young, Miss, relationship with George (Booth), 177–78

Zekiah Swamp, 77, 78, 91, 97, 99–102, 119
Ziegen, Joseph, 138–39

About the Author

✦✦✦

W.C. Jameson is the award-winning author of more than eighty books. He is the best-selling treasure author in the United States, and his prominence as a professional fortune hunter has led to stints as a consultant for the *Unsolved Mysteries* television show and The Travel Channel. He served as an adviser for the film *National Treasure* starring Nicolas Cage and appears in an interview on the DVD. His book *Treasure Hunter: Caches, Curses, and Deadly Confrontations* was named Best Book of the Year (2011) by Indie Reader.

Jameson has written the sound tracks for two PBS documentaries and one feature film. His music has been heard on National Public Radio, and he wrote and performed in the musical *Whatever Happened to the Outlaw, Jesse James?* Jameson has acted in five films and has been interviewed on The History Channel, The Travel Channel, PBS, and *Nightline*. When not working on a book, he tours the country as a speaker, conducting writing workshops and performing his music at folk festivals, concerts, roadhouses, and on television. He lives in Llano, Texas.

Acknowledgments

✦✦✦

The publishing and successes of most of my books involve the contributions of a number of important people. It had been my good fortune to be associated with Taylor Trade Publishing and their efforts in facilitating the production of the Beyond the Grave series. Headman Rick Rinehart runs a classy operation, always responds to my e-mails in a timely manner, and has proven to be a congenial lunch companion.

Linking up with super literary agent Sandra Bond turned out to be one of the best decisions I've ever made during my more than four decades of literary pursuits. Somehow she has managed to place everything I send to her.

During the writing of *John Wilkes Booth: Beyond the Grave*, I have occasionally sought the expertise of others. A conversation with the crack researcher and crime scene investigator Steve Sederwall invariably yields insights that had previously eluded me. John Ferguson supplied the trigonometric calculation that helped to explain the shooting of the man in Garrett's barn.

I never send a manuscript to anyone before it has been worked over by Laurie Jameson, the best editor, poet, novelist, memoirist, gardener, and wife in the country.